T0355084

The First Jewish Environmentalist

The First Jewish Environmentalist

The Green Philosophy of A.D. Gordon

YUVAL JOBANI

OXFORD
UNIVERSITY PRESS

OXFORD
UNIVERSITY PRESS

Oxford University Press is a department of the University of Oxford. It furthers
the University's objective of excellence in research, scholarship, and education
by publishing worldwide. Oxford is a registered trade mark of Oxford University
Press in the UK and certain other countries.

Published in the United States of America by Oxford University Press
198 Madison Avenue, New York, NY 10016, United States of America.

© Oxford University Press 2024

Library of Congress Cataloging-in-Publication Data
Names: Jobani, Yuval, author.
Title: The first Jewish environmentalist : the green philosophy of
A.D. Gordon / Yuval Jobani.
Description: New York : Oxford University Press, [2024] |
Includes bibliographical references and index. | Contents: Introduction:
Why Gordon matters—Historical Background: What led Gordon to compose Man
and Nature?—Philosophical Foundations: Gordon's basic concepts and
main arguments—A Religion of Nature: On Gordon's religious
commitment to the environment—'The Return to Nature' Speech: Gordon
as an Environmental Prophet—Epilogue: What is to be done?
Identifiers: LCCN 2023032628 | ISBN 9780197617977 (hardback) |
ISBN 9780197617991 (epub) | ISBN 9780197617984
Subjects: LCSH: Gordon, Aaron David, 1856–1922. | Philosophy of nature. |
Ecology—Philosophy. | Labor Zionism.
Classification: LCC DS151.G6 J63 2023 | DDC 320.5801—dc23/eng/20230729
LC record available at https://lccn.loc.gov/2023032628

DOI: 10.1093/oso/9780197617977.001.0001

Printed by Sheridan Books, Inc., United States of America

For my son, Yonatan

Contents

Acknowledgments

This book reflects a long journey into Gordon's writings. It developed out of joint studies, thought-provoking conversations, and spirited debates on the philosophy of the "the true teacher." I would like to thank my colleagues and students who were particularly helpful in the process of researching and writing the book: Adam Afterman, Allan Arkush, Avner Ben-Amos, Hanit Benglas, Hanoch Ben-Pazi, David Biale, Asher Biemann, Kobi Dana, Hasia Diner, Jeremy Fogel, Céleste Gineste, Yemima Hadad, Motti Inbari, Svitlana Kobets, Anna Landa, Menachem Lorberbaum, Yehudah Mirsky, Iair Or, Haim Rechnitzer, Arieh Saposnik, Eugene Sheppard, Tali Tadmor-Shimony, Zvi Tauber, Gideon Tikotzky, Hava Tirosh-Samuelson, Yossi Turner, Michael Walzer, Douglas Weiner, Azzan Yadin, Yael Zerubavel, and Rafi Zirkin-Sadan.

My research assistant Eylon Weitzman generously devoted a great deal of time to discussing the thesis developed in this book. My special thanks to Ron Margolin and Yarin Raban for our many intensive hours of joint study of Gordon's works, the fruits of which have nuanced my entire analysis. At Oxford University Press, I especially would like to thank Cynthia Read and Steve Wiggins for their advice at various stages of this project.

My fellowship at the Katz Center for Advanced Judaic Studies at the University of Pennsylvania (2016–17) provided me with the time and resources needed to gather the relevant materials for this study and to begin examining them. I also received generous assistance from the Israel Science Foundation (Grant 889/22), from the Kelman Center for Jewish Education, and from the School of Jewish Studies at Tel Aviv University. I would like to thank the participants and organizers of the conferences and workshops where I presented various parts of this study. At the 23rd Annual Gruss Colloquium at the Katz Center for Advanced Judaic Studies I experimented with the second chapter, which was then published in the *Jewish Quarterly Review* 111: 3 (2021). Other chapters of the book were presented at the Workshop on Freethinkers at the German Historical Institute in Rome (2018), the 34th AIS in Berkeley, the 50th Annual Meeting of the AJS in Boston (2018), the 51st Annual Meeting of the AJS in San Diego (2019), and at a panel discussion on Jewish green thought at the University of Virginia (2021).

My parents, Moshe and Myriam, and my brother Itamar have been an unwavering source of support throughout the years. Finally, I am especially grateful to my beloved Keren and our amazing children Yonatan, Tom, and Uriah for their true love.

Abbreviations of Gordon's Writings and Bibliographies

GWA Aharon David Gordon, *The Writings of A. D. Gordon* [Heb.], 5 vols., ed.
Yosef Aharonovich, Tel Aviv: Hapoel Hatzair, 1925–1929

GWB Aharon David Gordon, *The Writings of A. D. Gordon* [Heb.], 3 vols., eds.
Hugo Bergman and Eliezer Shochat, Jerusalem: The Zionist Library,
1952–1954

GWT Aharon David Gordon, *Gordon: Selected Writings in One Volume* [Heb.], ed.
Nachman Teradyon, Tel Aviv: Stiebel, 1935–1936

GSE Aharon David Gordon, *Selected Essays*, trans. Frances Burnce,
New York: League for Labor Palestine, 1938

MN   Aharon David Gordon, *Man and Nature—Critical Edition* [Heb.], eds.
Yuval Jobani and Ron Margolin, Jerusalem: The Hebrew University Magnes
Press, 2020

T   Muki Tsur (ed.), *Higher than Loneliness: Letters to and from A.D. Gordon*
[Heb.], Tel Aviv: Hakibbutz Hameuchad, 1998

GB   Aharon David Gordon, *Bibliography* [Heb.], eds. Shmuel Lulav at el., 3 vols.,
Degania Alef: Gordon House 1979–1992

Figure 0.1. The beard of a prophet and a redeemer, dreamy eyes shining with a youthful sparkle. A portrait of Gordon by Avraham Soskin, undated. Israeli Benzion Collection. Album of Ben-Zion Israeli (Tchernomirsky), Yad Ben-Zvi Photo Archives.

1

Introduction

Why Gordon Matters

In light of the climate crisis, communities of faith must rethink their traditions and adapt them to the rapidly changing environmental reality. Such religious reflection is essential—no less than scientific investigation—if we are to address and manage our impact on the environment. It is in this spirit that *The First Jewish Environmentalist* sets out to introduce Gordon's green Jewish philosophy to a new generation of readers.

Hailed by Martin Buber as "the true teacher," pioneer, philosopher, and dreamer, Aharon David Gordon (Russian Empire–Land of Israel, 1856–1922) is increasingly being recognized as the first Jewish environmentalist. Long before global warming became a major threat, Gordon warned against the mounting dangers of human assault on nature and urged us to open ourselves to nature and reattune with it. Rather than trying to conquer nature, Gordon argued, we should merge with it; rather than being a master or slave of nature, we should become nature's friend and ally. Since childhood, nature fertilized and shaped Gordon's mindscape, as it eventually did his philosophical writings. Gordon's fresh insights on critical contemporary issues—such as ecology, gender, social justice, and postsecularism—have recently been inspiring not only a rapidly growing body of scholarly literature, but also communal readings and study among young readers whose imagination was captured by Gordon's thoughts and dreams.

Based on a wealth of recently published manuscript sources incorporated in the 2020 critical edition of Gordon's magnum opus *Man and Nature*, coedited by the author, *The First Jewish Environmentalist* demonstrates how Gordon's call for humanity to reorient itself toward nature is more timely and urgent today than ever before.

Introducing Gordon's ideas and setting them in their historical context, *The First Jewish Environmentalist* sheds new light on the interconnections between religion, culture, education, and the environment. Expanding his canonical status beyond the realm of Hebrew culture, *The First Jewish*

The First Jewish Environmentalist. Yuval Jobani, Oxford University Press. © Oxford University Press 2024. DOI: 10.1093/oso/9780197617977.003.0001

Environmentalist situates Gordon in the tradition of nature-intoxicated prophets such as Rousseau, Thoreau, and Tolstoy and extracts from *Man and Nature* empowerment and inspiration for seekers advocating the protection of our planet.

A multitude of billboards, all competing for the eyes and desires of passersby, have become an integral part of the transportation infrastructure throughout the world. In Israel, however, as opposed to almost every other country, it is illegal to place billboards by the side of intercity roads and highways. When one leaves the confines of the city, one therefore gains respite from the grasp of a hyperactive consumer society that relentlessly seeks to separate man from the nature that surrounds him. Few realize that the demand to banish billboards from the side of the roads was originally made by Aharon David Gordon in his philosophical magnum opus, *Man and Nature*.[1] Born in the Podolia region of southwestern Russia (in what is today the Ukraine) in 1856 and having died in Degania, Land of Israel/Palestine in 1922, Gordon composed the bulk of *Man and Nature* in the Land of Israel in the first decade of the twentieth century. His desire to rid the roadways of advertising became a living reality by means of the landmark 1966 billboard law, which was initiated by, among others, the prominent writer and parliamentarian S. Yizhar (pseudonym of Yizhar Smilansky; Israel, 1916–2006), for whom Gordon was a continual source of inspiration.[2]

Gordon's influence is obvious in several of the speeches given by the parliamentarians debating the billboard law proposal. Uri Avneri (Germany–Israel, 1923–2018), for example, a journalist and writer who was at the time leader of a small radical left-wing political party ("*Haolam Hazeh—Koah Hadash*"), claimed that

> contact with nature is an abundant source of inspiration for man, in particular for the urban man. When leaving his city, he is influenced, whether

---

[1] MN, XV: 231.

[2] Gordon remained a steadfast point of reference throughout Yizhar's life. The significance of Gordon's presence is already obvious in Yizhar's first published story *Ephraim Goes Back to Alfalfa* (1938), in which Gordon's call to return to nature is clearly reflected in the hero's yearnings. In his late novel *Tsalhavim* Yizhar quotes from, and engages with, Gordon's *Man and Nature*. See S. Yizhar, *Tsalhavim* [Heb.], Tel Aviv: Zmora Bitan, 1993, pp. 134–135. See also Dvir Tzur, *Between Home and the Field, between Man and Space: Space and Place in S. Yizhar's Novels Preliminaries and Tsalhavim* [Heb.], Jerusalem: Hebrew University Magnes Press, 2015, pp. 198–214; Yuval Jobani and Gideon Katz, "In the Convoy and alongside It: A Study of S. Yizhar's Works on Education and Literature," *Contemporary Jewry*, 36: 2 (2016), pp. 203–224.

consciously or not, by the landscape that surrounds him. His joy of life is renewed; his roots in the landscape of his land are deepened. The sight of the mountains and the valleys, the streams and the groves, recharges the batteries of his spiritual powers.[3]

In the longest and most dramatic speech of the debate, S. Yizhar, who later described himself as "Gordon's last follower,"[4] stated that

both sides of the road are in fact the grand and free garden of every man [. . .] what is or is not in them, their cleanliness or corruption—affects the passersby, even if they pass by hastily in their cars, and even when they are sleepy and not paying attention to what lies outside, but merely catch inadvertent glimpses.[5]

But S. Yizhar, as the following literature survey demonstrates, was not the last student of the "teacher of truth."[6]

Literature Survey

The centenary of Gordon's death in 2022 offered a good vantage point for surveying—as if from a bird's eye view—the vast, diverse, and rapidly

---

[3] "Debate of Billboard Law," in *Knesset Protocols* [Heb.], Jerusalem: Government Print, 1965, vol. 44, p. 56. On this debate and its repercussions on contemporary petitions opposing the placement of billboards on the Ayalon Highway, see Daniel Mishori, "Signs and Sovereignty: Court Appeals against Highway Billboards as a Struggle over the Commons" [Heb.], *Maasei Mishpat*, vol. 1 (2008), pp. 109–126.

[4] See Helit Yeshurun, "Telling the Finite with the Infinite—An Interview with S. Yizhar" [Heb.], *Hadarim—Journal on Poetry*, vol. 11 (1994), p. 218.

[5] "Debate of Billboard Law," pp. 57–58.

[6] See Martin Buber, "The True Teacher: In Memoriam A. D. Gordon" (1923). In this short essay, as well as the four others dedicated to Gordon, Buber expressed profound admiration for Gordon as a model of self-realization. All of Buber's essays on Gordon have been incorporated in a special section of the extended edition of Buber's *Paths in Utopia* [Heb.], ed. Avraham Shapira, Tel Aviv: Am Oved Press, 1984, pp. 253–264. For an analysis of Buber's attitude to Gordon, see Avraham Shapira, "Revival and Legacy: Martin Buber's Attitude to A. D. Gordon," *Journal of Israeli History: Politics, Society, Culture*, 18: 1 (1997), pp. 29–45. For comparisons of Gordon's and Buber's thought, see Hagar Lahav, "Postsecular Jewish Theology: Reading Gordon and Buber," *Israel Studies*, 19: 1 (2014), pp. 189–213; Ron Margolin, "The Implicit Religiosity of Nietzsche's Heresy: On A. D. Gordon and Martin Buber's Reading of Nietzsche" [Heb.], *Iyyun: The Jerusalem Philosophical Quarterly*, vol. 64 (2015), pp. 418–430; Shapira Avraham, "Whole Systems in Twentieth-Century Jewish Thought: Buber and Gordon—Between Parallelism and Supposed Influence" [Heb.], *Teuda: Studies in Judaica*, vols. 16–17 (1990), pp. 697–722; Shalom Ratzabi, *Anarchy in "Zion": Between Martin Buber and A. D. Gordon* [Heb.], Tel Aviv: Am Oved, 2011.

growing body of literature on Gordon's life, thought, and legacy. Even the incomplete three volumes of Gordon's bibliography (GB), which do not cover the literature published on Gordon after 1992, contain more than 2,000 items. Mapping out such a vast sea of literature is no small task. Yet it is possible to divide the literature on Gordon into four major waves. By its nature, such division is not rigid, nor is it exhaustive, and its aim is only to delineate major trends in the literature on Gordon.

The First Wave (1922–1928): The Emergence of an Icon

In his final notes, written on his deathbed in Degania, Gordon requested that his close friends not write or talk about him during the first year of mourning for him. "Those who want to pay tribute to me," he wrote, "should respect me with silence."[7] Paradoxically, his request only further contributed to the already ongoing process of elevation of Gordon into an icon of twentieth-century Hebrew culture. Through a massive surge of reminiscences and appreciations published in the first years after his death, the pioneers of the Second Aliyah offered for the generations to come a probing portrait of Gordon's extraordinary personality and dramatic life that culminated in his religious attitude toward the agricultural cultivation of the Land of Israel. Indeed, throughout the years since his death Gordon's charismatic personality never ceased to capture the imagination of the Hebrew republic of letters and to inspire young people.[8]

---

[7] GWA, V: 230.

[8] The Hagiographic-like literature on Gordon is vast. See, for example, the special issue of *Hapoel Hatzair* marking the tenth Anniversary of Gordon's death (3: 16–17, January 29, 1932); *Arakhin: An Anthology in Memory of Gordon*, [Heb.] editor not indicated, Tel Aviv: Gordonia Maccabi, 1942; Mordecai Kushnir (ed.), *A.D. Gordon: Reminiscences and Appreciations* [Heb.], Tel Aviv: Histadrut HaOvdim, 1947. This body of literature echoes the Hasidic's "Praise Literature" (*Sifrut HaSvachim*) on one hand, and the extensive usage of hagiographic material by nineteenth-century Russian writers on the other hand. See Margaret Ziolkowski, *Hagiography and Modern Russian Literature*, Princeton: Princeton University Press, 2014. See also the comprehensive and detailed survey of Gordon's impact on Hebrew culture in the first half of the twentieth century in Leah Pelled, *The Reception of Aharon David Gordon's Philosophy and Personality in Hebrew literature and Periodicals (1904–1948)* [Heb.], PhD thesis, Jerusalem: The Hebrew University, 2004.

The Second Wave (1929–1969): Canonization and Contextualization

Following the completion of the publication of the first edition of Gordon's writings in 1929 (GWA), Gordon's work began to attract scholarly attention and critical acclaim. Martin Buber (Vienna-Jerusalem, 1878–1965) and Hugo Bergman (Prague-Jerusalem, 1883–1975) were among the first to recognize the canonical stature of Gordon's writings and to enshrine him in the pantheon of Jewish philosophers.[9] In their path-breaking studies they read Gordon's works through the prism of their own intellectual world and research interests, highlighting his affinity to philosophers and thinkers such as Henry Thoreau (Concord, Mass., 1817–1862), Friedrich Nietzsche (Röcken–Weimar, 1844–1900), Georg Simmel (Berlin-Strassburg,1858–1918), Henry Bergson (Paris, 1859–1941), and Carl Gustav Jung (Switzerland, 1875–1961), all of whom warned against the dire consequences of intensified processes of rationalism, urbanization, and alienation from nature in modern times. Buber and Bergman were joined by other prominent scholars of the time—such as Nathan Rotenstreich (Galicia-Israel, 1914–1993)[10] and Josef Schächter (Galicia-Israel, 1901–1994)[11]—in approaching Gordon's philosophy as a distinct and innovative strand of the critique of modern culture.

The Third Wave (1970–2006): Gordon and the Jewish Tradition—Influences and Contribution

While not denying Gordon's debt to Western philosophical tradition, in his seminal study *The Individual* published in 1970,[12] Eliezer Schweid (Israel, 1929–2022) turned to in-depth exploration of Gordon's unique dialogue with the Jewish tradition. Inspired by Schweid's study, Avraham Shapira provided

---

[9] See Buber, *Paths in Utopia*, pp. 253–264. Among Bergman's numerous works on Gordon are his essays "Aharon David Gordon and New Spiritual Trends," *Hapoel Hatzair* 43: 20 (1951), pp. 9–10 (part 1); Bergman, "Aharon David Gordon," 43: 21 (1951), 12–13 (part 2); Hugo Bergman, "The thought of Gordon on Man and Nature—A New Perspective," *Molad* 4: 22 (1950), pp. 220–226; and his monograph, *Aharon David Gordon: The Man and His Thought* [Heb.], Jerusalem: World Zionist Organization, 1952.

[10] Nathan Rotenstreich, *The Nation in the Philosophy of Gordon* [Heb.], Jerusalem: World Zionist Organization, 1952.

[11] Josef Schächter, *The Philosophy of Aharon David Gordon* [Heb.], Tel Aviv: Dvir, 1957. During this period, Shlomo Bardin published the first monograph in English on Gordon entitled *Pioneer Youth in Palestine*, New York: Bloch, 1932, based on his doctoral dissertation at Columbia University.

[12] Eliezer Schweid, *The Individual: The World of A.D. Gordon* [Heb.], Tel Aviv: Am Oved, 1970.

a comprehensive survey of the Kabbalistic and Hasidic sources of Gordon's thought,[13] and Strassberg-Dayan offered an in-depth comparison of Gordon's thought to that of Rabbi Kook's (1865–1935) spiritual, religious, and moral philosophy.[14] The scholarly effort, during this period, yielded a nuanced understanding of the ways in which concepts, arguments, and poetic images from the Jewish tradition were woven into the fabric of Gordon's writings.[15]

The Fourth Wave (2007–): A Philosopher for Our Time

The last few years have seen a renewed interest in Gordon, which is expressed not only in a significant wave of papers and books published about him,[16] but also in public readings and communal study of his writings organized by young people whose interest in Gordon is not academic, but spiritual, existential, and cultural.[17] Despite the century that has

[13] Avraham Shapira, *The Kabbalistic and Hasidic Sources of A. D. Gordon's Thought* [Heb.], Tel Aviv: Am Oved, 1996.

[14] Sara Strassberg-Dayan, *Individual, Nation and Mankind: The Conception of Man in the Teachings of A.D. Gordon and Rabbi Abraham I. Hacohen Kook* [Heb.], Tel Aviv: Hakibbutz Hameuchad, 1995. For a comparison between Gordon and Kook see also Yehudah Mirsky, *Towards the Mystical Experience of Modernity: The Making of Rav Kook, 1865–1904*, Boston: Academic Studies Press, 2021, pp. 343–346.

[15] Among the numerous studies in this direction one could mention Gideon Shimoni, "The Jewish Identity of A.D. Gordon" [Heb.], in Shimoni, *The Zionist Ideology*, trans. Smadar Miloh, Jerusalem: Hebrew University Magnes Press, 1995, pp. 283–285; Yehoyada Amir, "Towards 'a Life of Expansion': Education as Religious Deed in A. D. Gordon's Philosophy," in Yisrael Rich and Michael Rosenak (eds.), *Abiding Challenges: Research Perspectives on Jewish Education—Studies in Memory of Mordechai Bar Lev*, London: Freud, 1999, pp. 19–63. See also Zvi Zameret, "Berdyczewski, Brenner and Gordon on the Sabbath" [Heb.], *Iyunim Bitkumat Israel* (Thematic Series), 2008, pp. 451–468.

[16] Numerous papers and chapters in books dedicated to Gordon have been published in recent years and they cannot all be mentioned here. The following books have all been published in the last fifteen years and are wholly dedicated to Gordon: Shai Horev, *A Man of Morals and of Labor: The Worldview and Ideological Place of Aharon David Gordon in the Context of the Ideological Leadership of the Labor Party* [Heb.], Haifa: Duchifat, 2013; Einat Ramon, *A New Life: Religion, Motherhood and Supreme Love in the Works of Aharon David Gordon* [Heb.], Jerusalem: Carmel, 2007; Eliezer Schweid, *The Foundation and Sources of A. D. Gordon's Philosophy* [Heb.], Jerusalem: Bialik Institute, 2014; Eilon Shamir, *For the Sake of Life: The Art of Living According to Aharon David Gordon* [Heb.], Tel Aviv: Hakibbutz Hameuchad, 2018; Ehud Fuehrer, *New Man in a Jewish Form: A New Reading in A. D. Gordon's Philosophy* [Heb.], Ramat-Gan: Bar Ilan University Press, 2019; Joseph Yossi Turner, *Quest for Life: A Study in Aharon David Gordon's Philosophy of Man in Nature*, Boston: Academic Studies Press, 2020; Naama Shaked (ed.), *If We Seek Life: Anthology* [Heb.], Jerusalem: Kvish Ehad, 2021.

[17] In recent years, dozens of young people have convened to mark Gordon's *yahrzeit* (anniversary of death) with various special events held in, among other places, the urban Kibbutz Beit Israel, Kefar Rupin (February 2017), and at the Alliance House in Jerusalem (February 2017, February 2018, and January 2019), as well as with online events (February 2000, February 2021). In addition, a three-day festival was held in September 2022 in Gilo Forest, Jerusalem, to mark the centenary of Gordon's death.

passed since his death, Gordon, the thinker and the dreamer, still inspires young people.[18] The younger generation of Gordon's readers are increasingly utilizing Podcasts and WhatsApp groups in order to discuss and circulate his philosophy and legacy.[19] Indeed, Gordon's philosophy and views on issues such as ecology,[20] gender,[21] religious renewal,[22] education,[23] political criticism, and social justice[24] remain a vibrant presence in contemporary Hebrew culture.

[18] The recent nonacademic literature on Gordon's life and teachings is vast. See, for example, Galila Ron-Feder-Amit, *A.D. Gordon: A Life Narrative* [Heb.], Ben Shemen: Modan, 2017, and Shaked, *If We Seek Life: Anthology.*

[19] See, for example, Nadav Halperin's radio podcasts on Gordon in the Israeli Public Broadcasting network Kan Tarbut (February and May 2021), https://www.kan.org.il/Podcast/item.aspx?pid= 21002;   https://omny.fm/shows/kan-tarbut-specials/71071072-ae8c-49f5-bf9a-ad09013982f4. Hundreds of WhatsApp users are subscribed to groups dedicated to the study of Gordon's writings, created in May 2021 by Gavriel Shiff. See also Einat Ramon, "A.D. Gordon (10-Year Anniversary of Gordon's Death)" [Heb.], *Makor Rishon*, January 26, 2022.

[20] Fred Dobb, "Four Modern Teachers: Hirsch, Kook, Gordon, and Buber," in A. Waskow (ed.), *Torah of the Earth: Exploring 4,000 Years of Ecology in Jewish Thought*, Woodstock, Vt.: Jewish Lights Publishing, 2000, vol. 2, pp. 21–41; Samuel Bloomfield, "Gordon and His Thought in the Context of the Problems of Ecology in Our Time" [Heb.], in Menachem Zohary et al. (eds.), *Hebrew Thought in America*, Tel Aviv: Yavne, 1973, vol. 2, pp. 268–275; Avner De-Shalit, "From the Political to the Objective: The Dialectics of Zionism and the Environment," *Environmental Politics*, 4: 1 (1995), pp. 70–87; Alon Tal, *Pollution in a Promised Land: An Environmental History of Israel*, Berkeley: University of California Press, 2002, chap. 2; Asaf Shamis, "Reclaiming AD Gordon's deep eco-nationalism," *Nations and Nationalism*, 29:1 (2023), pp. 85–100. For a general discussion of Jewish environmentalism see Hava Tirosh-Samuelson (ed.), *Judaism and Ecology: Created World and Revealed Word: Religions of the World and Ecology*, Cambridge, Mass.: Harvard University Press 2002.

[21] See Ramon, *A New Life*; Einat Ramon, "A Woman-Human: A. D. Gordon's Approach to Women's Equality and His Influence on Second Aliya Feminists," in Ruth Kark, Margalit Shilo, and Galit Hazan-Rokem (eds.), *Jewish Women in Pre-State Israel: Life History, Politics and Culture*, Waltham: Brandeis University Press, 2008, pp. 111–121; Gad Ufaz, "The Woman and the Family in the Philosophy of A. D. Gordon" [Heb.], *Iyunim Bitkumat Israel: Studies in Zionism, the Yishuv and the State of Israel*, vol. 8 (1998), pp. 602–613.

[22] Moti Zeira, "Aharon David Gordon as a Shaper of Culture" [Heb.], *Iyunim Bitkumat Israel: Studies in Zionism, the Yishuv and the State of Israel* (Thematic Series), 2008, pp. 345–355; Einat Ramon, "Religion and Life: The Renewal of Halakhah and the Jewish Religion in the Works of Aharon David Gordon" [Heb.], *Zmanim: A Historical Quarterly*, vol. 72 (2000), pp. 76–88.

[23] Gad Ufaz, "The Source of the Concept of 'Self-Education' in A. D. Gordon's Thought" [Heb.], *Devarim*, vol. 2 (1999), pp. 59–71; Reuven Garber, "Man and Nature: On Gordon's Doctrine of Sustainability and Its Application in Spiritual Education" [Heb.], *BaMichlala*, vol. 21 (2002), pp. 35–54; Leah Pelled, "The Concept of Self-Education in A. D. Gordon's Teachings" [Heb.], *Hahinuch Usevivo*, vol. 11 (1989), pp. 27–37; Eliezer Schweid, "The Philosophical-Educational Structure of the Thought of A. D. Gordon" [Heb.], *Iyyun: The Jerusalem Philosophical Quarterly*, vol. 46 (1997), pp. 393–414.

[24] See Ratzabi, *Anarchy in "Zion"*; Eliezer Schweid, *New Gordonian Essays: Globalization, Post-Modernization and the Jewish People* [Heb.], Tel Aviv: Hakibbutz Hameuchad, 2005; Joseph Yossi Turner, "National Individuality, Universal Humanity and Social Justice in the Thought of Aharon David Gordon" [Heb.], *Daat*, vol. 81 (2016), pp. 369–388; Fuehrer, *New Man.*

Overview of the First Jewish Environmentalist: Gordon's Green Jewish Philosophy

In the vision and the imagination of early twentieth-century Hebrew culture, the return of Jews to the motherland was associated with their return to nature. However, as the next chapter demonstrates, the meaning and the implications of that return to nature were the subject of heated debate among the Jewish pioneers in pre-independent Palestine. Indeed, Gordon wrote the first chapter of *Man and Nature*, which bears the book's title and delineates its conceptual framework, as a critical response to *Life and Nature* (1909) by Yehuda Leib Metmann, the founder of the Hebrew Gymnasium. In his *Man and Nature*, Gordon came out against Metmann's educational vision, which called for gaining control of nature in the Land of Israel by means of rigorous scientific investigation, in the spirit of the Baconian slogan "knowledge is power." Gordon perceives the limitless exploitation of nature, against which he repeatedly argued, as a product of the Enlightenment's demystification of, and alienation from, nature. Instead of dominating nature, Gordon argued, we should strive to harmoniously integrate our lives with nature out of a deep sense of responsibility toward it.

Chapter 3 turns to explore the philosophical foundations of MN and Gordon's basic concepts and main arguments. Providing us with a grand synoptic view of existence in its entirety, Gordon's philosophical system embraces the unity of ontology, ethics, religion, and aesthetics. The aim of this chapter is to shed new light on the dialectical infrastructure and main concepts of Gordon's timely and much needed call for humanity to reorient itself toward nature. Its main argument is that Gordon upheld the principle of contradiction as the organizing principle of existence and the driving force of life. Accordingly, he argued that the good life is grounded in a dialectic interplay between opposites such as egoism and altruism, conscious and unconscious, individualism and collectivism, and between our tendency to detach ourselves from nature in order to understand it and our tendency to unify with nature in order to experience it. In the vein of the Hegelian dialectic, which had a profound impact on the Russian intellectual landscape of the second half of the nineteenth century, Gordon argued that nature in general and man in particular are not destroyed by the contradictions embodied in them but are, rather, shaped by them. This is the "Supreme truth," as he puts it, "without which there is no place for supreme thought, supreme poetry and supreme life" (MN, XI: 206).

Although Gordon gradually disengaged himself from the "shackles" of the halakha (the Jewish ceremonial law), as chapter 4 demonstrates he never distanced himself from the Jewish tradition. Schooled in an Orthodox Eastern European community, Gordon knew the Jewish tradition well and worked within it, even though he was moving beyond its established rituals toward the liminal sacred realm where man and nature merge. By attributing religious significance to the cultivation of the Land of Israel, Gordon substituted a hoe for phylacteries (*tefillin*), and the sacred silence of the tiller of the land for the traditionally verbal prayer. Placing Gordon in the tradition of nature-intoxicated thinkers and writers such as Rousseau, Thoreau, and Tolstoy, chapter 4 explores the unique array of concepts, arguments, and poetic images that Gordon contributed to the canon of environmental literature and ecocriticism.

In his last days, Gordon depicted himself as continuing the Jewish tradition of the "Prophet and the Mad Spiritual Man" (GWA, V: 226–227). Gordon's portrait, taken by the photographer Avraham Soskin (Russian Empire–Israel, 1881–1963), clearly shows the beard of a prophet, and his dreamy eyes, which captured the imagination of the young pioneers of the Second Aliyah (see Figure 0.1). Chapter 5 provides a close reading of Gordon's well-known prophetic "Return to Nature" speech, which ends the first chapter of MN. In this speech, Gordon weaves fragments, idiomatic phrases, paraphrases, and metaphors from the classical Jewish corpus of the Bible, Talmud, Midrashic literature, and Kabbala. This richness of language lends a distinctly prophetic character to Gordon's speech as well as the validity of religious admonition. In addition, chapter 5 broadens the canvas against which we can better understand the depth and scope of the impact of Gordon's green philosophy on Jewish culture. The chapter explores the various ways in which rural collective communities in the Land of Israel were inspired by Gordon to renew and invent Jewish ecological rituals and practices. For example, the young pioneers restored and refined the ancient "first-fruits" ceremony during the festival of Shavuot and invented planting ceremonies during the celebration of Tu Bishvat (New Year of the trees) during the 1920s.

Deeply committed to Jewish national renewal but fully aware of the dangers inherent in nationalism, Gordon offered an alternative nonstatist, pacifist vision of Zionism. Viewing domineering and aggression in the spheres of politics and gender as a transfiguration of human domineering and aggression against nature, Gordon's Zionism called for the establishment of small, independent, and gender equal agricultural communities, which cohabit peacefully with their Arab neighbors. In these communities, animals would be protected, cared for, and not treated as if their value were reducible to their usefulness to humans. Indeed, it is the vulnerability and helplessness of animals, Gordon argued, that turns our treatment of them to a litmus test of our morality. A staunch vegetarian, Gordon ceased to wear phylacteries while praying because they are made of cow leather. By examining Gordon's call for animal liberation, the epilogue of the book highlights the significance of Gordon's legacy in a time of unprecedented environmental turmoil and extracts from Gordon's engagement with the Jewish tradition insights and inspiration for green seekers of all faiths.

2

Historical Background

What Led Gordon to Compose *Man and Nature*?

A philosophical work, like any other cultural effort, does not come into being in a vacuum but expresses, even if at times contradictorily, the spirit of its time, reflecting the lights and shadows of the culture, or the aggregate of cultures, in which it was created. *Man and Nature* is not, in this context, an exception. Its first two chapters were published in the years 1910 and 1913, respectively, in *Hapoel Hatzair*, the journal of the Zionist Labor Party, of which Gordon was the spiritual leader, even though at the time, in a characteristic act of defiance, he did not actually join the party as a member.[1]

Like the other chapters of the book, which were published only in the late 1920s, after Gordon's death, the first two chapters can be understood as a distinct and innovative Hebrew version of the critique of modern culture that, since Rousseau, constitutes one of the central and important branches of modernity itself.[2] Indeed, Gordon must be placed in the wider context of the profound ambivalence, which gradually intensified during the nineteenth and early twentieth centuries throughout Europe and North America, toward the processes of industrialization and urbanization.[3] Moreover, as we shall see,

---

[1] Hapoel Hatzair was a moderate socialist Zionist party that was established in 1905 by members of the Second Aliyah in order, among other goals, to promote physical work by Jews living in the Land of Israel in fields such as agriculture and construction. Following Victor Turner's observations and terminology, Ramon characterizes Gordon's leadership as "liminal," which is typical of spiritual leaders living at the margins of the social structure and independently from constraints relating to status or economic situation. See Ramon, *A New Life*, p. 3; and Victor Turner, *The Ritual Process: Structure and Anti-Structure*, Ithaca: Cornell University Press, 1979, pp. 108–111. Gordon's actual influence on Hapoel Hatzair was rather limited. Meir Chazan, for example, demonstrated in this context that Gordon's influence on concrete events between 1909 and 1921, in which the issue of the use of force was raised in the New Yishuv [the organized Zionist community in pre-independent Palestine], was rather restricted. See Meir Chazan, "Activism and Moderation Regarding the Use of Force: Brenner, Gordon and Hapoel Hatzair" [Heb.], *Iyunim Bitkumat Israel: Studies in Zionism, the Yishuv and the State of Israel* (Thematic Series), 2008, pp. 239–261. For a cautious evaluation of Gordon's influence on the Hashomer Hatzair movement, see Avivah Halamish, "The Dialectic Influence of A.D. Gordon on Hashomer Hatza'ir" [Heb.], *Cathedra: For the History of Eretz Israel and Its Yishuv*, vol. 114 (2004), pp. 99–120.

[2] Peter Gay, *Modernism: The Lure of Heresy*, New York: WW Norton & Company, 2010, pp. 3–20.

[3] The literature is vast. See, for example, Jan Marsh, *Back to the Land: The Pastoral Impulse in England 1880–1914*, London: Quartet Books Limited, 1982; T. J. Jackson Lears, *No Place of*

The First Jewish Environmentalist. Yuval Jobani, Oxford University Press. © Oxford University Press 2024.
DOI: 10.1093/oso/9780197617977.003.0002

Gordon's *Man and Nature* echoes various moral and aesthetic conceptions of nature as they were crystallized in imperial Russia at the turn of the twentieth century.[4] In particular, Gordon was inspired by the Narodnik's embrace of the peasant as the guardian of virtue who was able to hearken to the voice of nature and resist the evils and alienation of civilization.[5]

Gordon, therefore, was clearly influenced, whether directly or indirectly, by various ideas characteristic of the turn of the century and accordingly sought to emphasize the importance of the unconscious as opposed to the conscious, of experience as opposed to rational thought, and to re-examine the relationship of the individual vis-à-vis society.[6] Furthermore, in *Man and Nature* Gordon can be understood as having tried to enrich the Zionist vision and imagination with the religious significance Leo Tolstoy (Russia, 1828–1910) attributed to the cultivation of the land. Tolstoy, as Rina Lapidus puts it, was perceived by Gordon as "the prophet of a new religion, the religion of those who return to manual labor and through it renew themselves

---

Grace: Antimodernism and the Transformation of American Culture 1880–1920, Chicago: The University of Chicago Press, 1994; John Alexander Williams, *Turning to Nature in Germany: Hiking, Nudism, and Conservation 1900–1940*, Stanford: Stanford University Press, 2007.

[4] As Douglas Weiner has demonstrated in his classic study *Models of Nature*, by the turn of the twentieth century three main trends could be identified in the Russian conservation movement: utilitarian, scientific, and aesthetic ethical. In the framework of the utilitarian approach only "useful" fauna, such as animals that could be exploited for food or commercial purposes, was protected, while "harmful" fauna, such as wolves, for example, could be hunted year round without restriction. According to the scientific approach, "virgin" nature must be protected since its scientific investigation is necessary in order to rationally develop methods and tools useful for contemporary agriculture. Lastly, the cultural, aesthetic, and ethical approach yearned to return to a pastoral golden age that preceded modernism and industrialism. For a detailed description and comparison of these models, see Douglas R. Weiner, *Models of Nature: Ecology, Conservation, and Cultural Revolution in Soviet Russia*, Pittsburgh: University of Pittsburgh Press, 2000, pp. 10–18, 229–237. On various conceptions of nature in imperial Russia see, among others, Jane Tussey Costlow, *Heart-Pine Russia: Walking and Writing the Nineteenth-Century Forest*, Ithaca: Cornell University Press, 2013; Christopher David Ely, *This Meager Nature: Landscape and National Identity in Imperial Russia*, DeKalb: Northern Illinois University Press, 2002; Oleg Yanitski, *Russian Environmentalism: Leading Figures, Facts, Opinions*, Moscow: Mezhdunarodnyje Otnoshenija Publishing House, 1993, pp. 9–12; Philip Rust Pryde, *Conservation in the Soviet Union*, Cambridge: Cambridge University Press, 1972, pp. 9–13; and Anton Yu Struchkov, "Nature Protection as Moral Duty: The Ethical Trend in the Russian Conservation Movement," *Journal of the History of Biology*, 25: 3 (1992), pp. 413–428. A comprehensive comparison of Gordon's *Man and Nature* and various conceptions of nature in imperial Russia lies beyond the boundaries of the present study, but references will be provided throughout.

[5] See Isaiah Berlin, "Russian Populism," in Berlin, *Russian Thinkers*, New York: Penguin Classics, 2013, pp. 240–272; Richard Wortman, *The Crisis of Russian Populism*, New York: Cambridge University Press, 2008.

[6] See, in this context, Bergman's comparison of Gordon's thought to that of thinkers such as Bergson, Jung, and Nietzsche in his "Introduction to Man and Nature," GWB, II: 13–27.

and their people."[7] So, for example, Gordon's description of the religious experience of the tiller of the land in the first chapter of *Man and Nature* (MN, I: 32–33) echoes the lofty description in *Anna Karenina* (1878) of Konstantin Levin's spiritual mindset while toiling in the fields of his estate alongside his peasants.[8] Indeed, this sanctification of the agricultural ethos was an integral part of Gordon's attempt to bridge the cultural divide between the "last Jews" and "the first Hebrews."[9] Gordon, furthermore, also engaged in depth with Nietzsche's philosophy of the will to power, a philosophy that had a decisive influence on the young pioneers of the Second Aliyah, with whom Gordon, the "elder," maintained a kind of Socratic relation until the end of his life.[10]

Following his immigration to the Land of Israel Gordon experienced a dramatic existential and religious transformation that led him, among other things, (i) to change a clerical job he despised for an agricultural job that he perceived as a calling; (ii) to turn himself from a permanent resident in a small provincial village, into a pioneer in a new country, who frequently moves around in search of a job and a community that would enable him to fulfill the moral values he embodied and advocated; (iii) to turn himself from an intellectual who only follows the emergence of the pioneer movement in

---

[7] Rina Lapidus, "Introduction to Gordon's Translation of Tolstoy's *What Is Art?*" [Heb.], *Iyunim Bitkumat Israel: Studies in Zionism, the Yishuv and the State of Israel* (Thematic Series), 2008, p. 357. Gordon opposed Tolstoy's hostile attitude toward Judaism and the Jews, and his sweeping rejection of progress. However, in Gordon's thought, as well as in his linguistic style and even in his dress and exterior appearance, Tolstoy's influence is clearly visible. Indeed, Gordon proposed to name the boulevard of palm trees in Degania after Tolstoy, though his proposal was rejected. Still, Gordon writes, "when I walk along this boulevard, which I do every night . . . I am talking to the old-young man from Yasnaya Polyana . . . "; Nathan Bistritzky, *In the Secret of the Myth* [Heb.], Tel Aviv: Yachdav, 1980, p. 82. See also Jacob Fichman, "Introduction to the volume of Gordon's letters and notes" [Heb.], GWB, III: 23–24.

[8] Leo Tolstoy, *Anna Karenina*, trans. R. Pevear and L. Volokhonsky, New York: Penguin Classics, 2000, III: chaps. 3–4, pp. 172–178. See also Rafi Tsirkin-Sadan, "Tolstoy, Zionism, and the Hebrew Culture," *Tolstoy Studies Journal*, vol. 24 (2012), pp. 27–29. Tsirkin-Sadan also suggests that Gordon might have been influenced by Tolstoy's internalization of the thought of Wilhelm Heinrich Riehl (Germany, 1823–1897), who was among the leading thinkers of the German Völkisch movement. The significance Riehl attributed to symbols such as the land, the village, and the peasant is particularly relevant in our context.

[9] To use Berdyczewski's (Russian Empire–Berlin, 1865–1921) terminology. See Micha Berdyczewski, "Destruction and Construction (Meditations)" [Heb., 1897], in Berdyczewski, *The Writings of Micha Berdyczewski*, ed. A. Holtzman, Tel Aviv: Hakibbutz Hameuchad, 1996, vol. 5, pp. 110–114. See also Shapira, *Kabbalistic Sources*, pp. 42–44.

[10] In this respect, as with others, Gordon had to struggle with the influence of Nietzsche on the young pioneers of the Second Aliyah. For a survey of the impact of Nietzsche on Hebrew culture in the first half of the twentieth century, see Jacob Golomb, *Nietzsche, Zionism and Hebrew Culture* [Heb.], Jerusalem: The Hebrew University Magnes Press, 2002; Golomb, *Nietzsche in Zion*, Ithaca: Cornell University Press, 2004. See also Menachem Brinker, "Nietzsche's Influence on Hebrew Writers of the Russian Empire," in Bernice Glatzer Rosenthal (ed.), *Nietzsche and Soviet Culture: Ally and Adversary*, Cambridge: Cambridge University Press, 2010, pp. 393–413.

the Yishuv, to one of its leading activists, thinkers, and writers; (iv) following his arrival in the Land of Israel, to become a vegetarian; and later on to become a vegan. Moreover, (v) in this period his commitment to the halakha is gradually undermined.[11]

All that has been discussed so far, however, relates to the general context within which Gordon acted and from which he shaped his own original philosophical thought. But was there a specific event or text in reaction to which he began writing his most significant work, *Man and Nature*? The prevailing answer in Gordon scholarship is negative. It is commonly assumed that while Gordon's shorter essays and writings respond to events or significant polemics of his time (such as, for example, the "Brenner Affair,"[12] the war of languages,[13] and the controversy surrounding volunteering for the Jewish legion[14]), he did not compose *Man and Nature* in direct response to a specific event or text but, rather, as a philosophical study, intentionally kept distant from the events of the hour. Avraham Shapira sums up this interpretative consensus well when he states that

most of Gordon's works were not written as abstract studies or literary publications. They contain a passion to respond to concrete situations and the "problems of the hour." Through these writings, his worldview appeared and developed. [. . .] Except for his only systematic work—*Man and*

[11] See Yael Gordon, "My Father prior to His Arrival in Eretz Israel" [Heb.], T: 28–38; Leah Pelled, *The Reception of Aharon David Gordon's Philosophy and Personality in Hebrew Literature and Periodicals (1904–1948)* [Heb.], PhD thesis, Jerusalem: The Hebrew University, 2004, p. 12; Joseph Yossi Turner, *Quest for Life: A Study in Aharon David Gordon's Philosophy of Man in Nature*, Boston: Academic Studies Press, 2020, pp. 13–33.

[12] See, for example, Gordon, "On the Support (an open letter to my friends the workers)" (1911), GWA, I: 60–63. For a general discussion see Nurit Govrin, *The Brenner Affair: The Fight for Free Speech (1910–1913)* [Heb.], Jerusalem: Yad Izhak Ben-Zvi, 1985; Menachem Brinker, *Up to the Tiberian Alley: Narrative Art and Social Thought in Brenner's Work* [Heb.], Tel Aviv: Am Oved, 1990, pp. 157–190; Anita Shapira, *Yosef Haim Brenner: A Life*, Stanford: Stanford University Press, 2014, pp. 198–204.

[13] See, for example, letter 20 to the Committee for the Enhancement of Hebrew Language Education (1913–1914), GWA, V: 29–30. For a general discussion see Nathan Efrati, *The Evolution of Spoken Hebrew in Pre-State Israel 1881–1922* [Heb.], Jerusalem: The Academy of the Hebrew Language, 2004, pp. 144–149; Iair Or, *Creating a Style for Generation: Language Beliefs in The Hebrew Language Committee's Discussions, 1912–1928* [Heb.], Tel Aviv: Ov Press, 2016, pp. 129–162; Yosef Lang, *The Life of Eliezer Ben-Yehuda* [Heb.], Jerusalem: Yad Ben Zvi, 2008, vol. 1, pp. 309–350.

[14] See, in this context, his article "In Memoriam (LeZikaron)" (1918), GWA, IV: 180–191. See also Chazan, "Activism and Moderation," pp. 247–251. For a general discussion of the debate on volunteering for the Jewish Legion, see Anita Shapira, *Land and Power: The Zionist Resort to Force, 1881–1948*, Stanford: Stanford University Press, 1999, pp. 85–95. See also Derek J. Penslar, *Jews and the Military: A History*, Princeton: Princeton University Press, 2013, pp. 196–200; Ze'ev Tsahor, "The Controversy amongst the Eretz-Israel Labour Parties Concerning Enlistment in the 'Jewish Legion'" [Heb.], *Cathedra: For the History of Eretz Israel and Its Yishuv*, vol. 3 (1977), pp. 30–39.

Nature—Gordon always aspired to respond [. . .] to the complexities of the "renewed life."[15]

Schweid, who viewed *Man and Nature* as a kind of "philosophical diary" that was written gradually and recorded Gordon's thoughts "in the course of his efforts to adapt to the life of a pioneer in the Land of Israel,"[16] also stated that

> among all of his [Gordon's] many essays, only one attempt (the comprehensive *Man and Nature*) to systematically develop his worldview can be found. [. . .] He usually would not devote his essays to theoretical issues for their own sake, but rather reacted to various events preoccupying the labor movement in the Land of Israel.[17]

Ramon identifies the urge that led Gordon to write *Man and Nature* with his attempt to suggest a "response to the uncritical drift of the younger generation after Nietzsche's thought";[18] however, like other scholars, she too does not point at one specific event or text that led Gordon to write his *Man and Nature*.

As opposed to the accepted position in Gordon scholarship, I will claim here that the first chapter of his *Man and Nature*, which bears the book's title and delineates its conceptual framework, was written as a direct and critical response by Gordon to *Life and Nature*, a pamphlet composed by Dr. Yehuda Leib Metmann (Russian Empire–Land of Israel, 1869–1939). This pamphlet was published in Jaffa in 1909, eleven months before Gordon anonymously published his "Man and Nature: Meditations and Dreams of a Radical" in *Hapoel Hatzair*, a piece that was to become the first chapter of his book.[19] In

---

[15] Shapira, *Kabbalistic Sources*, pp. 24–25.

[16] Eliezer Schweid, *The Individual: The World of AD Gordon* [Heb.], Tel Aviv: Am Oved, 1970, p. 63.

[17] Eliezer Schweid, "The Reunion between the Scientific and the Existential Perspectives in Gordon's Thought" [Heb.], *Alpayim: Journal for Contemporary Thought and Literature*, vol. 23 (2002), p. 154. See also Schweid, "The Philosophical-Educational Structure of the Thought of A. D. Gordon" [Heb.], *Iyyun: The Jerusalem Philosophical Quarterly*, vol. 46 (1997), pp. 393–393.

[18] Ramon, *New Life*, p. 74. Ramon also notes that the last parts of MN and the articles that Gordon published in the last eight years of his life, in which he responds to ideological and political events, actually constitute one literary unit (*New Life*, p. 87).

[19] The two editions of Gordon's writings (GWA and GWB) omit the subtitle of the article as well as several short passages from the original version on which I am here relying, and that was printed in *Hapoel Hatzair* on October 5, 1910. It is possible that Gordon's subtitle echoes Rousseau's *Reveries of a Solitary Walker* (1782). Although Gordon does not refer explicitly to Rousseau, he shared several of his philosophical positions. For example, Gordon argued that the intensification of urban life leads to the intensification of "the lust for power, wealth, honor and sex as an end in itself, as well as the other manifestations of the parasitic life" (MN, IV.4: 104). A similar argument can be found in Jean-Jacques Rousseau, *Emile, or On Education*, trans. Allan Bloom, New York: Basic Books, 1979, p. 468.

his pamphlet Metmann announces the establishment of the Nature Society in the Land of Israel, which was designed to reside and function alongside the Hebrew Gymnasium that Metmann had founded in 1906. But what were the purposes of this society? From what circumstances did it emerge? And why was Gordon, who is known for his passionate appeals to preserve and protect nature, so vehemently opposed to a society dedicated to the study of nature in the Land of Israel? In order to answer these questions, we will first introduce Yehuda Leib Metmann and the Society of Nature that he founded shortly after his immigration to the Land of Israel.

Metmann's *Life and Nature*

A few months after Gordon's arrival in the Land of Israel, the day following the holiday of Sukkot, Metmann reached the port of Jaffa.[20] Like Gordon, Metmann was born in the Podolia region of southwestern Russia (in what is today the Ukraine).[21] Both Metmann and Gordon had received a traditional Jewish education; Metmann studied at the Mir yeshiva and was even ordained as a rabbi, while Gordon had studied with private teachers, except for a short period at a yeshiva in Vilna.[22] As opposed to the thousands of Jews who made their way to the Land of Israel out of nonideological concerns,[23]

[20] Dov Haviv-Lubman, "The Man Who Swam against the Current" [Heb.], *HaBoker*, April 6, 1939, p. 2. On Metmann see also Hanit Benglas, *Judah Leib Metmann-HaCohen: Founder of the First Hebrew Gymnasium* [Heb.], MA thesis, Tel Aviv: Tel Aviv University, 2015; Hanit Benglas-Kaufman and Yuval Dror, "Dr. Yehuda Matman-Cohen: Founder of the Herzliya Gymnasium and Urban Zionist Entrepreneur of Hebrew Education and Culture in Europe and Israel (1869–1939)" [Heb.], *Dor Ledor—Studies in the History of Jewish Education in Israel and the Diaspora*, vol. LV (2021), pp. 38–84; Shlomo Haramati, *The Pioneer Teachers in Eretz Israel* [Heb.], Tel Aviv: Israel Ministry of Defense Press, 2000, chap. 11; Shalom Levin, "Yehuda Leib Metmann-HaCohen" [Heb.], in I. Bartal, Y. Keniel, and Ze'ev Tzachor (eds.), *The Second Aliyah*, Jerusalem: Yad Ben Zvi, 1997, vol. 3, pp. 523–524.
[21] More than five million Jews were living in the tsarist empire in the beginning of the twentieth century, constituting about half of the Jewish population at the time. See Gur Alroey, *An Unpromising Land: Jewish Migration to Palestine in the Early Twentieth Century*, Stanford: Stanford University Press, 2014, chap. 1.
[22] Levin, "Metmann," p. 253; Yoseph Aharonovich, "Biographical Notes on Gordon," in GWB, I: 55–57. Yoseph Aharonovich (Russian Empire–Land of Israel, 1877–1937) does not indicate in which Vilna yeshiva Gordon studied.
[23] According to Yoseph Aharonovich and Yael Gordon (Gordon's daughter; Russian Empire–Israel, 1879–1958), after his parents' death, Gordon was not yet determined to immigrate to the Land of Israel, and he considered the possibility of becoming a Hebrew-Zionist teacher in "America"—a term that could refer to either the United States or Argentina, where Jewish agricultural settlements were established at the time following the initiative of Baron Hirsch. His wife, however, Feige Tartakov-Gordon (Russian Empire–Land of Israel; date of birth unknown, died 1909), vehemently refused to immigrate to a country other than the Land of Israel. See Aharonovich, "Biographical Notes," pp. 62–64; Yael Gordon, "My Father prior to His Arrival to Eretz Israel" [Heb.], T: 37; Ramon,

both Gordon and Metmann, who had been profoundly inspired by Ahad Ha'am (pseudonym of Asher Zvi Hirsch Ginsberg; Russian Empire–London–Land of Israel, 1856–1927),[24] immigrated to the Land of Israel out of deeply Zionistic motives. Both of them already had families when they immigrated. Indeed, they both were experienced, mature men when they first set foot in Jaffa, that "dirty Asian town," as Gordon called it (see Figure 2.1).[25]

However, in spite of these similarities, Metmann and Gordon had radically different personalities, worldviews, and Zionist visions. Accordingly, they forged very different lives for themselves in the Land of Israel. Metmann was an energetic and versatile educator and entrepreneur, while Gordon was a "radical dreamer and thinker."[26] Metmann was enthusiastic about urbanism and saw it as a means to ensure the prosperity of the New Yishuv, while Gordon recoiled from it, repeatedly warning of its perils and the dangers it posed to the national revival project. Metmann had immigrated to the Land of Israel with a doctorate in linguistics from the University of Bern and had later acquired experience and training as an educator at Bern's Freies Gymnasium. Gordon was an autodidact who surrounded himself not with diplomas but with classical Jewish books, scientific treatises, and periodicals, even when he worked in the fields. Indeed, Nechama Pohatchevsky (Russian

New Life, pp. 45–46; see also Zvi Zameret, "Aharon David Gordon," in Ze'ev Tsahor (ed.), _The Second Aliya: Biographies_ [Heb.], Jerusalem: Yad Ben Zvi, 1997, p. 124. Alroey, who examined the letters sent by the Jewish immigrants to various information bureaus for travelers to Palestine in the early twentieth century, concluded that "Zionist ideology played a very limited role in immigration to Palestine." Alroey, _An Unpromising Land_, p. 234.

[24] On the immense significance the "discovery" of Ahad Ha'am's writing had on Gordon prior to his arrival to the Land of Israel see Aharonovich, "Biographical Notes," pp. 60–61; Schweid, _The Individual_, pp. 28–31. Following the Brenner affair (1910), Gordon's enthusiasm cooled and he wrote to Yoseph Aharonovich: "I respect Ahad Ha'am very much, even though I am not one of his _hasidim_ [a follower of a rabbi], as I am not a _hasid_ at all." Letter 4 to Yoseph Aharonovich (1910–1911), GWA, V: 170. Unlike Gordon, Metmann had close ties with Ahad Ha'am, both ideologically and personally. In 1899, when Ahad Ha'am returned to Odessa from a visit to the Land of Israel, he gave a lecture in which he pointed to the lack of intellectuals and free professionals in the Yishuv. According to Fania, Metmann's wife and partner in the establishment of the Hebrew Gymnasium, this lecture by Ahad Ha'am led Metmann to establish the Association of the Revival Army, whose goal was to create a stratum of young intellectuals in the Yishuv. See Rachel Elboim-Dror, _Hebrew Education in Palestine—Vol.1: 1854–1914_ [Heb.], Jerusalem: Yad Ben Zvi, 1986, p. 242. See also Haramati, _Pioneer Teachers_, pp. 118–119; Levin, "Metmann," p. 253.

[25] Gordon, "First Letter from the Land of Israel (from a personal exchange of letters by an immigrant)" (1904), GWA, II: 216. In 1904 when they immigrated to the Land of Israel, Gordon was forty-eight years old and Metmann was thirty-five. Gordon died eighteen years after his immigration to the Land of Israel and was buried in 1922 in Kibbutz Degania Aleph, which had been his home during the last years of his life. Metmann died at the age of seventy in 1939 and was buried at the old cemetery in Tel Aviv, to which he had returned after moving to Ramat Gan for several years.

[26] This is how Gordon describes himself in the subtitle of his article "Man and Nature," which was printed by _Hapoel Hatzair_ on May 10, 1910.

Figure 2.1. Jaffa Port, 1912. Gordon arrived here when he immigrated to the Land of Israel in 1904. In his letters Gordon expressed his horror at Jaffa's poor sanitation conditions, arguing that the land's inhabitants have no understanding of its nature. Photographer: Leo Kann. Album of the photographer Leo Kahn, Yad Ben-Zvi Photo Archives.

Empire–Land of Israel, 1869–1934), a farmer, writer, and activist for women's rights in the Land of Israel, describes Gordon in his guard booth in Rehovot surrounded with books, journals, and articles: "We found in his possession," she writes, "science books in five languages: Hebrew, Arabic, Russian, French, and German. A few dictionaries in these languages, notebooks and papers written on both sides were lying on the floor. And the 'uncle' [Gordon] guarded, learned, and wrote all day and all night."[27] In the Land of Israel, Gordon lived as a laborer-intellectual, while Metmann functioned as a versatile cultural entrepreneur. Indeed, Metmann was involved in, among other things, the founding of Tel Aviv and Ramat Gan,[28] the establishment

---

[27] Nechama Pohatchevsky, "Night and Day in the Rehovot (a kind of letter)" [Heb.], *Hapoel Hatzair*, July 30, 1908, p. 13.
[28] Metmann was also the one who gave Ramat Gan its name. See Levin, "Metmann," p. 253.

and management of a bank,[29] and the establishment of a newspaper.[30] But his most significant legacy was the establishment of the Hebrew Gymnasium, which is why he was rightly called the "father of secondary education in the Land of Israel."[31]

Still, even if Gordon and Metmann seem to have woven parallel trajectories, five years after their immigration their paths crossed when Gordon wrote "Man and Nature: Meditations and Dreams of a Radical" (1910) as a critical response to Metmann's *Life and Nature* (1909), in which Metmann announced the founding of the Society of Nature in the Land of Israel (hereafter: the Society of Nature). Let us now turn to the examination of Metmann's pamphlet, the circumstances in which it was written, the worldview it reflects, and the educational goals it sets forth for the Hebrew culture emerging in the New Yishuv at the time.

Metmann's *Life and Nature* was published in 1909. It was printed by Atin, a secular printing press that had been established in Jaffa three years earlier.[32] Its front-page states that it was published by the "Nature Society." In fact, this society had been founded a year earlier by Metmann in Bern, under the name of "Akademischer Verein zur Förderung der Naturkunde in Palästina" (the Academic Society for the Advancement of Nature Studies in Palestine). On the occasion of the Bern academy's founding, Metmann had given a lecture to the members of the Academic Zionist Society in Bern (where he himself had been active before his immigration to the Land of Israel in 1904).[33] This lecture, "Zur Regenerationsarbeit in Palästina" (On the Revival Work in Palestine), which was published as a pamphlet in 1908, is rather similar to *Life and Nature*, which he was to publish in Hebrew a year later in Jaffa.[34]

---

[29] Metmann was one of the founders of the Sharon Bank and its first chairman. This bank was established in order to offer loans for the purchase of the first homes in Ramat Gan. See Benglas, *Metmann*, p. 94.

[30] In 1933–1934 Metmann published a weekly journal for new immigrants called *Ha-Ivri* (The Hebrew). See Levin, "Metmann," p. 254. Metmann was an enthusiastic activist for the revival of the Hebrew language. About a year after he arrived in the Land of Israel, he was already promoting (at a meeting of the Jaffa Teachers Union) the idea of creating "a whole new grammar that will help the student learn the [Hebrew] language"; quoted in Or, *Creating a Style for the Generation*, p. 333. In the last years of his life Metmann published a comprehensive essay on the Hebrew language in the Mishnah period. See Benglas, *Metmann*, p. 88.

[31] See Haramati, *Pioneer Teachers*, p. 117. See also Arieh Bruce Saposnik, *Becoming Hebrew: The Creation of a Jewish National Culture in Ottoman Palestine*, New York: Oxford University Press, 2008, pp. 117–118.

[32] Nurit Govrin, "Journalism in Embryonic Tel Aviv—the Story of Three Pioneering Periodicals" [Heb.], *Kesher*, vol. 39 (2009), p. 36.

[33] See Levin, "Metmann," p. 253.

[34] Leo Metmann, *Zur Regenerationsarbeit in Palästina: Vortrag gehalten im akademischen Zionistenverein Bern*, Bern: Verlag des A. Z. V., 1908. The founding of this society was described by Ben-Avraham in an article published in the newspaper *Hatzvi* in March 1909. See Ben Avraham,

Life and Nature is divided into three parts. The first and central part, on which we will be focusing, describes the circumstances of the society's establishment and the rationale guiding its activities as well as its goals. The second part consists of the society's regulations, and the third and last part provides the society's lecture program for the year 1909 in Jaffa.

Metmann opens *Life and Nature* by expounding the philosophical foundations of the newly established Society of Nature. These passages are not the systematic and organized elucidation of a coherent and crystalized philosophical position. They form, rather, a free and associative presentation of various philosophical ideas and positions, which Metmann relies on in order to justify the establishment of his new society, which he portrays as one devoted to a thorough and comprehensive scientific investigation of the nature of the Land of Israel and the dissemination of knowledge about it among the people of the Yishuv. Despite the eclectic nature of Metmann's writing, it is clear through its pragmatic-empirical vision that he seeks to set the Society of Nature on Enlightenment foundations. Accordingly, Metmann declares at the beginning of his pamphlet that scientific research is intended to harness nature to improve the lives of human beings. Metmann argues that in the preceding one hundred years, scientific research has made a "great victory," revealing "new worlds" to man, and providing "new sources of sustenance" for tens of thousands of hard-working laborers.[35] Metmann also uses the Platonic image of knowledge as light, which gave the Enlightenment its name,[36] writing that the Society of Nature has set itself the goal of spreading the light of scientific knowledge to the "darkest corners."[37] He himself held a series of lectures at the time on scientific subjects in Jaffa and the agricultural colonies in the Land of Israel.[38]

"The Activities of the Academic Society for the Advancement of Nature Studies in Eretz Israel (special article)" [Heb.], *Hatzvi*, November 3, 1909, p. 2. The pamphlet published in German in Bern is longer and more detailed than the one published in Hebrew in Jaffa, as the former is addressed to those who do not have a thorough and direct knowledge of the settlements in the Land of Israel. Philosophically, however, it is grounded in the same arguments presented in the Hebrew version, which, as we shall see in the following section, prompted Gordon to write his "Man and Nature."

[35] Yehuda Leib Metmann, *Life and Nature* [Heb.], Jaffa: Atin, 1909, p. 1.

[36] As, for example, the allegory of the cave in Plato's *Republic*. Historian John Pocock has argued that even though the metaphor of light was used in the eighteenth century, the concept of "enlightenment," as a distinctly defined concept, crystallized only after the eighteenth century, which was to become identified with the Enlightenment more than any other century. See J. G. A. Pocock, "Perceptions of Modernity in Early Modern Historical Thinking," *Intellectual History Review*, 17: 1 (2007), p. 79.

[37] Metmann, *Life and Nature*, p. 1. Later in the pamphlet, Metmann writes about the possibility of "enlightening the eyes of the world" through scientific research. See *Life and Nature*, p. 7.

[38] Ibid., p. 1.

In fact, the very act of establishing a research society aimed at accumulating and disseminating knowledge is inspired by the Enlightenment ethos seeking to establish and nurture scientific research societies independent of the university's ivory towers.[39] Metmann argued that making knowledge accessible to wider sections of the public created a revolution in the "spiritual and moral world of man." This revolution, he thought, distanced man from "delusions and superstitions, which were an impediment to humanity," and will eventually "purify man's soul, simplify the curvature of his heart, purify his feelings and desires until he will be rightly called 'the best of creatures.' "[40]

In order to promote the primacy of the natural sciences over all other branches of scientific inquiry, Metmann relies on the statement that "knowledge of nature is the mother of all sciences," which he attributes to "Baco," without providing any further reference. Metmann is here referring to Francis Bacon (London, 1561–1626), who in nineteenth-century German discourse was referred to as "Franz Baco,"[41] and to his declaration in the first part of his *Novum Organum* (1620) that "natural philosophy has to be regarded as the great mother of the sciences."[42] The presence of Baconian philosophy is evident in Metmann's pamphlet. Like Bacon, to whom the statement "knowledge is power"[43] is attributed, Metmann believed that through knowledge of nature man would be able to control nature and to improve himself as well as society at large. Knowledge of nature, Metmann argues, requires reliance on the senses:

> a sharp eye to see with, an ear to listen to every soft rustle, a tongue to taste, a nose to smell; these are the means through which to develop in the student the talent of perception, and awaken his power of thought, because all

[39] See Kieron O'Hara, *The Enlightenment: A Beginner's Guide*, London: One World, 2012, pp. 120–121.

[40] Metmann, *Life and Nature*, p. 1.

[41] See, for example, the title of the book by Kuno Fischer (Germany, 1824–1907), the historian of philosophy: *Franz Baco von Verulam*, Leipzig: Publisher Not Indicated, 1856. Other spellings—like "Bako"—were also used.

[42] Francis Bacon, *The New Organon*, eds. Lisa Jardine and Michael Silverthorne, Cambridge: Cambridge University Press, 2000, book 1, lxxix, p. 64.

[43] Bacon's precise statement was *ipsa scientia potestas est* (knowledge itself is power). See Francis Bacon, *Meditationes Sacrae* (1597), in James Spedding et al. (eds.), *The Works of Francis Bacon*, Boston: Brown, 1860–1864, vol. 14, p.79. The first known reference of the exact phrase *scientia potentia est* appeared in the Latin edition of *Leviathan* (1668) by Thomas Hobbes (England, 1588–1679), who served as Bacon's secretary. See Hobbes, *Leviathan, or the Matter, Fornme, & Power of a Common-Wealth Ecclesiasticall and Civill Harmondsworth*, ed. C. B. Macpherson, London: Penguin, 1968, p. 151.

of man's knowledge comes from his senses, *"nihil in intellectu nisi prius in sensu."*[44]

In this too, Metmann follows Bacon, a towering figure in empiricist philosophy and a foundational thinker in the history of British positivist pragmatism, which sought to distance itself from conceptual abstraction and speculation. Like Bacon, Metmann too thought of the acquisition of knowledge as a means of generating human welfare rather than an end in and of itself. Accordingly, he emphasizes the usefulness and pragmatism of science.

Moreover, if Bacon's *Novum Organum* gave the Society of Nature a philosophical and methodological toolbox, I would argue that Bacon's *New Atlantis* gave the Society its utopian horizon.[45] In this influential work, Bacon describes an English ship lost at sea that finds safe haven in New Atlantis, a state previously unheard of. In this utopian state, Bacon's vision of bettering man and human society through the promotion of science and scientific inquiry becomes fully realized. The central institution of New Atlantis is a scientific institute for the exploration of nature ("Solomon's House") whose purpose is "the enlarging of the bounds of Human Empire, to the effecting of all things possible."[46] Bacon describes in detail the enormous facilities, laboratories, and equipment available to the thirty-six scientists at Solomon's House. Among other things, Bacon portrays the botanical gardens and animal pens available to researchers.[47] In Solomon's house, Bacon stresses, existing knowledge is not memorized, but instead new knowledge is generated out of intensive empirical investigation.

Closeness to nature stands out as a dominant theme in Bacon's utopia. It characterizes not only the scientific investigation in New Atlantis but also the everyday life of the local people on the island, as well as their religious cults. Bacon, for example, describes in detail the usage of various plants and fruits in local family celebrations. The Englishmen who arrive to New Atlantis and

---

[44] Metmann, *Life and Nature*, p. 2. Literally: nothing in the intellect unless first in sense (the senses). This is the organizing principle of empiricism, the varieties of which can be found in the work of Aristotle (Greece, 384–322 BCE), Thomas Aquinas (Italy, 1224/25–1274), John Locke (England, 1632–1704), George Berkeley (Ireland–England, 1685–1753), and David Hume (Edinburgh, 1711–1776).

[45] The book, which Bacon apparently did not finish, was published only after Bacon's death. See Francis Bacon, *New Atlantis*, in Susan Bruce (ed.), *Three Early Modern Utopias*, New York: Oxford University Press, 1999, pp. 149–186 (subsequent citations will be to this edition). See also the introduction to the Hebrew translation by Menachem Fisch, in Francis Bacon, *New Atlantis* [Heb.], trans. Israel Cohen, Tel Aviv: Hakibbutz Hameuchad, 1986, pp. 5–18.

[46] Bacon, *New Atlantis*, p. 177.

[47] Ibid., pp. 177–183.

are invited to these festivities note with astonishment that they have never encountered celebrations in which "nature did so much preside."[48]

In the context of Metmann's Society of Nature, two points are particularly noteworthy. First, New Atlantis is located outside of Europe, symbolically far from the prejudices and superstitions that prevail there and that distance human beings from scientific inquiry and truth. Moreover, the atmosphere in New Atlantis is distinctively biblical. The name of its capital, Bensalem, for example, echoes the name of Jerusalem, the ancient capital of King Solomon, after whom the research institute of the island, Solomon's House, is named.

The people of Atlantis think of King Solomon as a preeminent scientist and even attribute to him a legendary book titled *Natural History*, in which he supposedly explored "all plants, from the 'cedar of Libanus' to the 'moss that groweth out of the wall,' and of all things that have life and motion."[49] Thus, Bacon identifies the return to nature with the return to the "Promised Land." In Bacon's utopia, the advancement of science and the flourishing of humanity go hand in hand with the return to an authentic biblical life. In one of the exchanges with Yavin, a Jewish merchant and scholar who is familiar with the local residents, his English interlocutor declares, "I confess the righteousness of Bensalem was greater than the righteousness of Europe."[50]

Second, Solomon's House, the flagship institution of scientific inquiry in New Atlantis, is portrayed by Bacon not as a university, but as an independent scientific research society. Indeed, this tiny, but vibrant, association of thirty-six scientists is aimed at offering an alternative to the prevalent stagnation at the universities, which Bacon harshly criticized.[51] New science, argues Bacon, requires the establishment of new research institutions where the finest researchers will enjoy the best conditions for scientific research.

Solomon's House, as meticulously portrayed by Bacon in *New Atlantis*, might have served as an ideal for Metmann when he established his Society of Nature in the hope that "various professors and scholars will lend their hand to help this society with advice and action."[52] In accordance with Bacon's Atlantis, Metmann sought to knit together the return of the Jews to their homeland and the return of the Jews to nature. To this end, he argued, new

---

[48] Ibid., p. 173.

[49] Ibid., p. 167.

[50] Ibid., p. 174. Indeed, Bacon had an ambivalent attitude toward the Jews. See also Claire Jowitt, "'Books Will Speak Plain'? Colonialism, Jewishness and Politics in Bacon's New Atlantis," in B. Price (ed.), *Francis Bacon's New Atlantis*, Manchester: Manchester University Press, 2018, p. 144.

[51] Basil Montagu, *The Life of Francis Bacon*, London: William Pickering, 1833, p. 10.

[52] Metmann, *Life and Nature*, p. 6.

educational institutions must be established in the Land of Israel, institutions that will shape the new Jew in the spirit of the Enlightenment and foster the scientific investigation of nature. "Our nation," writes Metmann, "has had many scholars, mathematicians, and philosophers even in the darkness of exile, but we have had no scholars of natural history."[53]

Indeed, in the Hebrew Gymnasium founded by Metmann, and in which he was responsible for the study of nature, students were encouraged to study nature through direct and intense contact.[54] The main objective of the Society of Nature (at least in the early stages of its establishment) was to provide the Hebrew Gymnasium with the scientific equipment it needed, including a library and a collection of exhibits from the natural world of the Land of Israel. As indicated in the regulations of the Society of Nature, "until it will be possible to establish a special building for the Society of Nature, everything that belongs to it (laboratory, library, etc.) will be located in the Hebrew Gymnasium under the management of the teacher of natural history there [i.e., Metmann himself]."[55]

Photographs taken in the Hebrew Gymnasium in the second decade of the twentieth century show various scientific items, some of which apparently belonged to the Society of Nature (see, for example, Figure 2.2).[56] In the classrooms intended for the study of natural history, geography, and geology, one can clearly see

> maps, scientific pictures, drawings of landscapes and botanical patterns, embroidery sampler patterns, reliefs and portraits. These items were hung on the walls densely, randomly, and at different heights. Books, stuffed animals [. . .] fossils, stones and minerals, measuring tools, laboratory tools and pottery were scattered inside cabinets with glass windows or on open shelves and tables.[57]

---

[53] Judah Leib Metmann, "Nature Study in High School" [Heb.], in Baruch Ben Yehuda (ed.), *The Story of Herzliya Gymnasium*, Tel Aviv: The Herzliya Gymnasium Publishing, 1970, p. 87.

[54] Metmann, *Life and Nature*, p. 5.

[55] Ibid., p. 11.

[56] *Hatzvi* newspaper, for example, reported a delay in the delivery of books and scientific instruments that had been bought and sent to the Land of Israel by the Society for Nature, immediately after its establishment in Bern in 1909. See Ben Avraham, "The Activities of the Academic Society," p. 126.

[57] Michal Chacham, "Herzlia's Crocodile: The Gymnasium's Art and Nature Classrooms," in Guy Raz (ed.), *Gymnasium Days: The Herzliya Hebrew Gymnasium 1905–1959* [Heb.], Tel Aviv: Eretz Israel Museum, 2013, pp. 53–63. See in particular the photographs on pp. 58, 59, 62, and 63. As Metmann noted, in its early years, the gymnasium did not yet possess the instruments required for the scientific investigation of nature. But this shortage, he writes, "brought us a lot of benefit in retrospect. We were forced to teach about nature in the outdoors, and this study helped both the teacher

Figure 2.2. Nature class with Dr. Yehuda Leib Metmann, Hebrew Gymnasium, mid-1910s. Photo: Avraham Soskin. Nadav Mann, Bitmuna. The Herzliya Hebrew Gymnasium archives. The Pritzker Family National Photography Collection, The National Library of Israel.

As Michal Chacham points out, this eclectic display is reminiscent of the Renaissance cabinets of curiosities (*Wunderkammern*). Like these small private collections of objects, which were the predecessors of modern museums, the classrooms of the Hebrew Gymnasium were packed with a mixture of nature objects (*naturalia*), artificial objects created by humans (*artificialia*), and scientific instruments (*scientifica*).[58]

and student tremendously." Later, he writes, "One of our friends, who came from Siberia, brought us a box full of different minerals and a simple, old microscope. [. . .] The students were delighted and excited! How great was the wonder of looking at a world of tiny animals struggling against each other in a single drop of murky water. No paintings and pictures, but real animals which cannot be seen with naked eyes"; Metmannn, "Nature Study in High School," pp. 88–89. See also Udi Michelson and Aharon Lapidot (eds.), *One Hundred Years of Gymnasia* [Heb.], Tel Aviv: The Hebrew Gymnasia Herzliya, 2004, p. 15. In 1908, instruments and scientific equipment were purchased from abroad. However, some of the items, such as stuffed animals, pictures, and paintings of plants and animals did not provide the information required to investigate the local nature. Therefore, additional items were purchased from the collection of Israel Aharoni, widely known as the "first Hebrew zoologist," who researched and documented the local animals. See Chacham, "Herzlia's Crocodile," p. 57. See also Metmann, "Nature Study in High School," pp. 89–90.

[58] Chacham, "Herzlia's Crocodile," p. 54.

Beyond Metmann's commitment to the rigorous scientific investigation of nature, his claim is that direct contact with the nature of the Land of Israel ensures not only its rational understanding but also a strong emotional attachment. "Only when the nation returns to nature, and studies the nature of the land of the forefathers," says Metmann, "will the cords of the souls be tied to the environment. . . . We should not shy away from telling the truth: natural love for the land,[59] a love that is not based on rationality, but on healthy emotions connected to the environment—we do not yet have."[60]

Influenced by the Western European Gymnasiums curriculum,[61] Metmann argued that one must learn from these institutions how a scientific investigation of nature instills love and attachment to the homeland in the student's subconscious. "The schools in the enlightened countries," declares Metmann,

> create an emotional attitude toward nature not by impressive lectures and proofs of logic, but through a combination of sensory learning, intellectual understanding and awakening emotions in the unconscious realm of the student's psyche. In this way, one creates in human beings the feeling that is the ground of patriotic sentiment, even before one recognizes the existence of this sentiment. Our students would also have such healthy souls if in our school more time would be devoted to a more in-depth study of nature.[62]

The acquisition of the "healthy love" of nature through its scientific investigation is presented by Metmann as a means to ensure that the students will return to the Land of Israel upon completion of their higher studies abroad. "Many of those who went abroad to study," he pointedly writes, "forgot to return to their land."[63] The background to this statement is twofold. On the one hand, Metmann made special efforts in order to obtain international recognition for the graduation certificate of the Hebrew Gymnasium.[64] This

---

[59] In the expanded German edition of the pamphlet, Metmann uses the expression *Liebe zur Heimat* (Love for the Homeland). See Metmann, *Zur Regenerationsarbeit in Palästina*, p. 14.

[60] Metmann, *Life and Nature*, p. 3.

[61] See also Metmann, "Nature Study in High School," p. 88. The curriculum of the Hebrew Gymnasium in its early years was greatly influenced by the curriculum of the Freies Gymnasiun in Bern where Metmann acquired experience and training as an educator before immigrating to the Land of Israel. See Benglas, *Metmann*, chap. 4.

[62] Metmann, *Life and Nature*, p. 4.

[63] Ibid., p. 3.

[64] See Nirit Reichel, "The First Hebrew 'Gymnasiums' in Israel: Social Education as the Bridge between Ideological Gaps in Shaping the Image of the Desirable High School Graduate (1906–48)," *Israel Affairs*, 17: 4 (2011), p. 608.

recognition, which was obtained in 1910, enabled the graduates of the gymnasium to study at universities abroad (which was crucial, as the Hebrew University and the Technion had not yet been established). On the other hand, Metmann made special efforts to ensure that gymnasium graduates who continued their studies abroad would return to the Land of Israel—both those who were born in the Land of Israel and those who came to study at the gymnasium from abroad due to restrictions imposed on the admission of Jewish students to gymnasiums throughout the Russian Empire.[65]

Metmann sought to plant the "patriotic sentiment" in the souls of his students in the following two ways: first, by organizing educational excursions, in which students would "collect everything that comes to hand—from snails, seashells and seaweeds to seasonal flowers; fish, lizards, bats, etc."[66]; second, by means of what he calls "the Hebrew nomenclature," by which he means the Hebrew naming of flora and fauna in the Land of Israel.[67] The cultivation of patriotism by exploring the motherland and by developing relevant terminology in the national language were characteristic of the nineteenth-century European national movements that inspired the pioneers of Hebrew education in the Land of Israel.[68]

In conclusion, in his *Life and Nature*, Metmann presents the scientific investigation of nature as a means of promoting two distinct interests of the Yishuv. The first is to improve the living conditions of the pioneers. A rigorous investigation of the nature of the land itself, Metmann claims, will assist the pioneers in their efforts to "improve the soil, improve the plants and the animals, clean the air [. . .] and ease their work."[69] The second interest that the scientific investigation of nature serves is the creation, nurturing, and strengthening of what Metmann refers to as "the patriotic sentiment."[70] The scientific investigation of nature ties the young generation to the homeland and assures its loyalty to the Yishuv in spite of the great challenges facing it. Metmann, who was well aware of the magnitude of the aims he set for his new Society of Nature, concludes the first part of his *Life and Nature* by

---

[65] Statistical data on the graduates of the gymnasium, in its early years, were published in 1921 in a detailed report prepared by Yosef Luria (Russian Empire–Land of Israel, 1871–1937), head of the Education Department of the World Zionist Organization. See Yosef Luria, *Education in the Land of Israel: Report (Booklet 2)* [Heb.], Tel Aviv: Education Department in Eretz Israel, 1921, pp. 19–20.

[66] Metmann, "Nature Study in High School," p. 89.

[67] Ibid., p. 91; see also *Life and Nature*, p. 8.

[68] Chacham, "Herzlia's Crocodile," pp. 65–66.

[69] Metmann, *Life and Nature*, p. 5.

[70] Ibid., p. 4.

paraphrasing the words of the Mishnah in tractate Avot (2.16): "He used to teach: It is not up to you to finish the work, but you are not free to give it up."[71]

Gordon's *Man and Nature* as a Response to Metmann's *Life and Nature*

Gordon published his article "Man and Nature: Meditations and Dreams of a Radical" eleven months after the publication of Metmann's *Life and Nature*.[72] Gordon's article was published anonymously in *Hapoel Hatzair* (Metmann, incidentally, published an advertisement for his gymnasium in the same issue).[73] Although neither Metmann nor his pamphlet is mentioned in "Man and Nature," Gordon's article is in fact a response to Metmann's piece. Indeed, Gordon quotes the motto of *Life and Nature* on the very first page of his article[74] and cites and paraphrases Metmann throughout, albeit without providing references.[75] More generally, as we shall see, Metmann's presence is also evident in the way Gordon chooses to unfold his philosophical arguments in "Man and Nature."

The claim that Gordon wrote his "Man and Nature" in response to Metmann's *Life and Nature* is a novelty in Gordon scholarship, and as such it requires clarification and elaboration. While I will claim that Gordon's "Man and Nature" responded to "Life and Nature," it was certainly not Gordon's sole impetus for writing it. Indeed, the ideas he communicated in the essay recapitulated thoughts that had been taking shape in his mind for years,[76] and that continued to occupy him throughout his life. Moreover, Metmann's

---

[71] *Mishnah Avot* in Shaye J. D. Cohen, Robert Goldenberg, and Hayim Lapin (eds.), *The Oxford Annotated Mishnah*, New York: Oxford University Press, 2022, pp. 724–725.

[72] Metmann's pamphlet was published in Jaffa in the Hebrew month of Tammuz 5669 (June 1909); Gordon's article was printed in *Hapoel Hatzair* in the Hebrew month of Iyyar 5670 (May 1910).

[73] *Hapoel Hatzair*, May 10, 1910 (III: pp. 13–14), section 14 (advertisements).

[74] Gordon quotes (in MN, I: 15), without providing a reference, the motto of *Life and Nature*, "We are not poor when we enjoy the nature spread before us all."

[75] Gordon also quotes, without providing a reference, the opening sentence of *Life and Nature*, "Know nature and be fond of it!" (MN, I: 29). In addition, when Gordon writes, "it is said that science lights up the eyes and expels the shadows of imagination and the mysteries of the old world" (ibid.), he is paraphrasing Metmann's remarks regarding the possibility of "enlightening the eyes of the world" through scientific research (*Life and Nature*, p. 7) as well as Metmann's opening remarks in his pamphlet in which he praises science and presents it as shedding light on "darkest corners" (*Life and Nature*, p. 1).

[76] Already in his "First Letter from the Land of Israel" (1904), Gordon complained that the settlers "do not understand the nature of the Land of Israel, they are so far away from it!" (GWB, I: 77).

pamphlet was certainly not the only voice of the period advocating a critical re-examination of the relation between man and nature.

In this context, one must mention two further books that were also titled *Man and Nature*. The first is by Y. H. Brenner (Russian Empire–Land of Israel, 1881–1921)—a translation and adaptation of *Der Mensch und die Natur: Einleitung zum Studium von Natur Wissenschaft* (Man and Nature: Introduction to the Study of Natural Sciences) by Moyshe Gormidor [M. Baranov] (Russian Empire–New York, 1864–1924), published in New York in 1903.[77] Brenner's adaptation was printed in 1910, as was Metmann's pamphlet, and both by Atin in Jaffa. Brenner's book was part of the La'am (For the People) series of books at Hapoel Hatzair Press. Indeed, Gordon himself contributed to this series of translations and adaptations of popular scientific pamphlets.[78] Brenner's version of Baranov's *Man and Nature* was a popular book that aimed at communicating science to the general public. It provided useful agricultural information to the settlers in the Land of Israel and was widely distributed in the New Yishuv.[79] In this book, as in Metmann's pamphlet, science is perceived as a tool that enables man "to control the forces of nature, and to subdue them for his benefit."[80]

Another *Man and Nature* was written by the American scholar and diplomat George Perkins Marsh (Woodstock, Vermont–Italy, 1801–1882). In his *Man and Nature; Or, Physical Geography as Modified by Human Action* (1864),[81] Marsh, one of America's first environmentalists, warned that by uncontrolled exploitation of nature, humans are destroying themselves and the planet. Marsh's book had a huge impact in the second half of the nineteenth century. Incidentally, Marsh wrote the book after a visit to Palestine, remarking that the fertility of the land was severely damaged due to "misgovernment and foreign and intestine war."[82] The book was translated into

[77] *Man and Nature* [Heb.], adapted by B. Zeira [nom de plume of Y. H. Brenner], Jaffa: Laam, 1909–1910.

[78] Letter 6 to Yoseph Aharonovich (October 5, 1911), GWB, III: 39.

[79] Zohar Shavit, "The Development of Hebrew Publishing in Erets Yisra'el" [Heb.], in Shavit (ed.), *The History of the Jewish Community in Erets Yisra'el since 1882* [Heb.], Jerusalem: Bialik Institute, 1998, vol. 1, p. 231.

[80] Brenner, *Man and Nature*, p. 4.

[81] See George P. Marsh, *Man and Nature; Or, Physical Geography as Modified by Human Action*, New York: Charles Scribner, 1864; reprint, Cambridge, Mass.: Belknap, 1965. On Marsh and his legacy see David Lowenthal, *George Perkins Marsh: Prophet of Conservation*, Seattle: University of Washington Press, 2009.

[82] Marsh, *Man and Nature*, p. 314. See also Alon Tal, *All the Trees of the Forest: Israel's Woodland from the Bible to the Present (Yale Agrarian Studies Series)*, New Haven: Yale University Press, 2013, p. 23. As Zerubavel argues, the centrality of afforestation to Zionist ideology was linked to the "decline narrative and the notion that the Land of Israel had once been covered by forests that were later destroyed by the Arabs and the Turks." Yael Zerubavel, *Desert in the Promised Land*, Stanford: Stanford

Russian in 1866 and significantly contributed to the ecological awareness that developed in the Russian Empire in the second half of the nineteenth century.[83] So Anton Chekhov (Russian Empire–Germany, 1860–1904), for example, echoes this growing ecological awareness when he declares in his play *The Wood Demon* (1889), "You have to be mad and barbarous to destroy that which you cannot create. [. . .] There are fewer and fewer forests [. . .] the climate becomes worse day by day and earth grows poorer and uglier."[84]

Both Gordon's lifelong preoccupation with the questions raised in his "Man and Nature" and the presence of other similarly titled books in Gordon's cultural milieu indicate that his work did not emerge solely as a reaction to Metmann's pamphlet. And yet, it also remains the case that it is in light of this pamphlet that Gordon formulated several of his main philosophical views. Therefore, a full and adequate understanding of Gordon's philosophy must take into account his engagement with Metmann.

As we saw earlier, Metmann's Society of Nature was to reside and function, at least initially, alongside the Hebrew gymnasium he founded at the time. Like Ahad Ha'am, Joseph Klausner (Russian Empire–Israel, 1874–1958), and other major Zionist intellectuals of the period,[85] Gordon was thrilled by the founding of the world's first Hebrew gymnasium. "The Hebrew Gymnasium," he writes enthusiastically to Brenner, "is a real gymnasium, which, despite all of its shortcomings, is not inferior to any other gymnasium in the most enlightened states."[86]

University Press, 2018, p. 71. See also Zerubavel, "The Forest as a National Icon: Literature, Politics, and the Archeology of Memory," *Israel Studies*, 1: 1 (1996), pp. 60–99.

[83] See Weiner, *Models of Nature*, chap. 1.
[84] Anton Chekhov, *The Wood Demon: A Comedy in Four Acts*, in Chekhov, *Ten Early Plays by Chekhov*, trans. A. Szogyi, New York: Bantam Books, 1965, p. 109. On the cultural construction of Russia's landscape during the nineteenth century, see Ely, *This Meager Nature*; Costlow, *Heart-Pine Russia*.
[85] Ahad Ha'am and Klausner visited the Hebrew Gymnasium (first in 1911 and again in 1913) to examine it closely and took part in the polemic over the incorporation of biblical criticism in its curriculum. The polemics over its educational curriculum and vision did not diminish the sense of achievement in establishing the Hebrew Gymnasium. To the contrary, as Elboim-Dror suggests, it "stimulated cultural life in the country, stirred the spirits and stimulated thinking, criticism and self-awareness"; Elboim-Dror, *Hebrew Education in Palestine*, vol. 1, p. 252. See also Ahad Ha'am, "Two Domains" [Heb.], in Ha'am, *Collected Writings*, Tel Aviv: Dvir, 1947, pp. 415–420; Joseph Klausner, "A World Come into Being (Part II)" [Heb.], *Hashiloah*, 28 (1913), pp. 531–542; Joseph Klausner, "A World Come into Being (Part III)" [Heb.], *Hashiloah*, vol. 29 (1913), pp. 201–227. See also Allan Arkush, "Biblical Criticism and Cultural Zionism prior to the First World War," *Jewish History*, 21: 2 (2007), pp. 121–158.
[86] Gordon, "An Open Letter to Brenner" (1912), GWA, I: 107. Klausner also saw the schools of the Yishuv as "the new roots of life that are emerging [in the Land of Israel]." Klausner, "A World Come into Being (Part II)," p. 531.

Like labor or language, Gordon argues in his "Letters to the Diaspora," a school encompasses one's self from all sides. Therefore, new schools, such as the Hebrew Gymnasium, create "a new life, a new man."[87] Nevertheless, the importance he attributed to the Hebrew Gymnasium, and his great appreciation for the educators who led it, did not deter Gordon from criticizing Metmann's pamphlet.[88] Gordon, however, chose not to refer to Metmann explicitly, limiting himself to paraphrases as well as indirect references and quotations instead.

Gordon anchors his critique of Metmann's approach to nature in a basic philosophical distinction that stands at the heart of his philosophy, between two modes of human existence. In the first mode, man stands *opposite nature* and regards nature as a means for advancing his goals, while in the second mode man stands *within nature*, aspiring to merge with it. Gordon rejects the first exploitative mode, one clearly central to Metmann, and advocates the second.

The first mode of existence, intensified by the phenomenal achievements of modern science and legitimized by the Enlightenment, presupposes a separation between man and nature; within it man is striving to derive from nature the greatest possible profit and pleasure. In the context of discussing this mode of existence, Gordon quotes (without providing a reference) the motto of *Life and Nature*: "We are not poor when we enjoy nature which is spread before us all."[89]

The exploitation of nature against which Gordon writes can be perceived as a product of the alienation of man from nature, which is itself a product of the process of secularization and demystification of nature attributed to the Enlightenment. As Weiner points out, Russian revolutionary intelligentsia and various Marxist streams of thought inherit this philosophical impulse of the Enlightenment and of positivism.[90] According to this view, nature can

---

[87] Gordon, "Letters to the Diaspora," fourth letter, undated, GWA, II: 278–279. On Gordon's philosophy of education see Pelled, "Self-Education in A. D. Gordon's Teachings."

[88] In addition to his duties at the Hebrew Gymnasium, Metmann was in charge of botanical studies at Dr. Pickholtz's Agricultural School in Petah Tikva, established in 1912. See Yosef Lang, "The Agricultural School in Petach Tikva headed by Dr. Pickholtz 1912–1925" [Heb.], *Dor Ledor: Studies in the History of Jewish Education in Israel and the Diaspora*, vol. 39 (2011), pp. 24–25.

[89] MN, I: 15.

[90] Weiner, *Models of Nature*, pp. 233–234. Gordon, just like the Narodniks, disapproved of Marxism, just as he disapproved of the Enlightenment and positivism. Indeed, as Turner points out, "[Gordon] was vehemently anti-Marxist and even saw himself as the primary alternative to the predominantly Marxist World Union of Poalei Tzion." Joseph Yossi Turner, "Philosophy and Praxis in the Thought of Aharon David Gordon," *The Journal of Jewish Thought and Philosophy*, 24: 1 (2016), p. 132, n. 42. For the Narodniks, to embrace Marxism meant to betray their bond with the peasants

be controlled only through the rational understanding of its laws. However, cognitive understanding, as Gordon points out, separates the subject from the object of cognition. Therefore, the cognitive understanding of nature only intensifies human alienation. "As man takes more from nature," Gordon states, "he is drifting away from it [...] shrinking within his walls like a turtle in its shell."[91]

In "Man and Nature," Gordon ties his critique of science to his critique of art. This linkage should be understood in light of the common function of science and art as providers of meaning to the natural world that was "rediscovered" following the process of modernization. To take one example from the early modern era, landscape painting, as Christopher David Ely notes, "originated in the most urbanized parts of Renaissance Europe—Italy and the Low Countries."[92]

Now, Gordon sees art and science both as key drivers of the process of alienation from nature as well as distinct products of that alienation. "Science seeks out the visible light of nature, while art seeks out its hidden light. Nevertheless," Gordon writes,

> they both do not force man to step out of his shell, to ask for a wide and open space, to ask for eternal life. Both seem to be seeking to shrink nature and push it into the laboratories and cabinets of curiosities [hadre ha-maskit], and by doing so they uproot the last roots of the human soul from nature.[93]

Facing nature in the spirit of the Enlightenment—as an object intended to satisfy human interests—promotes the primacy of the scientific inquiry over all other modes of interaction with nature. Indeed, as we have seen, Metmann's main goal in providing the students of the Hebrew Gymnasium with scientific knowledge of nature in the Land of Israel was to enable them to gain control of nature and to empower them to manipulate it to the advantage of the New Yishuv, in the spirit of the Baconian "knowledge is power."

To Gordon, treating nature as an object is wrong and harmful. It is wrong because man interacts with nature not only through cognition (hakarah) but

---

and to replace nature's moral purity with the rude forces of modern economy. See Wortman, *The Crisis of Russian Populism*, pp. 192–193.

91 MN, I: 21.
92 Ely, *This Meager Nature*, p. 10.
93 MN, I: 21.

also through experience (*havayah*). "The being of the world, the infinite nature, enters into the soul of man," Gordon states, "through two sides: through that which man understands and feels, and through that which he cannot understand or feel but only live."[94] Gordon's notion of *havayah*, in which man becomes one with nature, cannot be captured by science or logic. Yet it is existentially crucial to Gordon. Therefore, he continually sought to endow it with a status equal to that of cognitive understanding. Furthermore, Gordon attributed to experience (*havayah*) a religious dimension and accordingly thought of this mode of being as an end rather than a means.[95] This aspect of his thought stands in stark contrast to Metmann, who, as we saw earlier, aimed to transform his student's emotional attachment to nature into "patriotic sentiment."[96]

Gordon argues that the primacy of cognitive understanding over life experience in man's interactions with nature is evident in a wide array of physical and psychological disabilities that characterize modern man. In order to present these disabilities clearly and precisely, Gordon clings to the traditional dichotomy between the "natural" and the "cultural" man. The strength and instincts of natural man, he argues, faded away as man increasingly distanced himself from nature. His physical senses, the first mediators with the external world and the primal source for his knowledge and emotions, gradually became weaker and poorer as his participation in the cultural world increased. Accordingly, in comparison with the natural man, the cultured man hears and sees less but suffers more pain and is sick more often (MN, I: 22).

The psychological damage of culture is even more destructive to man's soul and inner life than it is to his physical senses and strength. In the psychological sphere, Gordon writes,

the stream of life became even drier and the stream [of vitality] that flows from nature to the human soul became remarkably weaker. Love of one's fellow man, family love, love of friends, the virtue of compassion—all of those things fade away as man becomes more "progressive." (MN, I: 22)

---

[94] MN, I: 18.

[95] MN, I: 19–20. A general parallel might be drawn to the Narodnik's "direct feeling" (*neposredstvennoe chuvstvo*). The latter concept was used by Georgi Valentinovich Plekhanov (Russian Empire–Finland, 1856–1918), one of the leaders of Russian populism, in order to signify the peasant's natural comprehension of morality, gained without the external guidance of culture. See Wortman, *The Crisis of Russian Populism*, pp. 75–76.

[96] Metmann, *Life and Nature*, p. 4.

The last remains of natural emotions are undermined by egotistical rationality, on the one hand, and by the primal desires on the other. Gordon writes,

> even the simplest emotion—that of the love between man and woman, [an emotion] which usually does not require any special inspiration, is fading away. It is very rare today to find a natural love, a deep love, a love which is as strong as death, as it was once called. (MN, I: 22)

The damage caused to the natural emotion of love reflects, Gordon argues, the degree to which modern man has been torn from nature. His alienation is such that he has lost that which for Gordon is his most basic and natural talent, namely, "the talent of living" (MN, IX: 185).

There is, to the best of my knowledge, no record of Metmann's reaction to Gordon's harsh criticism of *Life and Nature*—perhaps because he was immersed at the time in the administrative and educational work related to the founding of the Hebrew Gymnasium. Unlike Gordon, Metmann was a man of action, not of philosophical contemplation. And while the gymnasium that he founded became a beacon of Zionist culture, his pamphlet in the end had no resounding significance. However, even if the pamphlet's sole contribution was to galvanize Gordon into writing his *Man and Nature*, it has done more than enough to earn it a place of honor in the history of ideas of twentieth-century Hebrew culture.

3

Philosophical Foundations

Gordon's Basic Concepts and Main Arguments

In *Man and Nature* Gordon grounds the infinite multiplicity and diversity of nature and human culture in one basic unity. This unity is not simple or contradiction free, but it provides Gordon's philosophy with a classical center of gravity, which enables him to engage and respond to ideas and concepts associated with fin de siècle life philosophy (*Lebensphilosophie*), such as the "will to power," the unconscious, and art as the locus of truth. Presenting a grand synoptic view of existence in its entirety, Gordon's philosophical system unites ontology, ethics, epistemology, religion, and aesthetics. Even if it is less complex than other philosophical systems in the history of philosophy, such as the monumental philosophical systems of Plato (Athens, 429?–347 BCE) or Spinoza (Amsterdam–The Hague, 1632–1677), it suggests one of the principal ways for understanding existence in its entirety, man's place within it, and the path to the good life. Gordon's metaphysics, which is the main focus of this chapter, provides a roadmap to his philosophical and spiritual landscape. As such, it is the key to understanding his unique approach to nature, man, and the interaction between them.

The aim of this chapter is to shed new light on the metaphysical infrastructure and main concepts of Gordon's timely crucial call for humanity to reorient itself toward nature. Its main argument is that Gordon upheld the principle of contradiction as the organizing principle of existence and the driving force of life. Accordingly, he argued that the good life is grounded in a dialectic interplay between opposites such as egoism and altruism, conscious and unconscious, individualism and collectivism, as well as between our tendency to detach ourselves from nature in order to understand it and our tendency to experience nature in order to unite with it. This is the "Supreme Truth," as Gordon puts it, "without which there is no place for supreme thought, supreme poetry or supreme life" (MN, XI: 206).

The First Jewish Environmentalist. Yuval Jobani, Oxford University Press. © Oxford University Press 2024.
DOI: 10.1093/oso/9780197617977.003.0003

Gordon's Spiral Writing Style in MN

Martin Buber met Gordon only once, at the 1920 Prague Conference, where Gordon delivered the opening speech "People-Man,"[1] which would become his most influential speech, and Buber was one of the central speakers.[2] Nevertheless, after Gordon's death in 1922, Buber published several short notes on Gordon, which are full of subtle and thought-provoking observations.[3]

In his notes, Buber attributes to Gordon two unique characteristics. *First*, Gordon had direct and unmediated contact with nature. "A man like Gordon," declares Buber,

> seems to engage with natural forces directly, without the mediation of social patterns. He is a rarity among us. Just as Gordon is independent of society, so is he independent of history. . . . No one could match him in this regard; no one like him can be found.[4]

Indeed, as we shall see, Gordon's philosophy gives a theoretical expression to the primacy and immediacy of his walk in the world. As such, his philosophy can be compared, but not reduced, to other philosophies. *Second*, Buber argues that Gordon belongs to a rare breed of thinkers and great teachers "who do not fully and explicitly specify the details and subtleties of their philosophy. They speak of it casually, as if they did not discover anything new— in simplicity and honesty appropriate to trivial things, even though they speak about things of eternal value."[5]

When Buber argued that Gordon's philosophy was not fully developed, Gordon's MN had not yet been published. Buber was therefore referring only to essays and articles published during Gordon's lifetime. In these writings, which include the first chapter of MN, Gordon, as we saw in the previous chapter, responds to remarkable events or polemics of his time, such as the establishment of the *Nature Society in the Land of Israel*, the "Brenner Affair,"

---

[1] See GWA, II: 33–39.

[2] Shapira, "Revival and Legacy," p. 32. The Prague Conference was a world assembly of Zionist Labor parties associated with *Hapoel Hatzair*. Buber's notes on Gordon have been incorporated in Buber's *Paths in Utopia*, pp. 253–264.

[3] Buber, *Paths in Utopia*, pp. 253–264.

[4] Buber, "The Dream Fulfiller (*HaMagshim*)" [1942], in *Paths in Utopia*, p. 256.

[5] Buber, "*The True Teacher*" [1926], in *Paths in Utopia*, p. 256. The first version of this note was written in 1923 shortly after Gordon's death.

the war of languages, and the controversy surrounding volunteering for the Jewish legion.

In sharp contrast to his essays and articles, in MN, which metaphorically resembles the forest glade of his mindscape, Gordon openly exposes the metaphysical core of his philosophical system. However, even in MN Gordon's writing is not strictly systematic. At the beginning of his magnum opus, to take one example, he does not provide his readers with a clear and thematic presentation of his ontology and epistemology, from which he derives his various positions on ethics, aesthetics, philosophy of religion, and political philosophy. Nor does he provide his readers with explicit and clear definitions of the organizing concepts and principles of his philosophical system such as "expansion" (*hitpashtut*), "contraction" (*tzimtzum*), and "hidden intellect" (*sechel neelam*).[6]

Instead of proceeding with his argument in linear, geometrical order, Gordon adopts a spiral writing style, in which he repeatedly discusses a particular topic in various places and contexts, each time repeating his thoughts while illuminating them from a new angle. In such a helical, spiral model of thinking, as pointed out by Hart, our thinking "does not return to the thing thought at the beginning of thought's motion but to another point in the spiraling plane of thoughts sought, hence an expansion of phenomenological field of both thinker and 'thing' thought."[7] Gordon's spiral writing style requires the reader to synthesize all the parts of MN in order to understand it. In other words, a proper understanding of Gordon's position on a certain issue must take into account all his references to it throughout MN. The status and role of contradictions in Gordon's philosophy, which will be thoroughly discussed in the next section, will provide us with a fine illustration of Gordon's spiral writing style.[8]

One can argue, at least partly, that Gordon's spiral writing style stems from the fact that he never completed the writing of MN, and that what he left in our hands (except for the first two chapters of the book, which were published in his lifetime) is nothing more than a collection of drafts of unedited and

---

[6] The concept *havayah* (experience) is an exception. Gordon coined the Hebrew word *havayah* and in this context defined it. See MN, VI: 143, ibid., n. 4.

[7] Ray Hart, *God Being Nothing: Toward a Theology*, Chicago: The University of Chicago Press, 2016, p. 15.

[8] Gordon's use of the metaphor of water that fish live in is another example of Gordon's tendency to repeat motifs in his writing while expanding their meaning. While in the first chapter of MN this metaphor denotes nature in the narrow physical sense (MN, I: 16), in the sixth chapter Gordon expands its meaning and uses it to denote nature in the broad metaphysical sense, which he calls "life of expansion" (MN, VI: 150–151; ibid., n. 12).

unfinished work. However, it seems that the avoidance of an orderly and systematic presentation of his thought is principled. Gordon himself declares that in MN he does not aim to "offer a philosophical position grounded in an exact scientific method, but only to give expression to simple human meditations" (MN, VI: 143, n. 4). It is in this vein that he even apologizes for innovating the technical philosophical term of *havayah* (experience) to clarify his thoughts and meditations (MN, VI: 143, n. 4). The spiral writing style also fits well with Buber's impression that for Gordon philosophy was more of a spontaneous way of life than a theoretical study of it.[9] So in a sense, even within his central philosophical work, Gordon tends to discuss abstract matters casually, without a systematic approach. Gordon's lively and free style continues to appeal to scholars and young nonacademic readers alike, but it does not facilitate the study of the metaphysical core of his philosophy. By joining together the various metaphysical claims scattered throughout MN, this chapter aims to demonstrate that the principle of contradiction is the organizing principle of existence according to Gordon. As such, it is not only the theoretical key to the main concepts of his philosophical system—such as "experience," "the hidden intellect," and God—but it is also the existential key to the supreme life. Therefore, any journey into "the dreams and meditations of a radical"—to borrow the subtitle of MN—must take its point of departure in an in-depth exploration of the place and role of contradiction in Gordon's philosophical system.

Before we turn to examine the role of contradiction in Gordon's philosophy a short note regarding Gordon's usage of Kabbalistic terminology is in order. Gordon elaborates his thought by freely employing Kabbalistic concepts, such as *yetzirah* (formation), *tzimtzum* (contraction), *hitpashtut* (expansion), *tiferet* (adornment), *sechel neelam* (hidden intellect), and *ein sof* (infinity).[10] Gordon continues to use traditional religious terms known

---

[9] "Gordon is no teacher of oratory but a teacher of life," declared Buber, "and what he articulates is no mere attitude but the very reality of his life"; Buber, "A Man Who Realizes the Idea of Zion (On A.D. Gordon)," in Buber, *On Zion: The History of an Idea,* trans. Stanley Godman, London: East and West Library, 1973, p. 161 (translation slightly altered).

[10] See, for example, MN, III: 23–25 (see also ibid., n. 8), MN, IX: 175 (See also ibid., n. 2), MN, II: 42 (See also ibid., n. 7). Gordon explicitly criticizes the kabbalistic notion of *ein sof* (MN, V: 129–130; see also ibid., n. 7), and from his remarks one can detect criticism of the schematism of the Kabbalistic thought (MN, IX: 181; see also ibid., n. 8). Shapira extensively discusses the Kabbalistic traces in Gordon's writings. See Shapira, *The Kabbalistic and Hasidic Sources.* Schweid, on the other hand, calls for caution against overreduction of Gordon's thought to the Kabbalistic tradition since Gordon, as he puts it, "did not continue the Kabbalistic tradition. He only wove it into the new fabric of the Jewish Enlightenment (*haskalah*) and adapted it to entirely different life experience." Eliezer Schweid, *The Individual: The World of A.D. Gordon* [Heb.], Tel Aviv: Am Oved, 1970, p. 111. In this vein, Fuehrer pointed out the fundamental difference between the meaning of the concept of reduction (*tzimtzum*)

to his intended audience (i.e., young pioneers whose traditional upbringing had made them well versed in Jewish religious literature), while pouring into them new and revolutionary content. The numerous references to Kabbalistic literature lends, as we will see later, a distinctly prophetic-religious character to Gordon's philosophy.

The Metaphysical Contradiction between the Principle of Contraction and the Principle of Expansion

The concept of "contradiction" (*stira*) in Gordon's philosophy has so far not received the full attention it deserves. This neglect is puzzling, given the centrality of this concept to Gordon's philosophy and the numerous times it occurs in MN. In this context, it should be noted that the number of occurrences of the concept of contradiction in MN is the same as the number of occurrences of the concept of "the hidden intellect" (*sechel neelam*), which gained the status of a distinct Gordonian concept and as such was extensively discussed in the literature on MN.[11] In fact, as we shall see, the concept of contradiction re-emerges in MN as it re-emerges in existence itself, which is by nature and essence—according to Gordon—full of "infinite contradictions and negations" (MN, III: 61).

The best entry point into Gordon's notion of contradiction can be found in the following passage from the third chapter of MN, in which Gordon explores the characteristics of human cognitive understanding and its limitations. "The 'I' who knows, to the extent that he knows," declares Gordon,

in Lurianic Kabbalah and the meaning of it in Gordon's philosophy. According to Fuehrer "the concept of reduction (*tzimtzum*) in Lurianic Kabbalah relates exclusively to God . . . and to the way God marginalized His presence to make room for the world. In contrast, Gordon relates the concept of contraction to human life and uses it . . . to signify fragmentation, differentiation, and separation of one part from the whole. It has a completely different meaning . . . Gordon only borrowed the word *tzimtzum* while signifying it with a totally different meaning to the one it had in Lurianic Kabbalah"; Fuehrer, *New Man*, pp. 139–140.

[11] Both concepts appear thirty-six times in MN; Gordon also refers twice in MN to the "the intelligence of the hidden" (*secheliyoutuo shel ha'neelam*). On the "hidden intellect" in MN see, for example, Shalom Ratzabi, *Anarchy in "Zion": Between Martin Buber and A. D. Gordon* [Heb.], Tel Aviv: Am Oved, 2011, pp. 198–209; Avraham Shapira, *The Kabbalistic and Hasidic Sources of A. D. Gordon's Thought* [Heb.], Tel Aviv: Am Oved, 1996, pp. 118–132; Ehud Fuehrer, *New Man in a Jewish Form: A New Reading in A. D. Gordon's Philosophy* [Heb.], Ramat-Gan: Bar Ilan University Press, 2019, pp. 47–52.

sees in the world and life an infinite number of contradictions and negations, and sees himself, to the extent that he seeks to reconcile the contradictions, caught in dire straits (*kaf hakela*)[12] moving from one contradiction to the next one which is deeper and wider, until finally he is struck by the abysmal, fundamental contradiction that encompasses all contradictions" (MN, III: 61)

Two fundamental claims for the understanding of the place and role of contradictions in Gordon's philosophical system are embedded in this passage: (I) From an epistemological viewpoint existence contains infinite contradictions. Even if we approach existence through cognitive understanding and maintain the most consistent instruments of thought, existence reveals itself, time after time, as involving contradictions. (II) The contradictions in existence interconnect with each other and with the most basic and primal contradiction embedded in existence, which Gordon refers to as "the abysmal, fundamental contradiction that encompasses all contradictions" (MN, III: 61).

The first statement is not self-evident, as it is possible to argue that reason reveals the coherence of what appears to be fragmented and incoherent. Moreover, the second statement does not necessarily derive from the first statement, as it is possible to argue that even if reason reveals contradictions in existence, these contradictions are unrelated in any way, and they certainly are not various expressions or modes of a single basic metaphysical contradiction. Nevertheless, Gordon insists that existence contains infinite contradictions stemming from one basic contradiction that is the organizing principle of existence.[13]

Gordon, therefore, cast the multiplicity of contradictions into a systematic architectural structure, which leans on a single fundamentally profound contradiction from which all other contradictions in existence stem. But what is the "abysmal, fundamental contradiction that includes all contradictions" (MN, III: 61)? Which contradictions are derived from it? And why at all is the principle of contradiction perceived by Gordon as the organizing principle of existence in general, and in human life in particular? Answering these questions requires gathering various claims scattered throughout MN

---

[12] In the Kabbalah literature *kaf hakela* is perceived as the last stage before hell (*gehenom*), and in some sources it is presented as even worse than hell. See Yehuda Liebes, *Sections of the Zohar Lexicon* [Heb.], PhD thesis, Jerusalem: Hebrew University, 1976, pp. 380–384.

[13] See, for example, MN, III: 58–59, VI: 151–153, VII: 157, XVI: 241–242.

while taking into account Gordon's spiral writing style, which was discussed earlier.

Gordon's main metaphysical claim in his philosophical system is that all existing beings are subordinate to two metaphysical principles that contradict each other. The first principle is the principle of contraction (*tzimtzum*), and the second principle is the principle of expansion (*hitpashtut*). The principle of contraction indicates the natural yearning of all existing beings to prefer themselves over other existing beings and, consequently, to strive, out of metaphysical necessity, to "contract" into themselves all that is outside them. The instinctive drive of animals, for example, to protect themselves from other animals and utilize them to satisfy their natural needs, follows, according to Gordon, from the principle of contraction (MN, III: 60).

The second metaphysical principle is the principle of expansion. This principle indicates the natural yearning of all existing beings to expand the boundary of their being toward other existing beings. This is done through concern for or empathy with others, and even by giving preference to other beings. An outstanding example of this, which appears in several places in MN, is "the mother animal who gives her life to save the fruit of her womb" (MN, IV.3: 102).[14] In rescuing her offspring, Gordon argues, the mother is driven "by an inner force to sacrifice her soul to save that which is more important to her than her own soul" (MN, IV.3: 102).[15] By prioritizing the life of her offspring over her own life, the entity of the mother—"daughter of Eve *(Hava)* or daughter of an animal *(haya)*"[16]—expands, due to metaphysical necessity, into the being of her offspring.[17]

[14] See also MN, IX: 175–176; XII: 210–211. The example of the mother animal who sacrifices her life to save her offspring appears several times in Gordon's writings. See, for example, "From the private letters of a settler and worker in the Land of Israel to his friend in the Diaspora (third letter)" [1914], GWB, II: 344; "An examination of the difference between Judaism and Christianity" [date not indicated], GWA, III: 202, 207. In this essay Gordon also claims that the term *havayah* (experience), which he coined, relates to *hava* (Eve) "because she was the mother of all living" (Genesis 3: 20). See GWA, III, p. 277. Unless otherwise indicated, all quotations of the Hebrew Bible are taken from *Tanakh: The New JPS Translation According to the Traditional Hebrew Text*, Philadelphia: Jewish Publication Society, 1985

[15] An extreme example of maternal sacrifice in the natural world is provided by certain species of spiders in which the mother allows her offspring to eat her while she is still alive. See Ayelet Shavit, *One for All? Facts and Values in the Debates over the Evolution of Altruism* [Heb.], Jerusalem: Hebrew University Magnes Press, 2008, pp. 72–73.

[16] "An examination of the difference between Judaism and Christianity" [date not indicated], GWA, III: 202.

[17] The idea that altruism is a central feature of the natural world and humanity was much elaborated upon the turn of the twentieth century by the Russian anarchist and naturalist Peter Kropotkin (Russia–England–Russia, 1842–1921). In his influential *Mutual Aid: A Factor of Evolution* (1902), which is based, among other things, on studies he conducted in Siberia and Norway, Kropotkin argued that animals do not struggle with each other but, rather, help each other to cope with the

The metaphysical contradiction between contraction and expansion is clearly manifested in nature, which is an arena of struggle and conflict on the one hand, and a locus of collaboration and harmony on the other hand.

In the "worldly creation," as Gordon puts it, there is

> on the one hand, infinite disintegration, infinite contraction, leading to a war of all against all, large and small . . . hence the absence of any unity, any intelligent order, any perfection; and on the other hand—absolute unity, a common law that pervades all worlds and all abysses, perfection, depth, and infinite light. (MN, VII: 157)

Before we turn to examine the various manifestations of the contradiction between the principle of contraction and the principle of expansion, it is important to consider two implications arising from the metaphysical character of this contradiction.

First, as a metaphysical contradiction, the contradiction between the principle of contraction and the principle of expansion applies to all existing beings: inanimate, vegetative, animate, and human (MN, III: 44–45). Thus, it is manifested, out of the same metaphysical necessity, not only in the animal world but also in the plant and inanimate world, even if it is far less visible in the latter from the point of view of human cognition. The principle of expansion, according to Gordon, is expressed through correspondence and cooperation between different elements in existence. As such, Gordon

---

extreme climate in which they live. "Fortunately though, competition is not the rule either in the animal world nor in mankind," declares Kropotkin, "natural selection finds better fields for its activity. Better conditions are created by the elimination of competition by means of mutual aid and mutual support. In the great struggle for life—for the greatest possible fullness and intensity of life with the least waste of energy—natural selection continually seeks out optimal ways to minimize competition. [. . .] Most of our birds gradually migrate southwards as winter approaches, or gather in great flocks and undertake long journeys—and thus avoid competition [. . .] When beavers over-populate a river, they avoid competition by separating into two parties—the older beavers head downriver, while the younger go upriver [. . .] 'Don't compete!—competition is always injurious to the species, and you have plenty of resources to avoid it!' That is the tendency of nature, not always realized in full, but always present. That is the watchword which comes to us from the bush, the forest, the river, the ocean. 'Therefore cooperate—practice mutual aid! That ensures greatest safety for all, the best guarantee of survival and progress, physical, intellectual, and moral.'" Peter Alekseevich Kropotkin, *Mutual Aid: A Factor of Evolution*, London: Penguin, 1972, p. 81. Slightly adapted from the original. Kropotkin's book was translated to Hebrew in 1921 by Moshe Ben Eliezer. At the turn of the twentieth century, as Weissblei points out, Kropotkin's articles and essays in Yiddish translation were published in hundreds of thousands of copies and circulated among members of the Jewish socialist and revolutionary movements in Russia and the United States. See Gil Weissblei, *The Revival of Hebrew Book Art in Weimar Germany* [Heb.], Jerusalem: Carmel, 2019, p. 307, n. 184. See also ibid., pp. 307–309. On Gordon's proximity to Kropotkin see also Dov Nir, "Peter Kroptkin and the Israeli Utopia" [Heb.], *Studies in the Geography of Israel*, vol. 12 (1986), pp. 11–21.

locates the principle of expansion not only in the animal world (which also includes man) but also in the celestial bodies, whose formation, annihilation, and movement occur in complete conformity to the common natural law (MN, III: 62). Nevertheless, as we shall see later, in the portion of existence known to us (MN, III: 45), the contradiction between the principle of contraction and the principle of expansion reaches its peak in man. Using a well-known Talmudic phrase to describe man's metaphysical standing, Gordon declares that man is "where heaven and earth touch one another" (Babylonian Talmud, Bava Batra 74A).[18]

Second, although the principle of contraction and the principle of expansion exclude each other, from a metaphysical point of view they are ultimately equivalent to one another. Both are organizing principles of existence, and as such their validity, scope of application, and ontological status are perfectly equal. Existence could not be what it is without one of them. Neither has, nor can have, any precedence or priority over the other, neither in moral value nor in any other respect.

The last argument requires special emphasis because Gordon, for reasons discussed below, seems to give in several places in the MN precedence to the principle of expansion over the principle of contraction. In the third chapter of MN, for example, the principle of contraction is presented in a negative light as a principle that incites in nature total war of all against all that has no end or respite. A war that brings to all that face it, and each thing indeed does face it—animals, humans, and entire peoples—"sorrow, anguish, all kinds of calamities, all kinds of terrible, cruel, dark ugliness" (MN, III: 62). The principle of contraction, declares Gordon, casts "shadow and filth over the entire breadth of the world" (MN, III: 62).

---

[18] This phrase is crossed out in the manuscript; see MN, VII: 157 n. 2. Gordon's reading of the Talmudic phrase "where heaven and earth touch one another" (Babylonian Talmud, Bava Batra 74A) is based on transference of the *axis mundi* symbolism from an external-physical realm to the internal-mental realm. According to this transference, which was central in Hasidism, heaven and earth touch one another not in the sacred site but in the sacred person (the *zaddiq*). For a comparative study of the image of *axis mundi* in various religions see Mircea Eliade, *Patterns in Comparative Religion*, Lincoln: University of Nebraska, 1996, pp. 366–385; Eliade, *The Sacred and the Profane: The Nature of Religion*, New York: Houghton Mifflin Harcourt, 1987, pp. 20–67; Emile Durkheim, *The Elementary Forms of Religious Life*, trans. K.E. Fields, New York: Free Press 1995 [1912], pp. 208–216. For application of Mircea Eliade's insights around the symbol of *axis mundi* to the holy man traditions of later Judaism, especially those of Kabbalistic and Hasidic masters, see Arthur Green, "The Zaddiq as Axis Mundi in Later Judaism," *Journal of the American Academy of Religion*, XLV: 3, 1977, pp. 327–347; Ron Margolin, *Inner Religion in Jewish Sources: A Phenomenology of Inner Religious Life and Its Manifestation from the Bible to Hasidic Texts*, trans. Edward Levin, Boston: Academic Studies Press 2021, pp. 541–542.

The principle of expansion, on the other hand, is presented by Gordon in several places in MN as a positive principle. In the twelfth chapter of MN, for example, he presents it as the organizing principle of the supreme life and states that

> to the extent that man frees himself to a greater degree from his turtle-like life of contraction, his soul merge with the life of the world, he is sanctified by a supreme, natural, worldly, cosmic holiness, by the sanctity of the supreme idea, and he gains supreme love. (MN, XII: 211)

Despite these assertions, as we shall see later, Gordon is absolutely committed to full equivalence between the principles of expansion and contraction and, accordingly, he states, "if both sides [contraction and expansion] act equally, life is complete, and thus the satisfaction with life is complete; but if one of them acts at the expense of the other, life is marred" (MN, IV.4:104).

Examining Gordon's justification and reasoning over the very existence of the contradiction between the principle of contraction and the principle of expansion requires a detailed examination of the expression of this contradiction in man's realm. The reason for this is that as a thinker with distinct existential leanings, most of Gordon's discussions of the place and role of this metaphysical contradiction are conducted with reference to its manifestations and implication in human and social life.

As a segment of nature, man expresses nature in a certain unique way. "Each person," as Gordon puts it, "is the 'I' of the world in a special and particular way" (MN, IV.4: 108).[19] As such, man "concentrates" or summarizes within himself, in his own unique way, existence as a whole (MN, IV: 72). Hence, the question "What is the self?" is in fact a restricted formulation of the more general question, "What is existence?" (MN, III: 47). Gordon, therefore, situates the question of the meaning of life in a broad metaphysical framework, anchoring the meaning of life in general and human life in particular in the meaning of existence in its entirety. In fact, this correspondence is grounded in an isomorphism between the structure of man and the structure of nature that resonates in the title of the book, *Man and Nature*. Moreover, as will become clear later in the discussion, for Gordon it is only the adherence to this structural correspondence that allows man a proper standing within nature.

---

[19] See also MN, VI: 155

In the human realm, the contradiction between the principle of expansion and the principle of contraction is manifested through the contradiction between what Gordon calls experience (*havayah*) and cognition (*hakarah*), respectively. Given Gordon's spiral writing style, in order to glean the full meaning of these concepts and their characteristics, we must bring together the various references to them throughout MN. Indeed, experience and cognition turn out to signal not only two modes of interaction with nature, but also the organizing principles of the two major eras in human history.[20] In the spirit of genealogical inquiry, which gained influence through the works of philosophers such as Jean-Jacques Rousseau (Geneva–France, 1712–1778) and Nietzsche, Gordon argues that man has undergone major and dramatic changes during history. Therefore, man, as we know him today, significantly differs from man in ancient times.[21]

In the first stage of human existence, man lives a life of expansion into nature. He experiences nature and himself as one unity, without recognizing himself as a differentiated entity that is separate and distinct from its natural surroundings. Man's life at this stage is organized by experience and not by cognition. Like the lives of other animals, man's life "is intermingled with the natural life, flowing along with it, commensurate with its fluctuations and dictates, and leaving no special impression" (MN, IV.1: 73).

The second stage in human history, which continues to this day, begins with the development of human cognition. At this point, the cognitive perception of nature tears man away from nature, shrinking him within himself. The cognitive perception of a particular thing requires moving away from it. "The cognitive perception," Gordon states, "is primarily a separation (*havdalah*), a certain distance" (MN, IV.1: 73). By distancing man from nature, cognition provides man not only with an understanding of nature

---

[20] See MN, IV.1: 71–78. In this passage Gordon still does not use the technical term *havayah* (experience), which he coins only later in the discussion (MN, VI: 143–144, ibid., n. 5).

[21] Progress and culture, Rousseau argues, have fatally harmed the natural man and almost completely corrupted him. In this vein Rousseau writes that "like the statue of Glaucus, which was so disfigured by time, seas and tempests, that it looked more like a wild beast than a god, the human soul, altered in society by a thousand causes perpetually recurring, by the acquisition of a multitude of truths and errors, by the changes happening to the constitution of the body, and by the continual jarring of the passions, has, so to speak, changed in appearance, so as to be hardly recognizable." Jean-Jacques Rousseau, "Discourse on the Origin and Basis of Inequality Among Men" in Rousseau, *"The Discourses" and Other Early Political Writings (Cambridge Texts in the History of Political Thought)*, trans. Victor Gourevitch, Cambridge: Cambridge University Press, 1997, p. 124. Like Rousseau, Nietzsche also anchors his notion of man in a thorough and comprehensive examination of the far-reaching changes and transformations that man has undergone throughout his history, and he devotes to this inquiry, among other essays, his *Genealogy of Morality: A Polemic* [1887].

but also with an understanding of himself. As such, it constitutes his self-consciousness as a distinct and separate entity. Just as experience signifies man's place within nature, cognition signifies man's place opposite nature (MN, IV.1: 75).

Gordon describes the transition from "a life of experience" to a "life of cognition" as "traumatic" in the original Greek sense of the term, which denotes damage or injury. Man's body and soul, Gordon argues, were fatally injured while being "torn from nature" (MN, I: 21). The shock man suffers when expelled from nature by his cognition is like the shock a fish suffers when pulled out of water. As a result, man lost his most basic natural talent: "the talent of living," in Gordon's words (MN, IX: 185).

The most poignant and easily identifiable consequence of what Gordon labels as the loss of "the talent of living" is the phenomenon of suicide. The high incidence of suicide at the turn of the twentieth century has become a source of growing concern and has attracted much theoretical and practical attention. In his groundbreaking 1897 work *On Suicide* Emile Durkheim (France, 1858–1917) argues that the high incidence of suicide is not caused by individual despair but by a social crisis that reflects abnormally high or low levels of social integration. We do not know what Durkheim's direct or indirect influence on Gordon was, but we know that Gordon was deeply troubled by the high rate of suicide among young pioneers in the Land of Israel at the beginning of the twentieth century. Like Durkheim, Gordon considered suicide to be a particular expression of a wider and more general problem.[22]

By definition, suicide is an unnatural death. An unnatural death, which, according to Gordon, results from an unnatural life.[23] Suicide is the final

---

[22] On the high suicide rates among young pioneers of the Second Aliyah, see Gur Alroey, "Pioneers or Lost Souls?—The Issue of Suicide in the Second and the Third Aliya" [Heb.], *Contemporary Jewry*, vol. 13 (1999), pp. 209–241, and Muki Tsur, *Doing It the Hard Way* [Heb.], Tel Aviv: Am Oved, 1976, pp. 27–44.

[23] In contrast to Gordon, the Stoics held that whenever the means to living a naturally flourishing life are not available to us, suicide is justified, as part of life in agreement with nature. The founder of the Stoic school, Zeno of Citium (Cyprus–Athens, 344–262 BCE) was said to have committed suicide because he had suffered a fall and had broken his toe. See Diogenes Laertius, *Lives of Eminent Philosophers*, trans. Robert Drew Hicks, Cambridge: Harvard University Press, 1965, VII, 28, p. 141. According to the Stoics, as Cicero (Roman Republic, 106–43 BCE) puts it, "It is the appropriate action to live when most of what one has is in accordance with nature. When the opposite is the case, or is envisaged to be so, then the appropriate action is to depart from life. This shows that it is sometimes the appropriate action for the wise person to depart from life though happy, and the fool to remain in it though miserable." Marcus Tullius Cicero, *On Moral Ends*, ed. Julia Annas, trans. Raphael Woolf, Cambridge: Cambridge University Press, 2001, Book III, p. 84. Adopting this Stoic stance, Nietzsche preached for the free death [*freien Tode*] and demanded that one be able to "die at the right time!" Friedrich Nietzsche, *Thus Spoke Zarathustra*, trans. Adrian Del Caro, Cambridge: Cambridge University Press, 2006, p. 53. In this respect, Gordon, as we saw earlier, had to struggle with Nietzsche's influence on the young pioneers of the Second Aliyah.

consequence, although certainly not the only or even the gravest consequence of modern lifestyle. It is preceded, as we saw in the previous chapter,
by a lengthy list of injuries caused not only to man's physical senses and
strength but also to his soul and inner life. The damage caused to the natural emotion of love (MN, I: 23), along with other factors, led to a negative
birth rate, which Gordon takes as conclusive evidence that culture organizes
for man a life that does not aim for life, not even in the most primal and
basic requirement for the physical continuation of the human species.
Consequently, not only does the number of family units decrease, but
also the ties between the members of the family—in both nuclear and extended families—weaken.[24] According to Gordon, all the emotions—sexual
emotion, parental emotion, and familial emotion—belong to the same sequence. The object of each one of these emotions is wider than the object of
the former, but its intensity and power tends to be weaker (MN, VII: 160).
These emotions are interconnected and interdependent. Therefore, the collapse of one leads to the collapse of all the others. Precisely as the collapse
of the individual leads to the collapse of the family, so the collapse of the
family leads to the collapse of society as a whole. This is because society,
according to Gordon, is the natural continuation of the family with the in-
termediation of the tribe in ancient times, or the nation in modern times.
Culture as we understand it, Gordon argues, damages social solidarity and
transforms society from a setting in which individuals support each other to
an arena in which individuals harm each other while trying to dominate one
another.[25] In a phrasing that might have come out of Hobbes's *Leviathan*
Gordon concludes that "Human life has been cut off from its source and
thus it is limited, poor, small, bland, empty and worthless" (MN, IX: 185).[26]

---

[24] More and more young pioneers chose not to establish a family and bring up children.
Consequently, Gordon argues, they suffer from early aging symptoms, "their ill eyes, sick teeth, and
early baldness . . . are clear indications for this"; "Lack of Family Life" (1918), GWB, I: 475. See also
Gordon's critique of asceticism in MN, VIII: 171–172 and his discussion of contraception methods
in MN, X: 190–191. See also T: 112–121; Gad Ufaz, "The Woman and the Family in the Philosophy
of A. D. Gordon" [Heb.], *Iyynim Bitkumat Israel: Studies in Zionism, the Yishuv and the State of Israel*,
vol. 8 (1998), pp. 602–613.

[25] Gordon grants society a status of a second-order organic entity. "The significance of social
life for the formation of the individual," he argues, "is much more crucial, and mainly much more
profound than what we use to think . . . social life provides the fundamental basis for the unique
development of the individual. All his life the individual is produced by society, and if he gives something to society, he is only giving back what he got from society" (MN, IV.4: 106). Gordon comes
close here to Durkheim's position in his *On Suicide*. See Emile Durkheim, *On Suicide*, trans. Robin
Buss, London: Penguin, 2006, pp. 142–143. In other matters, too, Gordon's positions are close to
Durkheim's; see, for example, MN, III: 56, n. 12; IV: 79 n. 7; IV: 96 n. 28.

[26] In one of the most celebrated passages in the literature of modern political philosophy Thomas
Hobbes argues that in the state of nature, there is "no Arts; no Letters; no Society; and which is

These observations might lead to the conclusion that Gordon opposes cognition since it tears man from nature and thus leads to a life of misery, and
he embraces experience since it unifies man with nature and as such leads
to the supreme life. Indeed, just as there are several instances in MN where
Gordon speaks in condemnation of cognition, there are instances in which
he speaks in favor of experience.

Gordon, for example, identifies the supreme life with "supreme love," which
he sees as a pure experience of the expansion of man into nature as a whole.

> "The supreme love"—Gordon declares—"is not the contraction of the 'I' of
> the lover to make room for the 'I' of the beloved, but on the contrary: the
> expansion of the lover's life into the beloved's soul, as, for example, a loving
> mother dedicates her soul to that of her children . . . to the extent that man
> frees himself to a greater degree from his turtle-like life of contraction, his
> soul merges with the life of the world, he is sanctified by a supreme, natural,
> worldly, cosmic holiness, by the sanctity of the supreme idea, and he gains
> supreme love." (MN, XII: 210–211)

Gordon's seeming preference for experience over cognition is also evident in Gordon's quasi-autobiographical account of the tiller of the soil,
who through his toil experiences being on the verge of complete fusion
with nature. This experience is so pure and dense, Gordon argues, that it
cannot be spelled out by words, nor can it be captured by thought; only
silence can express it (MN, I: 32–33).[27] "At certain moments you seem to
merge with infinity," Gordon writes, "then you would be silent. Not only
speech, but also poetry and even thought seems like a desecration at such

---

worst of all, continuall feare, and danger of violent death; And the life of man, solitary, poore, nasty,
brutish, and short"; Thomas Hobbes, *Leviathan, or the Matter, Forme & Power of a Common—Wealth
Ecclesiasticall and Civill*, Harmondsworth, London: Penguin, 1968, *XIII*, p. 186.

[27] See also MN, V: 137–138, IX: 182–183, XI: 196, XIV: 225. Following the Belgian playwright and
poet Maurice Maeterlinck (Belgium–France, 1862–1949), Gordon claims that language is meant to
hide more than to reveal. See Maurice Maeterlinck, "Silence," in Maeterlinck, *The Treasure of the
Humble*, trans. Alfred Sutro, New York: Dodd, Mead & Company, 1903, pp. 7–8. A remarkably similar critique of language appears in the well-known essay "The Explicit and Allusive in Language"
(1915) by Hayim Nahman Bialik (Russian Empire–Germany–Land of Israel, 1873–1934), which was
influenced by Nietzsche's *On Truth and Lies in a Nonmoral Sense* (1896). See Azzan Yadin, "A Web of
Chaos: Bialik and Nietzsche on Language, Truth, and the Death of God," *Prooftexts*, 21: 2 (2001), pp.
179–203.

moments where you discover the secret of silence and its sanctity" (MN, I: 33).[28]

In this vein, in the sixth chapter of MN Gordon ends his comprehensive and meticulous comparison between experience and cognition in the following clear-cut conclusion: "not only in terms of scope but also, and most importantly, in terms of depth, experience is superior to cognition" (MN, VI: 146). Only experience, Gordon argues, provides man with a free and intuitive expression of being one "with this worldly, eternal creation" (MN, VI: 146).

Yet this apparent preference of experience over cognition, which appears in various places in MN, stands in striking contrast with the core of Gordon's metaphysics. From a metaphysical point of view, as we saw earlier, Gordon is committed to absolute equivalence between experience and cognition. For even if experience is chronologically prior to cognition (see, e.g., MN, III: 52–53), it is not metaphysically superior to it. For experience and cognition are anchored in two basic principles of reality: expansion and contraction, respectively, neither of which has precedence or priority over the other. Experience and cognition, Gordon declares emphatically as he clings to the metaphysical infrastructure of his thought, are "double-faceted aspects of one life" (MN, V: 165).

At this point in the discussion, two questions arise. First, how is it possible to metaphysically justify the assertion that life is both experience and cognition, given that they contradict each other? Or more generally, what justification could Gordon have for arguing that existence is based on contradiction? After all, from a logical point of view, if existence is one, it is inconceivable that it would be a thing and its opposite at the same time. Second, if experience and cognition are metaphysically equivalent to each other, why is it that at various places in MN Gordon presents experience as superior to cognition? In the next section, we will try to answer these questions by turning to explore what Gordon calls the "hidden intellect" (*sechel neelam*) of existence, which is the organizing principle of existence.

[28] Tracing what he calls the "retreat from the word" in modernity, George Steiner describes as follows the sanctification of silence, ". . . we look out of language not into darkness but light"; George Steiner, "The Retreat from the Word," in Steiner, *Language and Silence*, London: Faber & Faber, 1967, p. 40.

The "Hidden Intellect" and the Meaning of Contradictions in Existence and Human Life

As man is a segment of nature, the contradiction between the principle of expansion and the principle of contraction, which is embedded within nature as a whole, is also embedded within man. These principles find expression in human experience and cognition, respectively. The principle of contraction and the principle of expansion are described by Gordon as psychological forces that act upon the human psyche and stimulate it, forces that "create in their repetitive action the very essence of human life" (MN, VII: 156). But in man one can find not only the very existence of the "abysmal contradiction" (MN, III: 61) but also the meaning and goal of this contradiction. Our proximity to ourselves allows us easier access to the essence and role of contradiction in existence. "This contradiction," as Gordon puts it, "which we do not know how to settle and do not know what it means in the life of the world, finds enlightenment and sufficient elucidation and explication in human life" (MN, VII: 157).

The good life or the supreme life, Gordon argues, is not free from contradiction between contraction and expansion but is, rather, based on it:

> The desired human life, the life, to which the human soul aspires . . . is nothing but a fusion of the two attitudes: an attitude towards a life of contraction and an attitude towards a life of expansion. Contradiction is nothing but the driving force, which, like any force that gives rise to movement, contains opposites. Man, who embodies nature in its highest degree, seems to stand on the boundary between the life of contraction and life of expansion. His soul is divided into two worlds, which complement each other: a world of infinite contraction and a world of infinite expansion. The rotational motion between these opposites gives birth to a higher light in the soul. Thus, the soul might live within all the manifestations of her 'I' into all the manifestations of being and into all the infinity of being, to feel herself as a kind of 'I' of the whole being and to take part in the works of creation and world leadership. (MN, VII: 157–158)

Through concise and condensed language, Gordon reveals in this passage the role of contradiction in human life and the life of the world. The supreme life, he argues, is constant movement between the selfish contraction of oneself and the altruistic expansion and opening of the self to its surroundings. This movement is anchored in the general principle in nature according to which every force that gives rise to motion involves opposites. The constant movement between contraction and expansion characterizes not only supreme human life but also the life of nature in its entirety. Through constant movement between contraction and expansion man is carried toward unification with existence, which is itself a movement between opposites.

The supreme life, then, is not a life in which man is called to "negate his own self and to prefer instead the self of others" just as it is not a life in which man is called to magnify and glorify his "I," "like a parasitic plant," at the expense of others (MN, VII: 158). The supreme life, Gordon argues, is a continuous pendulum motion alternating between withdrawing into one's self, and extending it and reaching out to others. To illustrate this point, let us go back to the example of the mother's devotion to her offspring, hailed by Gordon as an exemplary instance of life at its highest. A mother who will devote all of herself to her children while neglecting her own physical and psychological needs will end up harming not only herself but also her offspring, who will not be able to gain her support. If, however, she devotes herself to her own Self while neglecting or even exploiting her children, she will end up harming not only her offspring but also herself, since not fulfilling her motherhood will result in a feeling of emptiness and unworthiness. Only through a pendulum motion alternating between concentration on her own needs and tending to the needs of her children can she reach the verge of complete unification with existence in its entirety. This pendulum motion is necessary, according to Gordon, to maintain the natural balance of human life. Extreme selfishness evokes discontent and arouses in man a desire for altruism and concern for others. Whereas boundless giving of oneself exhausts the "I" and results in a need for reattachment to egoistic interests.

The highest form of giving, according to Gordon, is a giving out of abundance and expansion of the I and not out of its contraction and shrinking. Supreme giving leads to supreme love, in which, as we saw earlier, the "I" of the lover is expanded through the beloved, as in the case of loving mothers.

The love of the mother for the fruit of her womb, a love, which is the only ultimate reward for all her sorrow and anguish and devotion of soul—is the symbol of supreme love! Here is the most beautiful, deep, and holy emotion in all of creation, and in all the depths of life. This emotion is the undivulged secret of nature, revealable only to he who partakes in the act of creation, in eternal life. (MN, XII: 211–210)[29]

The principle of movement out of contradiction stands at the center of Gordon's perception of existence. As such, it has significant implications not only in the moral realm but also in the epistemological realm. Indeed, even the relationship between cognition and experience—as epistemological manifestations of contraction and expansion—is distinctively dialectical. On the one hand, cognition and experience "feed and make a living," as Gordon put it, from different and opposing sources. Cognition "makes a living" from nature through the mediation of the senses, which supply it, in an almost mechanical way, with a massive accumulation of facts (MN, X: 187 n. 1), whereas experience "makes a vital livelihood from cosmic life itself, as if the stream of life of the worldly nature flows directly, unmediated, into human nature" (MN, X: 187 n. 1). Yet it is precisely due to the difference and negation between cognition and experience that they "complement and enhance each other" (MN, X: 186 n. 1). The more closely one knows nature, the more he may experience nature, and vice versa.[30]

The more comprehensive our understanding of the laws of nature and its structure, the better our cognition of how the elements that constitute the unity of nature mutually correspond. This cognition, Gordon argues, may enhance and enrich the experience of our "unification with everything" (MN, X: 186 n. 1). However, the experience may also increase and enrich cognition. For cognition may draw from the depth of man's world of experience new material for its investigations. Cognition, as Gordon puts it, "engages, processes and illuminates this material, actualizing its potential" (MN, X: 188 n. 1).[31]

---

[29] In identifying the secret of life with motherly love Gordon is close to Bergson, who argued in his *Creative Evolution* (1907) that "we have this sudden illumination before certain forms of maternal love, so striking, and in most animals so touching, observable even in the solicitude of the plant for its seed. This love, in which some have seen the great mystery of life, may possibly deliver us life's secret. It shows us each generation leaning over the generation that shall follow. It allows us a glimpse of the fact that the living being is above all a thoroughfare, and that the essence of life is in the movement by which life is transmitted"; Henri Bergson, *Creative Evolution: Humanity's Natural Creative Impulse*, trans. Arthur Mitchell, New York: The Modern Library, 1944 [1907], p. 128.

[30] In the eighth chapter of MN Gordon presents the final goal of culture as the mutual development of scientific cognition and religious experience. In this, he stands against a prevailing tendency to treat science and religion as two conflicting or at least incompatible branches of culture. See also MN, VIII: 168–169; ibid., n. 10; IX: 173–174.

[31] Gordon's position here falls in line with the study of the subconscious that was developed by Sigmund Freud (Austria–London, 1856–1939) and Jung. Still, Gordon's strong reluctance to reduce a person's psychic world to his sexual desires (MN, I: 24) and his deep religiosity bring him closer to Jung than to Freud. Gordon's claim that experience precedes cognition (MN, VI: 143–144) is also

Figure 3.1. Wooden bridge over the outlet of the Jordan River from the Sea of Galilee, 1920s. On the opposite bank Degania can be seen, the settlement where Gordon spent his final years, and where he was laid to rest. Photo: Yaacov Ben-Dov. Album of Ben-Zion Israeli (Tchernomirsky), Yad Ben-Zvi Photo Archives.

In his call for a rational inquiry of man's world of subconscious experience, Gordon precedes the "depth psychology" that developed after his death. This precedence is evident in his words to his daughter, Yael, on his deathbed in Degania (see Figure 3.1). In a special issue of *Hapoel Hatzair*, published on the tenth anniversary of Gordon's death, Yael recounts that in his last days he drafted his essay "Idea or Illusion" [1922], which was intended to preface

consistent with Jung's claim that our consciousness emerges from the depths of our subconscious and feeds from it. See, for example, Carl Gustav Jung, *Memories, Dreams, Reflections*, New York: Vintage Books, 1989, pp. 42–56. Jung's claim that under the individual subconscious one can find collective subconscious may also be consistent both with Gordon's concept of the "I" (MN, IV.4: 106) and his genealogy of religion, which is developed in the fourth chapter of MN. In this context, Bergman argued that unlike Freud, who above all feared the outburst of the id, Gordon was chiefly afraid that the extreme restraint of the "I" will result in a depletion of man's psychic world; Bergman, "Introduction to Man and Nature," GWB, II: 18. On the polemics between Freud and Jung over the libido and the subconscious that led in 1913 to a rift between them, see Anthony Stevens, *Jung: A Very Short Introduction*, New York: Oxford University Press, 2001, pp. 18–25; Peter Gay, *Freud: A Life for Our Time*, New York: WW Norton & Company, 2006, pp. 225–243.

the complete edition of all his writings. Her father, she writes, described the main idea of this essay, as follows:

> A Day will come, and man will deepen the exploration of his soul. Since he diverted his thought to the nature outside himself, his soul remains, to this day, almost entirely obscure to him. Man has made significant and ground-breaking discoveries in natural sciences, marvelous innovations in science and technology. However, it is only when man explores his soul that he discovers within himself powerful hidden forces that enrich humanity and evolves humanity's inner psychological culture to match the progress in science and technology. He compared humanity, in this sense, to an individual, who at the dawn of his life explores the surrounding environment and diverts his attention away from his inner world. Only when he is older . . . he begins to pay attention to his soul as well as to his inner world . . . Gordon described to me with great enthusiasm the glorious future of man when he discovers the treasures of his soul, and how his hidden light will break through to illuminate and improve human relations until they reach the level of "New Heaven and New Earth."[32] Finally, he would add, if we believe in the possibility of such great progress of the human spirit in the future, we must begin to direct our life towards this great future . . .[33]

Cognition and experience—Gordon summarizes his position—participate in "a circular process. The more cognition develops and expands, so too experience develops and expands, and vice versa. When a man knows more, his experience [makes him] strive to live more, to live a full and new life at every moment" (MN, IX: 173). Moreover, as this repetitive circular interaction between cognition and experience expresses the all-encompassing repetitive circular interaction between contraction and expansion, it "reveals the hidden light in life" (MN, X: 190)[34]

"The hidden" (neelam) is a concept that indicates the insight according to which existence contradicts itself in order to maintain its identity with itself. This insight lies beyond the realm of cognition because it deviates from the law of contradiction, according to which nothing can be at once a thing

[32] Compare Isaiah 65:17.
[33] Yael Gordon, "Memoirs and Impressions," *Hapoel Hatzair*, January 29, 1932, III: 16–17, p. 14. See also, in this context, Bergman's comparison of Gordon's thought to ideas associated with depth psychology in GWB, II: 17–20; Fuehrer, *New Man*, pp. 70–71.
[34] See also "Idea or Illusion" [1922], GWA, V: 224–225.

and its opposite. However, Gordon argues that even though the "the hidden" cannot be known—it can be lived: "Man does not comprehend in his mind and will never comprehend the hidden, but he will live it as a moment of creation, of supreme union, of supreme correspondence" (MN, IV.5: 112). The knowledge of the "the hidden" cannot be achieved through the regular intellect based on the law of contradiction but only through the "hidden intellect" (*sechel neelam*), which provides us with the "absolute truth." According to the "absolute truth" or the "naked truth," existence is constructed from the logical contradictions it contains and on which it is founded. Without the "supreme truth," which stands above the "truth" of cognition, "there is no place for supreme thought, supreme poetry . . . supreme life" (MN, XI: 206).

In Gordon's philosophical system, "the hidden intellect" functions as a mediating concept between cognition and experience, which constitute the most fundamental dichotomy of life. As such, the "hidden intellect" is for Gordon the "geometric point" of existence "by whose motion all forms are formed" (MN, II: 42; see also V: 135).

Evidence of the significance Gordon attributes to the concept of the "hidden intellect" can be found in his decision to identify it with the concept of "God" in his philosophical system.[35] The "hidden intellect" or God gives meaning to contradictions inherent in existence by introducing the movement between them as the organizing principle of existence. As a meaning-giving concept, Gordon argues, the "hidden intellect" or God cannot be situated in the epistemological dichotomy between Being and Nothingness (MN, V: 129–130).[36] Just as the "hidden intellect" or God does not fall under the categories of time and space, neither does it fall under the categories of Being and Nothingness. Therefore, the question of whether the "hidden intellect" or God exists, Gordon argues, is meaningless. In the same vein, the declaration of the death of God is absurd. "The hidden will never die," declares Gordon, "even if all the thinkers and all the scientists in the world will argue that everything is visible and known and clear" (MN, IV.2: 94).[37]

[35] Gordon uses twice in MN the word "or" to indicate equivalence between the "hidden intellect" and God (MN, V: 134), and in addition he switches between the two concepts (MN, V: 133).

[36] "It is possible to call 'the hidden' God," Gordon declares, "but it cannot be called Being or Nothingness in the same way these concepts are used within the limits of cognition. It is clear that the blindness of 'the hidden' cannot be grasped by cognition more than its rationality. Therefore, it is possible to speak about 'hidden intellect,' but not in the same sense that the concept of 'intellect' has within the limits of cognition" (MN, IV.3: 100).

[37] Nietzsche's famous proclamation of the death of God (*The Gay Science*, section 125) does not prevent Gordon from attributing to him "a deep spiritual yearning for supreme morality" (MN, IV.2: 92). For Gordon, Nietzsche's heresy is a "great heresy" since it is anchored in a commitment to a comprehensive value system and self-overcoming. Nietzsche's engagement with the Absolute, even

The unique status of the "hidden intellect" or God necessitates approaching it with a unique terminology. Instead of asking whether the "hidden intellect" or God exists, one should ask whether he is *Moha*? The word *Moha* is coined in Hebrew by Gordon to denote that which lies beyond the dichotomy between Being and Nothingness. Unlike *Havayah* (experience), *Moha* did not become part of contemporary Hebrew although no alternative was ever proposed. The nearest English translation to Gordon's question is as follows: Is the "hidden intellect" required?

Gordon answers in the affirmative to this metaphysical question ("ethereal question," as he calls it). Cognition, he argues, cannot attain the "hidden intellect," because it "has no relation to space, time and so on" (MN, V: 132–133). Nevertheless, there is a certain closeness between cognition and the "hidden intellect" due to the fact that they both offer us a map of reality that allows us to navigate our lives more successfully (MN, V: 138).

While cognition perceives the organizing principles of particular things within existence, the "hidden intellect" perceives the contours of existence in its entirety. Even if cognition cannot perceive the "hidden intellect" as it perceives other objects and concepts, its closeness to the "hidden intellect" allows cognition to perceive or grasp it more softly. The "hidden intellect" is indeed "hidden," but it is also "intellect," and as such, it functions as the interface point between cognition and experience. Gordon is well aware of the logical absurdity ("logical embarrassment" as he calls it) of the concept of "hidden intellect" but argues that other alternatives for exploring what is beyond the limits of cognition—such as absolute coincidence or blind will—are even more absurd because they are wholly contrary to cognition and do not complete it like the "hidden intellect." The "hidden intellect," as opposed to blind coincidence, is "more logical, more plausible, and closer to life" (MN, V: 136), Gordon concludes.

All the excerpts examined earlier reveal the "hidden intellect" to be an *Aufhebung* (sublation) of the dichotomy of cognition and experience. These contradictory moments are reconciled in the higher synthesis of the "hidden intellect" where they are both preserved and changed through

if not accompanied by a belief in the existence of God, gives his philosophy according to Gordon a distinctly religious dimension. See MN, I: 26–28, VII: 160 n. 10; Friedrich Nietzsche, *The Gay Science: With a Prelude in German Rhymes and an Appendix of Songs*, trans. Josefine Nauckhoff and Adrian Del Caro, Cambridge: Cambridge University Press, 2001, pp. 119–120. See also Yuval Jobani, "The True Teacher: Jewish Secularism in the Philosophy of A.D. Gordon," in Jan Woleński, Yaron M. Senderowicz, and Józef Bremer (eds.), *Jewish and Polish Philosophy*, Krakow: Austeria Publishing House, 2013, pp. 198–216.

dialectical interplay. It is because the "hidden intellect" embraces existence as a whole, including all its inherent negations and contradictions, that Gordon identifies it, as we saw earlier, with the concept of "God" in his philosophy.[38]

Here the question posed in the previous section resurfaces: If experience and cognition are metaphysically equivalent to each other, why is it that at various places in MN Gordon presents experience as superior to cognition? The preference of experience over cognition might seem rhetorical; Gordon, it can be argued, acts here as one who attempts to straighten a crooked stick by bending it not merely straight, but beyond the line of straightness, so that when it relaxes it will remain straight. To free man from the suffocating grasp of cognition Gordon makes a special effort to consolidate and fortify the status of experience by presenting it as if it were superior to cognition, solely to regain the precious balance between cognition and experience or between contraction and expansion, which constitutes the very essence of the "supreme life of man" (MN, IV.7: 121).

A careful reading of MN, however, suggests a better answer. Gordon uses the concept of experience not only to denote the negation of cognition but also to denote the dialectical synthesis between cognition and experience, that is, to denote what he usually calls the "hidden intellect." In other words, Gordon uses the concept of experience in two separate ways. In the narrower sense—which was examined in detail earlier in this chapter—he uses the concept to refer to the concept of expansion. In the broader sense—which we shall explore next—he uses the concept to refer to the dialectical fusion of contraction and expansion. Each of these usages of the term "experience" (havayah) includes two layers: an ontological layer that signifies existence itself, and an epistemological layer that signifies how existence is perceived.

Gordon presents the broader sense of the concept of experience near the end of the sixth chapter of MN. The subordination of cognition to the law of contradiction, he states there, does not allow it to perceive "the transition from a life of expansion to a life of contraction" (MN, VI: 152), and vice versa. Indeed, cognition cannot perceive any other natural transition such as the transition from inanimate to plant or from life to death. It is the obligation of cognition to rationality that prevents it from perceiving "the moment in which a thing is in two states simultaneously, the moment in which a thing

---

[38] MN, IV.3: 100; V: 133; and V: 134. See also "Passing Thoughts and Meditations" (date not indicated), GWA, V: 187.

seems to move to two opposing sides simultaneously as if to say the moment in which life comes into being" (MN, III: 58)

Experience, on the other hand, connects and unites what from the point of view of cognition is separate and detached. As such, Gordon identifies experience with "the hidden intellect" (MN, VI: 153). Nature as "a place of transition" is the "ultimate secret" of Nature. "This secret," Gordon argues, "is hidden from cognition, and cognition has no chance of ever discovering it. The secret is concealed in experience, in the hidden intellect of man" (MN, VI: 153). The hidden intellect, as we have seen, indicates the constant movement in existence between contraction and expansion, which finds expression in the human sphere in a constant alternation between cognition and experience. As such, the hidden intellect is also the point of interface between the worldly nature and the individual. The hidden intellect of man is in fact part of the hidden intellect of existence as a whole. In this vein, Gordon writes that "the hidden intellect of existence seems to be giving up its right [to create life] to the hidden intellect of man" (MN, VIII: 169). Therefore, man's striving to express in his private life the fusion between his "hidden intellect" and the "hidden intellect" of existence in its entirety is "the source of all the supreme aspirations of the human spirit" (MN, VIII: 169).

In fact, it is only the broader meaning of the concept of experience that enables us to understand, from a systematic point of view, numerous statements appearing throughout MN (presented earlier in this chapter) in which Gordon seems to give preference to experience over cognition. Among the statements on which the broader meaning of the concept of experience sheds light is Gordon's assertion that "cognition is but a part of experience; it is a visible light that comes from the hidden light of the experience. Experience is life, the foundation for all human perception and all human light. It perceives the absolute generality of worldly existence and the absolute unification of all manifestations of being. Without experience, without life there is nothing" (MN, VIII: 167). Under the narrow meaning of the term "experience" this assertion cannot be understood. Cognition is an expression of contraction and as such cannot be part of the experience, which is an expression of expansion. Only the broader meaning of the concept of experience enables us to understand, from a systematic point of view, the preference of experience over cognition. As indicating the dialectical synthesis between cognition and experience (in its narrow sense), experience (in its broader sense) stands above cognition, which lacks such dialectical depth.

So far, we have traced the way in which Gordon articulates his philosophical positions under the classic dialectical pattern of thesis, antithesis, and synthesis. But Gordon does not place the dialectic pattern above any other philosophical principle or moral value. On the contrary, as emerges from an intriguing passage from the third chapter of MN, Gordon seeks to subject the pattern of dialectical thought to a moral standard higher than any metaphysical idea or principle. Indeed, as we shall see, Gordon seeks to give the dialectical pattern distinct moral content.

During the discussion on the inability of cognition to settle the question of the meaning of existence, Gordon argues that

> in the realm of abstract thought, powered by the very detachment from life, contradictions can serve as building blocks: thesis, antithesis, and synthesis, for within abstract realms of the unreal—like the realms of poetic, artistic imagination, or scholarly logic—contradictions appear as multi-faceted, multi-colored impressive phenomena. In [real] life however, beings suffer contradiction's destructive, even lethal consequences that cause sorrow, anguish, blood, and tears and prove to be a death potion rather than a life preserving potion. (MN, III: 67)[39]

In this important passage, which has been omitted by Bergman and Shochat in their standard edition of the works of Gordon, Gordon staunchly rejects the blind adoption of dialectical thought. Dialectical thinking, Gordon warns, may provide imaginary justifications for committing unequivocally immoral acts that bring about "sorrow, anguish, blood, and tears" (MN, III: 67). Following Tolstoy, Gordon highlights in this context his rejection of modern art, which involves, in his view, decadence and moral degeneration.[40] In this context Gordon came out against Marxists who employ Hegelian dialectic in order to justify violence unparalleled in its cruelty in all of human history.[41] In contrast to these positions, Gordon argues that

---

[39] Gordon's wording here echoes R. Yehoshua Ben-Levi's saying, "If you are worthy, it [the Torah] is a drug of life; if not, a drug of death" (Talmud Bavli, Yoma, 72b). The Late Hebrew term *Sam HaChaim* (the drug of life) resonates the Akkadian term *Shammu Balati* (the plant of life) that indicates a plant that can restore youth to a man, and it is parallel to the biblical term *Etz HaChaim* (tree of life). See Moshe David Cassuto, "*Etz HaChaim*" [Heb.], in *Encyclopaedia Biblica*, Jerusalem: Bialik Institute 1971, vol. VI, pp. 328–330.

[40] See, for example, MN, I: 28.

[41] See, for example, MN, IX: 185. On Gordon's interpretation of Marxism and his critique of it see Schweid, *The Individual*, pp. 143–148; Josef Schächter, *The Philosophy of Aharon David Gordon* [Heb.], Tel Aviv: Dvir ,1957, pp. 51–55; In this context Turner argues that "in his writings after World War I, Gordon's anti-Marxist stance must obviously be seen as a response to the Bolshevik Revolution

dialectical thought must be subordinate to life. In fact, like any other tool, the value of the dialectical pattern is determined by its use. It must be rejected and replaced when it harms and destroys life, and it should be embraced when it strengthens and builds life. Thus, unlike Nietzsche, for example, Gordon is unwilling to use any philosophical idea or program to legitimize actions that are beyond good and evil (MN, VII: 158; XIII: 214–215). Life stands above any theoretical system or scheme. Immoral acts lead to "sorrow, anguish, blood, and tears," that is, to the diminution of life. And as such, Gordon rejects as absurd any speculative attempt to justify such acts through the dialectical method.

Gordon's turn to the dialectical worldview enabled him to cope with the tensions and contradictions that had bruised and shaken his soul to the core. At the source of this upheaval was the sense of rupture he suffered as a result of his constant movement between his longing for an experiential union with existence and his aspiration to attain an intellectual grasp of it. The dialectical worldview has enabled Gordon to anchor his psychological struggles and spiritual aspirations in the metaphysical contradiction between contraction and expansion, and as such to give cosmic meaning to the drama of his personal life. Gordon discovered that instead of alienating to one of the two founding elements of the "I," the dialectical worldview allows him to fully realize both of them. The reason for this is that in their dialectical swinging pendulum movement, the experience and cognition do not harm or destroy each other but, rather, strengthen and build each other.

in Russia, as well as to the Marxist Zionist ideologies of the pioneering youth movement *Hashomer Hatzair*, led by Meir Yaari (Galicia–Israel, 1897–1987) and Yaakov Hazan (Russian Empire–Israel, 1899–1992), and the *Kibbutz Hameuhad* settlement movement led by Yitzhak Tabenkin (Russian Empire–Israel, 1887–1971). But Tabenkin, a devout Marxist, was already a prominent figure in the earlier period of the Second Aliyah, and the *Hapoel Hatzair* party, with which Gordon identified, was vehemently anti-Marxist and even saw itself as the primary alternative to the predominantly Marxist World Union of *Poalei Tzion*"; Joseph Yossi Turner, "Philosophy and Praxis in the Thought of Aharon David Gordon," *The Journal of Jewish Thought and Philosophy* 24: 1, 2016, p. 134, n. 42. According to Rotenstreich, in his critique Gordon relied on the mechanistic-deterministic reading of Marx, which perceives man in economic terms while ignoring the existential-spiritual dimension of human life. The reason for this is that Marx's early writings from the early 1840s, in which he reveals the humanistic and existential dimensions of his thought, were almost unknown in Gordon's lifetime. See Nathan Rotenstreich, "Discussions on Marx" [Heb.], in Rotenstreich, *Issues in Philosophy*, Tel Aviv: Dvir, 1962, pp. 232–236; Nathan Rotenstreich, "Interview with Muki Tsur," *Sdemot: Literary Digest of the Kibbutzim Movement*, vol. 61 (1976), pp. 71–73; see also Sara Strassberg-Dayan, *Individual, Nation and Mankind: The Conception of Man in the Teachings of A.D. Gordon and Rabbi Abraham I. Hacohen Kook* [Heb.], Tel Aviv: Hakibbutz Hameuchad, 1995, pp. 122–125. On the similarities between Gordon's concept of self-education and Marxist and neo-Marxist stances see Fuehrer, *New Man*, pp. 177–179.

Gordon's philosophical work strongly resonates with the Hegelian dialectic that was widely disseminated among and appropriated by Russian thinkers and intellectuals,[42] especially by members of the Narodnik movement whose call to "go to the people [*narod*]" has left a mark on Gordon.[43] Many of the young Russian intelligentsia who belonged to, or associated with, this revolutionary movement were torn between their longing for the purity and simplicity of peasant life and their attraction to scientific research, which they tried to harness to improve the lives of the peasants by eliminating disease, hunger, and scarcity. And in an attempt to grasp the rope at both ends they sought to reshape themselves as "educated-peasants" who combine, in the vein of the Hegelian dialectic paradigm, a rational cognition of nature and a religious fusion with it.[44] In this spirit, for example, the agronomist Alexander Nikolayevich Englegardt (Russia, 1832–1893) tried to establish in the late 1870s an exemplary agricultural commune on his modest estate in

[42] On the profound influence Wilhelm Friedrich Hegel (Stuttgart–Berlin, 1770–1831) had on the Russian intellectual life, and on the wealth of different and contradictory interpretations of his philosophy—mainly by liberal Westernizers, but also by conservative Slavophiles, see Andrzej Walicki, *The Slavophile Controversy: History of a Conservative Utopia in Nineteenth-Century Russian Thought*, trans. Hilda Andrews-Rusiecka, New York: Oxford University Press, 1975, pp. 287–455; Andrzej Walicki, *The Flow of Ideas: Russian Thought from the Enlightenment to the Religious-Philosophical Renaissance*, trans. Jolanta Kozak and Hilda Andrews-Rusiecka, Frankfurt am Main: Peter Lang, 2015, pp. 201–222. See also Isaiah Berlin, "A Remarkable Decade," in Berlin, *Russian Thinkers*, New York: Penguin, 2013, pp. 168–169.

[43] About three thousand members of the Narodnik movement responded to Herzen's call to "go to the people" but failed to integrate among the peasants, who treated them with suspicion and distaste. Following the government's harsh crackdown on the Narodniks after the assassination of Tsar Alexander II [Alexander Nikolayevich Romanov] in 1881 the movement disintegrated. The Narodniks were tried in mass show trials as part of their persecution; in the largest of these trials, which was held in 1877, 193 young revolutionaries were tried (seventy-five of them died, committed suicide, or lost their sanity during the trial). On the history and ideology of the Narodnik movement as well as the main figures of the movement see Berlin, "Russian Populism," in Berlin, *Russian Thinkers*, pp. 240–272; Richard Wortman, *The Crisis of Russian Populism*, New York: Cambridge University Press, 2008; James Billington, *Mikhailovsky and Russian Populism*, London: Oxford University Press, 1958; Venturi Franco, *Roots of Revolution: A History of the Populist and Socialist Movements in Nineteenth-Century Russia*, New York: Alfred A. Knopf, 1960; Yitzhak Maor, "The Popular Revolutionaries ('Narodniks') and the Jews" [Heb.], in Maor, *The Jewish Question in the Liberal and Revolutionary Movement in Russia 1914–1890*, Jerusalem: Bialik Institute, 1964, pp. 105–115; Jonathan Frankel, *Prophecy and Politics: Socialism, Nationalism, and the Russian Jews, 1862–1917*, Cambridge: Cambridge University Press, 1984; Rafi Tsirkin-Sadan, *Jewish Letters at the Pushkin Library: Yossef Haim Brenner's Thought and Its Connection to Russian Literature and Thought* [Heb.], Jerusalem: Bialik Institute 2013, pp. 49–56; Izhak Schnell, "Nature and Environment in the Socialist-Zionist Pioneers' Perceptions: A Sense of Desolation," *Ecumene*, 4: 1 (1997), pp. 69–85.

[44] Gordon's call for the establishment of a dialectical interaction between the individual and society also echoes modes of thinking prevalent in the Narodnik movement (MN, IV.4: 106). The Narodniki writer Nikolai Nikolaievich Zlatovratsky (Russia, 1845–1911), for example, argued that the old social order granted man community but deprived him of freedom (thesis), while the modern individualism that replaced it granted man freedom but deprived him of community (antithesis). Whereas in the third stage—which the Narodniks are struggling to achieve—these two elements, communality on the one hand and personal freedom on the other, will merge (synthesis). See Wortman, *The Crisis*

Smolensk province. In his commune young intelligentsia sought to acquire rural lifestyles while educating the peasantry and bringing to them the fruits of scientific inquiry to improve their living standard.[45]

I believe that if Gordon's dialectical sensitivity were to be traced backward, it would be found in the Bible. Beyond the influence of various Russian readings and appropriations of Hegel's philosophy, the dialectical thought of Gordon developed under the aegis of the Latter Prophets. The reason for this is that the roots of the Hegelian dialectic—in particular, Hegel's idea of "the cunning of history"—are not to be found in ancient Greek literature but, rather, in the biblical. As pointed out by Amos Funkenstein, Hegel's dialectical thought should be read as a metamorphosis of medieval (Jewish and Christian) versions of the original theodicy developed by the prophets of Israel in the face of the destruction of the First Temple. This theodicy adopted the dialectical contradiction as its organizing principle and clung to it in order to claim that the victory of the enemies of Israel and the destruction of the Temple are not to be taken as evidence of Yahweh's weakness and failure but, rather, as a manifestation of his power and control.[46] The enemies of Israel, although unaware of their rule, act in the service of God as an instrument of punishment and purification for the people of Israel. As Isaiah put it, "Ha! Assyria, rod of my anger, in whose hand, as a staff, is My fury! . . . Howbeit he meaneth not so, neither doth his heart think so" (Isaiah 10:5, 7).[47]

At the culmination of MN Gordon resorts to a prophetic style, weaving together a vast web of intertextual references to the Jewish canon. In the first chapter of MN, for example, Gordon establishes a prophetic tone of "a watchman unto the house of Israel" by repetitive use of the term "son of man"

---

of Russian Populism, pp. 118–119. On Zlatovratsky's life, work, and influence on the Narodnik movement, see Wortman, pp. 101–136.

[45] Englegardt's *Letters from the Country* [1872–1877] provides a colorful and insightful portrait of Imperial Russia's rural countryside after the great reforms of Alexander II. For a selection of Engelhardt's letters, which had an enormous impact on the circle of intelligence at the time, see Aleksandr Nikolaevich Englegardt, *Aleksandr Nikolaevich Engelgardt's Letters from the Country, 1872–1887*, trans. and ed. Cathy A. Frierson, New York: Oxford University Press, 1993. On Englehardt's life and thought, see also Wortman, *The Crisis of Russian Populism*, pp. 35–60.

[46] See Amos Funkenstein, "Maimonides: Political Theory and Realistic Messianism," in Funkenstein, *Perceptions of Jewish History*, Berkeley: University of California Press, 1993, pp. 131–155.

[47] While the translation of verse 5 is from the new Jewish Publication Society translation of the Hebrew Bible (1985), in verse 7 I preferred the King James translation, which renders the Hebrew more literally.

(*ben adam*), which is a characteristic term of the prophet Ezekiel.[48] But it is possible that even if he was not aware of it, it is most of all his embracement of the dialectical mode of thinking that expresses the deepest biblical infrastructure of his thought. The reason for this is that the Bible, as Gordon himself stated in another context, "is hidden so deeply in our souls, compressed beneath such a burden of all that we have received from others, that we do not always see it. [...] We think that by discovering in the Bible new ideas we interpret it; however, the opposite is true: the visible Bible is an interpretation of the hidden Bible that lies within our soul."[49]

[48] The term *ben adam* appears 107 times in the Bible, the majority (ninety-three times) appear in the Book of Ezekiel.

[49] "Third letter" [1914], GWA, IV: 315

4

A Religion of Nature

Gordon's Religious Commitment to the Protection of Nature

"It is widely believed that the time of religion is over, but in fact, and
in depth its time has not yet come." (MN, IV.5: 113–114)

The dawn of day. A group of young radicals who arrived in the Land of Israel
a short time ago from the Russian Empire emerge in an easy and confident
step from the last shadows of the night and its coolness. On this day, fate is in
their favor, for they managed to find work as pit diggers in almond tree plan-
tations. "The work is contract-based, with a set price paid for each pit," writes
one of the members of the group. "Each worker gets a row of pits and quickly
and vigorously digs his pits to earn many Matliks [low-value Ottoman
coins]."[1] Among the young laborers, most of them in their early twenties, a
noticeably older one stands out. He is of medium height, and although his
beard is gray, a youthful sparkle shines from his eyes. He was the "old man,"
as they nicknamed Gordon, who was already forty-eight years old when he
immigrated to the Land of Israel to work as a farmer, even though he had
never done any manual labor before. He looked like one of them, working
enthusiastically with all of his bodily and mental forces. However, he was different, and his work was different:

> Pioneers who finish digging their rows run with their hoes on their
> shoulders to secure new rows. After some time, the latecomers also run
> to grab new rows, but they are late—those who came before them had al-
> ready taken all the rows in the plantation until there were none left. A fierce

---

[1] Zvi Suchovolsky, "The Man and the Friend," in Mordecai Kusnir (ed.), *A.D. Gordon: Reminiscences and Appreciations* [Heb.], Tel Aviv: Histadrut HaOvdim, 1947, pp. 36–37.

The First Jewish Environmentalist. Yuval Jobani, Oxford University Press. © Oxford University Press 2024.
DOI: 10.1093/oso/9780197617977.003.0004

quarrel breaks out between the former and the latter. Inadvertently you suddenly look up and see Gordon standing in one of the first rows intently digging his pits, fashioning each like a perfect work of art with walls meticulously planed, beautifully smooth and straight. Gordon pays no attention, nor does he hear the quarrel; he is busy with his work of God. A pang of shame assaults your heart, and you retire from the quarrelsome crowd.[2]

Zvi Suchovolsky (Russian Empire–Israel, 1886–1968), who wrote this passage, emigrated from Bialystok to the Land of Israel at the age of eighteen and worked with Gordon in the vineyards and orchards of Petah Tikva and Rehovot. Suchovolsky asserts that the description of Gordon's work as religious work is not metaphorical but reflects Gordon's continued striving "to gain a new feeling through work" (ibid., p. 36).[3] Gordon's work, he maintains, was a kind of "pure prayer," during which he

did not notice anything around him, neither the landlord nor anyone else. He worked with awe and reverence, his meager body swaying back and forth at work, his thin hands powerfully rising and falling with every strike of his hoe, heavy beads of sweat dripping from his face on to his old beard and his eyes shining with some special flame, a holy flame! Even Gordon's moments of rest were immersed in holiness,

moments in which Gordon's facial expression reminded Suchovolsky of the "pure, calm and serene facial expression of an ultra-Orthodox Jew following his ancestor's religion on the Day of Atonement during the concluding service (*Ne'ila*), confident that he is indeed forgiven by God."[4] Gordon's photograph, taken in Degania in 1920, echoes Suchovolsky's description of Gordon's agricultural work as "pure prayer" (see Figure 4.1).
Similar descriptions recur in other accounts of pioneers who worked with Gordon. Mordechai Charizman (Russian Empire–Israel, 1884–1978), for

---

[2] Ibid., p. 37. Berl Katznelson (Russian Empire–Land of Israel, 1887–1944), who shared his tiny room in Kinneret with Gordon during WWI, notes that at the time of the Second Aliyah the number of pits each pioneer could dig in one day was known to all, and it was held as the "glory and honor" of each pioneer; Berl Katznelson, *The Second Aliya: Lectures for the Socialist Youth (1928)* [Heb.], eds. Anita Shapira and Naomi Abir, Tel-Aviv: Am-Oved, 1990, p. 93.
[3] Suchovolsky, "The Man and the Friend," p. 36.
[4] Suchovolsky, "The Man and the Friend," p. 36.

Figure 4.1. Gordon working in the vegetable garden in Degania, 1920. This photograph was taken probably without Gordon's consent. Gordon disapproved of photographs as bourgeois props, intended to gloss over reality and to idealize the hardship of the pioneers in the Land of Israel. Unknown photographer, courtesy of Degania Alef archive.

example, a writer and translator who was closely associated with Gordon during the time he lived in Ein Ganim, wrote that

One always felt inspired in his presence, in conversation—and even long afterwards—by the lasting impression that he had a God, the king of the world, whom he saw face to face, spirit to spirit, whom he loves, loves and worships with all his heart, with all his soul and with all his might . . . with a hoe.[5]

Indeed, Gordon regarded his hoe as a sacred object. He carefully guarded it in his room when he was not working, making sure to carry it wherever he went and used to lean on it while conversing with friends. In his last days, when he was forced to part from his "holy hoe" (as he used to call it) due to his severe illness, he took it as an omen indicating the end of his life story.[6]

Martin Buber placed these semi-hagiographic accounts on par with his philosophical system.[7] Buber argues that Gordon's life and deeds not only

[5] See Mordechai Charizman, "In Ein Ganim" [Heb.], in Kushnir, *Reminiscences and Appreciations*, p. 48. Tehiya Lieberson (Russian Empire–Israel, 1885–1949), a leading labor activist, described Gordon as "a true religious Jew . . . an enthusiastic and dedicated farmer who approached his work with reverence"; Tehiya Lieberson, *The Story of My Life* [Heb.], Tel Aviv: Mifaley Tarbut Vechinuch, 1970, p. 36. "Work was sacred to him," stated the poet Jacob Fichman (Russian Empire–Israel, 1881–1958), "it was for him the basis not only for the happiness of the individual but also for taking root in life and cleaving to nature, to God. . . . Work was for him a cosmic action which can unite all the separate atoms"; Jacob Fichman, "First to Redemption" [Heb.], in Kushnir, *Reminiscences and Appreciations*, pp. 141–142. The writer David Maletz (Russian Empire–Israel, 1899–1981) declared that Gordon was "one of the luminaries of the age, one of those spiritual men who were privileged to behold their God face to face. He revealed the source of light and vitality in everything and in himself. He revealed the supreme radiance that binds everything together in great secrecy and binds him with everything. The whole universe is in him, and he is in the universe. Enchanted and enshrined he stands within the universe, within nature, and his soul sheds its tough outer shells that crumble and fall away. His soul is new, big, bright, immersed in everything. Silence is praise to it. It is impossible to express it in words, even poetry desecrates it. Just lift the hoe and work, work, with all your soul, work is the great secret. Everything is united and bound together . . . since light and acceptance are in the soul within, and it casts its spell on everything"; David Maletz, "With A.D. Gordon (10-Year Anniversary of Gordon's Death)" [Heb.], in Maletz, *Around the Essence—A Profile of a Generation*, Tel Aviv: Mifaley Tarbut Vechinuch, 1970, p. 62. On Gordon's continued influence on Maletz see Nurit Feinstein, *Repercussions of Identity: The Third Aliya Writers Yehudah Ya'ari, David Maletz and Others, as Thinkers and Identity-Molders in Pre-State Hebrew Literature* [Heb.], Tel-Aviv: Hakibbutz Hameuchad, 2015, pp. 63–64.

[6] Gordon's use of the phrase "the sacred hoe" is mentioned in a letter from Berl Katznelson to Sarah Shmuckler (Russian Empire–Land of Israel, 1889–1919) and Leah Meron (Russian Empire–Land of Israel, 1888–1967). See Yehuda Sharett (ed.), *Katznelson's Letters (1915–1918)* [Heb.], Tel Aviv: Am Oved, 1961, vol. 1, letter 34, p. 111. On Gordon's strong attachment to his working tools, see Leah Pelled, *The Reception of Aharon David Gordon's Philosophy and Personality in Hebrew literature and Periodicals (1904–1948)* [Heb.], PhD thesis, Jerusalem: The Hebrew University, 2004, p. 51.

[7] Such semi-hagiographic accounts of Gordon can be found in abundance in memorial volumes on Gordon. See, for example, Kushnir, *Reminiscences and Appreciations* (which include the Charizman's and Suchovolsky's accounts of Gordon discussed earlier); *Arakhin: An Anthology in Memory of Gordon*, [Heb.], editor not indicated, Tel Aviv: Gordonia Maccabi, 1942; and the special volume of *Hapoel Hatzair* journal commemorating the ten-year anniversary of Gordon's death (*Hapoel Hatzair*, January 29, 1932, III: 16–17). As indicated in the first chapter, these accounts should be placed in the wider context of the Hassidic hagiographic literature on one hand and the centrality of hagiography in nineteenth-century Russian literature on the other. Leo Tolstoy, who had an ambivalent attitude toward hagiography, was himself the subject of hagiographic accounts by his followers. In this vein, Valentin Bulgakov (Russia, 1886–1966) presented Tolstoy as a kind of a saint whose every act or utterance encapsulates a significant spiritual meaning. See Valentin Bulgakov, *The Last Year of Leo Tolstoy*, trans. Ann Dunnigan, with an introduction by George Steiner, New York: Dial Press, 1971 [1911]. Gordon's contemporaries found much in common between Gordon and Tolstoy.

exemplify Gordon's philosophy but also are an integral part of it and, as such, are bound to inspire future generations. Indeed, Gordon's inspiring description of the religious experience of the tiller of the land in the opening of his Magnum Opus *Man and Nature: Meditations and Dreams of a Radical* is associated to this day with the portrayal of Gordon himself, as conveyed by his contemporaries.[8]

The figure of Gordon, the pioneer who substituted a hoe for phylacteries (*tefillin*), and the sacred silence of the tiller of the land for the traditionally verbal prayer, has secured the status of an icon in Hebrew culture. In recent years, as we have seen earlier, Gordon fascinates young people who search for non-halakhic Jewish renewal. However, the portrayal of Gordon as one who turned the toil of the land into a religious unification with nature poses a number of weighty questions and concerns. Is Gordon's call to return to nature actually a call to return to pre-monotheistic religious forms in which nature is perceived as the ultimate horizon of existence? Is Gordon placing the religious sphere within nature, rather than outside it? Why does Gordon identify the ultimate religious moment with work in nature rather than with simply being or wandering in nature, as did earlier nature-intoxicated prophets such as Rousseau in *Reveries of the Solitary Walker* (1782)[9] or Thoreau in *Walden* (1852)[10]? Does Gordon perceive religion as a private,

---

See, for example, Alexander Siskind Rabinovitz, "On Four Things" [Heb.], in Kushnir, *Reminiscences and Appreciations*, p. 130. See also Shimon Kushnir, *Men of Nebo* [Heb.], Tel Aviv: Am Oved, 2004, p. 52, 134.

[8] MN, I: 32–33; see also ibid., n. 25

[9] Approximately one hundred and thirty years before Gordon's MN, in his autobiographical short book written toward the end of his life, Rousseau documents his religious experience of immersion in nature during his stay on St. Peter's Island. Rousseau, who devoted his time to studying and cataloging the island's vegetation, declares in the spirit of eighteenth-century Romanticism, "The more sensitive the soul of the observer, the greater the ecstasy aroused in him by this harmony. At such times his senses are possessed by a deep and delightful reverie, and in a state of blissful self-abandonment he loses himself in the immensity of this beautiful order, with which he feels himself at one. All individual objects escape him; he sees and feels nothing but the unity of all things"; Jean-Jacques Rousseau, *Reveries of the Solitary Walker*, trans. Peter France, London: Penguin, 1980, p. 108. In contrast to Gordon, who embraces and elevates the work in nature, Rousseau speaks in praise of the "blissful indolence" in which he spends his days on the island; ibid., p. 90.

[10] About a hundred years after Rousseau, Thoreau documented similar experiences of religious immersion with nature that he had during the two years he spent at Walden Pond in Massachusetts. Thoreau strongly emphasizes that these experiences stem from his being in nature and not from working in it: "Sometimes, in a summer morning, having taken my accustomed bath, I sat in my sunny doorway from sunrise till noon, rapt in a revery, amidst the pines and hickories and sumachs, in undisturbed solitude and stillness, while the birds sang around or flitted noiseless through the house, until by the sun falling in at my west window, or the noise of some traveler's wagon on the distant highway, I was reminded of the lapse of time. I grew in those seasons like corn in the night, and they were far better than any work of the hands would have been. They were not time subtracted from my life, but so much over and above my usual allowance"; Henry David Thoreau, *Walden*,

non-institutional and nonhistorical matter? Can the individual, according to Gordon, come into direct contact with the Absolute, without any mediation of community, religious establishment, ritual, or dogma? The final and most pressing question is whether Gordon's philosophy is a Jewish philosophy, and if so, in what sense? Addressing these questions necessitates a comprehensive in-depth study of Gordon's philosophy of religion, as it emerges from the entirety of his writings, and in particular from his MN, in which religion occupies more space than any other subject or issue.

Gordon, as will be demonstrated in this chapter, argued that the religious phenomenon is at the core of existence in general and of human existence in particular. In this spirit, the philosopher Samuel Hugo Bergman, who edited the second edition of Gordon's works, argued that Gordon's message "is essentially a religious message."[11] We will begin our study of Gordon's philosophy of religion in this chapter at the point where religion itself begins, according to Gordon. To this end we will turn to explore how Gordon traces in MN the origins of the religious phenomenon in a study of what might be called, in Nietzschean terminology, a "genealogy of religion."

Gordon's Genealogy of Religion

The attempt to offer historical and psycho-philosophical narratives that explain how religion came into being gained ground in the nineteenth-century fin de siècle, and it is associated primarily with Friedrich Nietzsche's *Genealogy of Morals* (1887),[12] Durkheim's *The Elementary Forms of Religious*

Princeton: Princeton University Press, 1971, pp. 111–112. Before leaving for Walden Pond Thoreau writes in his journal, "I want to go soon and live away by the pond, where I shall hear only the wind whispering among the reeds. . . . But my friends ask what I will do when I get there. Will it not be employment enough to watch the progress of the seasons?"; Henry David Thoreau, *The Writings of Henry David Thoreau—Journal 1837-1846*, Boston and New York: Houghton, Mifflin, 1906, December 24, 1841; vol. 7, p. 299.

[11] Bergman, "Introduction to Man and Nature," GWB, II: 27.

[12] The emergence of historicism in the nineteenth century laid the groundwork for the introduction and spread of the method of genealogical inquiry that was primarily, and rightly so, associated with Nietzsche's radical and revolutionary use of it in his *Genealogy of Morals*. As Geuss argued, Nietzsche subordinated the genealogical method to the conception of history he outlined and elaborated in his early essay "On the Uses and Disadvantages of History for Life" (1872). According to this conception, history, like all other forms of knowledge, should serve and be subject to "life" and its organizing principle, i.e., the will to power. See Raymond Geuss, "Nietzsche and Genealogy," *European Journal of Philosophy* 2: 3 (1994), p. 285. On the emergence and the development of the method of genealogical inquiry in the nineteenth century see Mark Bevir, "What Is Genealogy?," *Journal of the Philosophy of History* 2: 3 (2008), pp. 263–275.

Life (1912),[13] and Georg Simmel's various essays on religion.[14] It is in this context that Gordon discusses the religious phenomenon in the fourth chapter of MN. This chapter opens with a genealogy of religion in which four stages can be distinguished. From this genealogy, which focuses on the psycho-philosophical origin of the religious phenomena, it can be concluded that religion expresses man's attempt to reunite with nature from which he has been torn during the process of his cultural evolution and the development of his rationality (MN, IV.3: 97). Let us turn now to the four stages of Gordon's genealogy of religion.

I. The first stage of the genealogy explores the pre-rational natural state of humanity and its existential characteristics. At this primal stage, Gordon argues, man is completely immersed in nature. Therefore, by definition, he does not and cannot have religion, which signifies, according to Gordon, a yearning for reunification with nature. Yet, and this is the main point, this ancient unity between man and nature laid the psychological foundation for the later emergence of religion, as it endowed man with "a mental preparation which precedes any idea of divinity" (MN, IV: 72). Hence, the study of the religious phenomenon must begin with the examination of the pre-religious natural state of man.

Like the lives of other animals, Gordon writes, the life of the natural man "is intermingled with the natural life, flowing along with it, commensurate with its fluctuations and dictates, and leaving no special impression. Within the world of nature in its entirety man did not appear as a special or distinct object" (MN, IV.1: 73). The unification of man with nature ensured his

---

[13] According to Durkheim, a comprehensive and thorough understanding of any moral or social institution or practice necessitates the tracing and examination of its most ancient and elementary forms. As he aptly puts it in the opening of his study on the origin of the taboo on incest, "in order to understand a practice or an institution, a judicial or a moral rule, it is necessary to trace it back as nearly as possible to its origin; for between the form, it now takes and what is has been, there is a rigorous relationship. Doubtless, since it has been transformed in the course of its development, the causal conditions on which it originally depended have themselves altered; but these transformations in turn depend on what the point of departure was"; Emile Durkheim, *Incest: The Nature and Origin of the Taboo* (1897), in Edward Sagarin (ed. and trans.), Incest: The Nature and Origin of the Taboo *by Emile Durkheim and* The Origin and Development of the Incest Taboo *by Albert Ellis*, New York: Lyle and Stuart, 1963, p. 13, translation slightly altered.

[14] See Georg Simmel, *Essays on Religion*, Horst Jürgen Helle and Ludwig Nieder (eds. and trans.), New Haven: Yale University Press, 1997. Simmel presents the rationale for the genealogical analysis of religion, as well as of other realms of human culture, in the following way: "All high and pure forms existed at first experimentally, as it were, in the germ, in connection with other forms; but in order to comprehend them in their highest and independent forms, we must look for them in their undeveloped states"; Georg Simmel, "A Contribution to the Sociology of Religion" [1898], in Simmel, *Essays on Religion*, p. 102

alliance with all other creatures in nature and endowed his life with perfection and eternity.

The unity of all beings in nature, Gordon argues, exists without their inten-
tion or knowledge, but out of the essence of the "worldly being in its entirety,
which encompasses and constitutes all that is to be desired and anything that
can be obtained" (MN, IV.1: 73). The perfection of all the creatures in nature
stems from the fact that they are parts of nature whose perfection as infinite
is absolute. "The supreme perfection," Gordon states, "involves the perfection of each and every part [of nature in its entirety]" (MN, VIII: 162).

The conception of perfection that Gordon adopts here overlaps the conception of perfection that Spinoza develops in his *Ethics* (1677).[15] According
to Spinoza, an object loses its perfection only when denied something that
pertains to its nature. Nature is infinite and, as such, lacks nothing. Therefore,
God *or* Nature (*deus sive natura*) and all the things that follow from God *or*
Nature, down to the very last one, are absolutely perfect. They are perfect because they express God *or* Nature. Gordon argues that the creatures in nature
are not only perfect but also eternal.[16] They are eternal not in the sense of

---

[15] In the framework of the immanent tendency in his philosophy, Spinoza claims that both God
and the things that follow from him are absolutely perfect. This claim is presented by Spinoza as the
conclusion of the following argument: Given that the cause constitutes the essence, nature, and definition of the effect (*Ethics*, I, A4; III.56, Dem; and I.8, Schol 2), and because God is "absolutely perfect" (*Ethics*, I.11, Schol II/54) and is also "the immanent cause" of all things in existence (*Ethics*, I.18,
II/63), it necessarily follows that all things in existence are also absolutely perfect. Spinoza collapses
entirely the theological barrier between God, which is by definition absolutely perfect, and the world,
which is a world of partiality, loss, and malfunction. Even a blind man, he argues, is an absolutely perfect finite mode of God. All that can be contained in him is contained in him, and all that is contained
in him is contained in him necessarily. If the existence of the blind man could have been different,
existence in its entirety would have differed, which would suggest a lack of perfection. It is possible
to relate to the blind man as lacking perfection only from our limited point of view, which compares
the necessary existence of things in reality to the existence of things as we want them to be. Yet the
hierarchy of perfections that we impose on the details of existence reflects only our judgments, which
are usually wrong about the benefit these details of existence afford us. The differentiation between
perfection and imperfection is relative, just like other differentiations of the power of imagination: "good, evil, order, confusion, warm, cold, beauty, ugliness" (*Ethics*, Appendix to I, p. 444, II/81).
Spinoza discusses the example of the blind man in *Letter 21 to Willem van Blijenbergh* (Dordrecht,
1632–1696). See Benedictus de Spinoza, *The Collected Works of Spinoza*, trans. and ed. Edwin Curley,
Princeton: Princeton University Press, 1985, vol. 1, *Letter 21*, p. 377. On Spinoza's conception of perfection see also Yuval Jobani, *The Role of Contradictions in Spinoza's Philosophy: The God-Intoxicated
Heretic*, New York: Routledge, 2016, pp. 63–83. On the proximity between Gordon and Spinoza see
also MN, VI: 147–148, n. 9; XII: 208–209, n. 1.

[16] Eternity of the Moment, the motif that Gordon employs here, as elsewhere, is a distinctly
Nietzschean motif. This is despite his profound critique of Nietzsche's concept of eternal return, to
which he devotes the second chapter of MN. See, for example, MN, I: 33, n. 26. See also the epilogue
to the critical edition of MN by Jacob Golomb, "The Agricultural Philosopher Aharon David Gordon
Goes to Work" [Heb.], in MN, pp. 276–286.

unlimited continuation of existence in time, but as part and parcel of existence itself, which is eternal being (MN, IV.1: 76).

As we saw in detail in the previous chapter, the state of nature is a state
of unity among the creatures in nature. This unity does not eliminate tension or conflict between the creatures in nature but is, rather, founded
on it. For nature in its entirety, as well as all that is within it, is subject to
the dialectical synthesis between two contradictory principles: the principle of contraction and the principle of expansion. On the one hand,
according to the principle of contraction every creature in nature prefers
itself over all other creatures in nature. Since every creature in nature
strives to "contract" into itself everything else, there is total war of all
against all in nature. On the other hand, according to the principle of
expansion the creatures in nature yearn to expand the boundary of their
being toward other creatures in nature through concern for or empathy
with them, and even by giving them preference. The most common and
significant example of the principle of expansion in Gordon's oeuvre can
be found in "the mother animal who gives her life to save the fruit of
her womb" (MN, IV.3: 102). This act clearly expresses the striving of one
creature (the mother) to expand into the being of another creature (her
offspring).[17]

The contradiction between the principle of contraction and the principle of expansion applies to all existing beings in nature, yet it does not

---

[17] Modern philosophers, such as Hobbes, Spinoza, and Locke, suggested a variety of descriptions
of the state of nature. Gordon is particularly close to the account of the state of nature suggested by
Rousseau in his *Discourse on the Origin and Basis of Inequality among Men* (1755). According to
Rousseau, the life of the natural man, like that of any other animal, is based on a balance and com-
plementarity between two opposite instincts or pre-rational principles: (i) self-love (*amour de soi*),
which is concerned with the satisfaction of basic physiological needs and self-protection; and (ii)
pity and empathy (*pitié*), which indicates a natural aversion to seeing or causing suffering of animals. Pity, argues Rousseau, "is so natural that even the beasts sometimes show evident signs of it. To
say nothing of the tenderness mothers feel for their young and of the dangers they brave in order to
protect them, one daily sees the repugnance of horses to trample a living body underfoot; an animal
never goes past a dead animal of its own species without some restlessness: Some even give them a
kind of burial; and the mournful lowing of cattle entering a slaughter-house conveys their impression
of the horrible sight that strikes them"; Jean-Jacques Rousseau, "Discourse on the Origin and Basis
of Inequality among Men," in Rousseau, *The First and Second Discourses*, trans. Victor Gourevitch,
New York: Harper & Row, 1990, pp. 160–161. In contrast with Hobbes, who had described the state
of nature as a state of war of all against all in which man is wolf to man, Rousseau argues that because
in the state of nature "the care for our own preservation is least prejudicial to the self-preservation
of others, it follows that this state was the most conducive to peace and the best suited to Mankind";
ibid., pp. 159–160. In the margin of his copy of Rousseau's essay, Voltaire (François-Marie Arouet
de Voltaire; Paris, 1694–1778) jotted down, "The savage is not evil but like a wolf he is attacked by
hunger." See George Havens (ed.), *Voltaire's Marginalia on the Pages of Rousseau*, New York: Haskell
House, 1966, p. 10.

paralyze them but, rather, activates them. This contradiction, Gordon argues, is "nothing but the driving force, which, like any force that gives rise to movement, contains opposites" (MN, VII: 157). On the one hand every creature in nature strives to protect and strengthen itself. On the other hand, it does not only bring into existence other creatures but also protects and takes care of them and in crisis situations and extreme cases even sacrifices its life for their sake. However, in order to have the power and resources to help others, one must repeatedly place oneself above all others. Life in nature, then, is perceived by Gordon as a continuous pendulum motion between the selfish contraction of oneself and the altruistic expansion and opening of the self toward its surroundings. This pendulum movement continues endlessly in nature because all creatures in nature maintain a dialectic interplay between their egoistic and altruistic tendencies.

Animals, including man in the state of nature, are not totally devoid of cognitive ability. However, the cognitive ability in the state of nature is limited and carefully adapted to the "needs of life [of each animal], and to its cosmic place, no less and no more" (MN, X: 188). The cognitive ability of the creatures in nature is intended to ensure the "existence of the individual and the species, as well as its integration "through the supreme, cosmic account . . . with all that lives and exists" (MN, X: 188).

Similarly, the surrender of the creatures in nature to their desires is limited and carefully adapted to the continuation of the existence of their species and does not deviate from it. In fact, Gordon concludes, "all the powers, emotions, desires, and cognitions of the animal," like those of man in the state of nature, "fulfill their purpose and perform their role successfully" (MN, X: 189).[18]

In the state of nature man was a friend to himself, to others, and to nature. He did not try to move from his place in the general order of nature. Compared with man of culture, the life of the natural man is primitive and restricted, as he is deprived of all the benefits and indulgences provided by scientific progress. At the same time, however, the natural man, and this was his greatest advantage, was independent and provided all his needs by his own strength. Unlike the man of culture, he was enslaved by nothing, not

---

[18] Gordon is close here to Rousseau, who argued that the creatures in nature maintain balance between their desires and needs and their physical and cognitive abilities. See Jean Jacques Rousseau, *Emile, or On Education*, trans. Allan Bloom, New York: Basic, 1979, part II, pp. 80–81.

by humans, nor by his desires that were limited to the continuity of the line of life (MN, IV.1: 77). Therefore, it is no coincidence that the state of nature is preserved in the collective memory of mankind as an ideal. "Evidence for this," as Gordon argues,

> can be found in the legends of all ancient peoples, which portray man, after his creation, as walking faithfully with God (or with the gods) as if walking with a merciful father (or with merciful fathers). Then, after eating from the tree of knowledge (or after attaining knowledge in some way), man was cut away from his world, banished from his garden of Eden and the earth was cursed because of him. (MN, IV.1: 78)

II. The second stage of the genealogy begins with the development of human cognitive ability. At this stage, Gordon emphasizes, man's rational powers are limited and rudimentary; human cognition is intermingled with the imagination and conducted mostly through association. Man does not yet have the faculties of abstraction, judgment, and criticism that he will acquire only with the full development of his reason. At this point, according to Gordon, "the human intellect is still folded beneath the horizon" and man conceives the world only through "the human imagination, which is the dawning of the intellect or a reflected light of the intellect" (MN, IV. 2: 79).

The reasons that led to the development of human cognition are unknown, but its results are obvious: man's increasing detachment from nature. "With the appearance of the first gleam of thought," Gordon argues, "the first crack between the human soul and the worldly creation was created" (MN, IV.1: 73). Man must move away and disengage from nature in order to conceive it, just as he must move away and disengage from any other object of his cognition. However, the existential impact of man's detachment from nature has severe and far-reaching implications.

Once man is torn from Nature, he is filled with a sense of "cosmic detachment and orphanhood" (MN, IV.2: 78). This existential trauma is the "ground for the rise of religion," which for Gordon is nothing but the "hidden yearning to mend and stitch together the tear, to cling to the entire worldly existence" (MN, IV.2: 78). This yearning is so intense that religion, Gordon states, serves to delineate the entire horizon of human existence. All human affairs, at this stage of the genealogy, are religious. Even the "human's animal needs are wrapped, so to speak, in a cloak of religion (sanctification of food by sacrificing portions of it to the deities, sanctification of sexual intercourse by associating it with religious purposes)" (MN, IV.2: 79).[19]

At this stage human cognition, too, is covered with a "cloak of religion." In trying to understand nature man repeatedly imposes himself on nature in order to unite with it. Human cognition is limited to the realm of the imagination at this stage. Thus limited, it is, according to Gordon, "a kind of mirror of man—of his 'self'—directed toward that which is outside him . . . in order to take it into himself" (MN, IV.2: 79). This is the psychological mechanism behind the personification of the forces of nature that leads man to perceive "all things in human form, as if everything lives, feels, thinks and acts as a human being" (MN, IV.1: 74). This is how man created the pantheon of his ancient deities:

> Seeing, for example, the sky once bright and delightful to his heart and once gloomy and deeply saddening; or seeing the sun once illuminating and warming the planets and giving them life and once searing his flesh and drying and burning every plant . . . once again it becomes clear and simple to him . . . all these objects are conscious living beings like him, although they are infinitely greater and stronger than him, more sublime than him and can do what he cannot . . . [this is how] the concept of hidden and spiritual substances was born in the human mind, in the beginning in the form of various spirits and demons, good and evil, and later in the form of gods, who actually are not completely different from humans. (MN, IV.2: 80)

Paradoxically, man populating his world with gods in order to reconnect with nature finds himself distanced even further from nature. The task of approaching nature is replaced by the task of approaching the gods "so that they will shower their abundant blessings on him. How to act so as not to provoke anger, or how to reconcile their anger?" (MN, IV.2: 81). The answer to this question becomes increasingly complex as man discovers that the gods, due to their human traits, engage in constant struggle and conflict among themselves. Approaching one God means moving away from another

---

[19] Gordon draws on the extensive fin de siècle anthropological and sociological literature of elementary religious forms. In this context it is possible to mention, for example, Durkheim's claim that while today religion occupies a smaller and smaller portion of social life, it originally embraced the entire human existence. See Emile Durkheim, *The Division of Labor in Society*, trans. W. D. Halls, Basingstoke: Macmillan 1984 [1893], p. 119.

God, which may harm him. Therefore, while man must try to reconcile with the gods, he must also establish peace between them.

But even if the religious world of man at this stage did not address his existential longing to reunite with nature, it did, however, broaden and improve his intellectual, emotional, and social skills. Religion taught man how to see himself both as a separate and distinct being, as an individual and independent agent in the world, and as an integral part of a whole greater than himself. Through continuous movement between the particular and the general, man developed the "skills of abstraction, specification and logical generalization" (MN, IV.2: 81) and acquired the emotional depth and richness that distinguishes him as a human being (MN, IV.2: 82). He also formed social collectives—such as the community, the tribe, and later the nation—in order to mediate between himself as a particular entity, and nature as a general entity. "Here," Gordon concludes, "the whole world of man is being formed, especially human consciousness, language, poetry, and the formation of the nation; everything is based on religion or involves religion" (MN, IV. 2: 83).[20]

The religious affiliation of the community to nature is mediated by the place where it is located and develops, and therefore the local landscapes, animals, and plants are always integrated into the religious worship. The members of the religious community worship "not only the heavens and the earth, the sun and the moon," but also the "local animals, birds, trees, and stones . . . the spirits of the fathers and other deceased relatives, etc." (MN, IV.2: 83–84). Each religious community creates for itself a local group of idols "that unites the community members with their natural environment into one living whole" (MN, IV.2: 84).[21] This unification with nature

---

[20] Gordon is close here to Durkheim's claim that religion is the seedbed of culture and human society. As Durkheim aptly puts it, "Religion contains in itself from the very beginning, even in an indistinct state, all the elements which in dissociating themselves from it, articulating themselves, and combining with one another in a thousand ways, have given rise to the various manifestations of collective life. From myths and legends have issued forth science and poetry; from religious ornamentations and cult ceremonials have come the plastic arts; from ritual practice was born law and morals. One cannot understand our perception of the world, our philosophical conceptions of the soul, of immortality, of life, if one does not know the religious beliefs which are their primordial forms. Kinship started out as an essentially religious tie; punishment, contract, gift, and homage are transformations of expiatory, contractual, communal, honorary sacrifices and so on"; Emile Durkheim, "Preface to the Second Volume of L'Année Sociologique" [1899], in Kurt H. Wolff, (ed.) *Emile Durkheim, 1858–1917: A Collection of Essays, with Translations and a Bibliography*, Columbus: The Ohio State University Press, 1960, pp. 350–351. See also Yuval Jobani, "The Secular University and Its Critics," *Studies in Philosophy and Education*, 35: 4 (2016), p. 340.

[21] In this passage too Gordon is close to Durkheim, who argued that religion's primary function is the creation, reinforcement, and maintenance of social solidarity. According to Durkheim, while the religious cult's apparent function is to strengthen the ties between the faithful and their god—the god being only a figurative representation of the society—they at the same time strengthen the ties

culminates in the holidays and festivals of the community and is celebrated by its members with enthusiasm and great joy.

III. The third stage of the genealogy of religion marks the transition from polytheism to monotheism. This development is described by Gordon as follows:

> As the human collective grew and became more distinct, unified, and organized—family to community, to tribe, to nation—religion became more beautiful, rational, and enlightened. Religion became less individual-istic, limited, and concrete and more general, comprehensive, and spiritual. And vice versa: as religion developed, so did the human collective; the ac-tion is reciprocal. (MN, IV.2: 84)

The transition from multiplicity to unity in the social sphere was accompanied by a transition from multiplicity to unity in the conception of the divine world. Consequently, the number of gods decreased, and their specific characteristics blurred as they become more and more united into one unified concept. "The closer human beings unite and organize into one body and one living soul, into one nation," Gordon declares, "the number of their main gods decreases, and they unite into one whole . . . the concept of the divine sheds its crude, particularistic, and materialistic character and gradually gains a purer, more encompassing, unified spiritual form" (MN, IV.2: 84–85; see also IV.3: 96–97).[22] Cleaving to the "sole and eternal di-vinity, which constitutes everything and is responsible for everything" (MN, IV.2: 85), unites man within himself, endows him with responsibility for

---

between the individual and the society of which he is a member"; Emile Durkheim, *The Elementary Forms of Religious Life*, trans. K. E. Fields, New York: Free Press, 1995 [1912], p. 227.

[22] One can find echoes of these ideas in Simmel's claim that the conception of God's unity is nothing more than an abstraction and an intensification of the conception of social unity controlled by the center. According to Simmel, "We do not simply accept our disconnected and manifold impressions of things but look instead for the connections and relations that bind them into a unity. We presuppose everywhere the presence of higher unities and centers for seemingly separate phe-nomena, so that we can orient ourselves amid the confusion in which they come to us. That human inclination is assuredly something that has grown out of social realities and necessities. Directly and appreciably, particularly in the clan, in the family, in the state, in every voluntary association, we find a whole made up of separate elements, which nevertheless is effectively controlled by the center. [. . .] The unity of things and interests with which we first become acquainted in the social realm finds its highest representation—and one separated, as it were, from all material considerations—in the idea of the divine; it occurs most completely, of course, in the monotheistic religions, but to a certain extent also in the lower religions"; Simmel, "A Contribution to the Sociology of Religion" (1898), in Simmel, *Essays on Religion*, pp. 110–111.

himself and for his world, and restores to him the perfection and eternity he lost upon leaving the state of nature. At this point religion reaches its highest and purest peak in which it achieves its ultimate goal, that is, the reunification of man with nature, thereby fulfilling the soul's powerful secret longing (MN, IV.2: 85).

The development of all the religions of "highly cultured peoples (the Greeks and Romans, for instance)" was supposed to lead from polytheism to monotheism, from "a multiplicity of manifest, concrete idols to a one-and-only God who is completely hidden" (MN, IV.2: 86). However, only among the Israelites did the conditions for the full development of religion mature, and only their religion developed into monotheism, which is the highest stage in the evolution of religion. Although among the Greeks and Romans, Gordon argues, "there have always been outstanding individuals, philosophers, poets, etc., who held advanced perceptions of the divine" (MN, IV.2: 87), the religion of their people remained pagan.[23]

Gordon briefly presents two hypotheses regarding the special conditions that led to the development of monotheism within the ancient people of Israel. According to the first hypothesis, in contrast to the people of Israel, the imperialist infrastructure of other highly developed cultures in the ancient world gave their religions a distinctly syncretic character, preventing them from developing into monotheism. The mixture of doctrines, rites and idols that characterize the "religions of all the ancient conquering peoples" (MN, IV.2: 85) produced only "mechanical unity" (MN, IV.3: 97) rather than organic unity or "cosmic unity" with nature (MN, IV.3: 97). The people of Israel, on the other hand, precisely because "they were not very strong, and unable to conquer other nations and assimilate and absorb them" (MN, IV.2: 87), obtained the conditions for the development of monotheism.

[23] Brenner, on the other hand, argues that even among the people of Israel, and not only in Greece, only outstanding individuals held true cognition of God. The masses, however, in all religions, have always been immersed in idolatry and superstition. In his controversial article "In Journals and in Literature" (1910) Brenner declares, "The masses never get to the core and eat only the peel, sometimes coolly sometimes enthusiastically, but always habitually and mechanically . . . it is well known that the ancient Greek philosophers fought against the religious doctrines of their time, fought for the celebrated monotheism no less than our prophets of Israel, and as such they were infinitely more religious than the priests and clergies, who were hostile to the philosophers. It is also well known that in theory and in regard to the elite, the love for humans and the appreciation of eternal values can be found, in all the scriptures of all faiths and religions. In regard to the masses, however, we find bondage and superstition and absurd laws as well as religion wars because of idols, statues, altars, houses of worship, customs, rituals, intrigues, and all kinds of absurd laws"; Yosef Haim Brenner, "In Journals and in Literature [The Vision of Conversion]" [Heb.], in Brenner, *Complete Works*, ed. Yitzhak Kafkafi, Tel-Aviv: Hakibbutz Hameuchad, 1985, vol. 3, pp. 476–487.

The second hypothesis links the unique living conditions of the desert, in which the Israeli nation was formed, to the development of the belief in one God.[24] The open, sparse, and monotonous desert landscape invites man to absorb "the entire worldly creation and its infinite expansion" (MN, IV.2: 87). For the desert is not rich in "forms, nuances and details" (MN, IV.2: 86) that might divert one's being away from expanding into existence in its totality and cause one to shrink into oneself. Moreover, to cope with its extreme climate, the desert's inhabitants must unite with each other and thus perceive the unity of nature and experience it.[25]

Gordon's reference to these two hypotheses is brief and concise not only because they offer only partial and overly rigid explanations for the development of monotheism within the ancient people of Israel, but mainly because his focus is philosophical rather than historical. Gordon's core concern is not how monotheism evolved out of religious forms that preceded it, but how monotheism in its purest form enables man to reunite with nature from which he was torn in the process of his intellectual and social development.

At the heart of Gordon's answer, as we shall see, is the ideal of the supreme responsibility of man to nature, which stems from the perception of the supreme unity of man and nature. The great empires of antiquity used their religions as political tools to forge artificial bonds of unity among the

---

[24] This idea seems to resonate with Ernest Renan's (France, 1823–1892) theory regarding the influence of desert landscape on the religious beliefs of the ancient Israelites, which is encapsulated in his well-known declaration "the desert is monotheistic" ("le désert est monothéiste"). See Ernest Renan, *Histoire générale et système comparé des langues sémitiques: Histoire générale des langues sémitiques*, Paris: Imprimerie impériale, 1863, vol. 1, p. 6. On the response of Jewish thinkers—such as Ahad Ha'am, Nachman Syrkin (Russian Empire–Berlin–New York, 1868–1924), Joseph Klausner, Rabbi Binyamin (pseudonym of Yehoshua Redler-Feldmann, Galicia–Israel, 1880–1957)—to Renan's account of the development of monotheism in ancient Israel see Hanan Harif, *For We Are Brethren: The Turn to the East in Zionist Thought* [Heb.], Jerusalem: The Zalman Shazar Center, 2019, pp. 135–144. See also Yaacov Shavit and Jehuda Reinharz, "Introduction" [Heb.], in Iganz Goldziher, *A Lecture on Orientalism: In Memory of Ernest Renan* [Heb.], eds. Yaacov Shavit and Jehuda Reinharz, Raanana: The Open University, 2016, pp. 9–58.

[25] This religious idealization of the desert echoes the well-known proclamation of the prophet Jeremiah: "I accounted to your favor the devotion of your youth. Your love as a bride, how you followed Me in the wilderness, in a land not sown" (Jeremiah 2:2). In his essay "On the Place [Ha'Makom]," which is dedicated to the perception of the place in Jewish and Israeli culture, Gurevitch argues that "the desert does not disappear with the settlement in the land, but persists as a living element, as the homeland of the idea"; Zali Gurevitch, *On Israeli and Jewish Place* [Heb.], Tel Aviv: Am Oved, 2007, p. 35. Yael Zerubavel, who studied in depth and in detail the cultural construction of the desert in Zionism and Hebrew culture, associates the Zionist pioneers' fascination with the desert with "the important European trend, articulating deep-seated concerns about the future of the West. A growing anxiety about the dehumanizing impact of technology [. . .] was paired with a fascination with the East and its traditional societies, which were seen as living in greater harmony with nature. The East thus appealed to Westerners as a place of refuge from the excessively technological modern West, a view that contributed to the appeal of the desert"; Yael Zerubavel, *Desert in the Promised Land*, Stanford: Stanford University Press, 2018, p. 36.

people they ruled. In contrast, the ancient religion of Israel was, according to Gordon, a natural religion that sought to reunite man with nature through the creation of an affinity between the individual and ever-expanding concentric circles that begin with the sexual relationship, continues in the family, tribe, nation, and humanity, and ends by incorporating the entire nature or cosmos.

The supreme responsibility toward nature, which derives from the attainment of supreme unity with nature, is perfectly compatible, according to Gordon, with the commandment "You shall be holy, for I, the Lord your God, am holy" (Leviticus 19:2). Out of this sense of responsibility, the religion of Israel developed its most sublime ideals, such as, "Love your fellow as yourself" (Leviticus 19:18), "Nation shall not take up Sword against nation" (Isaiah 2:4), "The wolf shall dwell with the lamb" (Isaiah 11:6), and "For the land shall be filled with devotion to the Lord as water covers the sea" (Isaiah 11:9) (MN, IV.2: 85).

The ancient religion of Israel, like any other religion, emerged out of and drew from particular circumstances and factors yet offered, according to Gordon, a comprehensive and universal way of life.[26] Therefore, general conclusions about the human condition can be extracted from the study of the Jewish religion. It is in this vein that Gordon chose to title his main philosophical book "Man and Nature" rather than "The Jew and the Land of Israel," although it does contain an extensive discussion of the renewal of Jewish life in the Land of Israel.

A crystalline formulation of the existential dimension of the Jewish situation can be found in "A Little Observation" (1911), an article published shortly after the publication of the first chapter of MN, in which Gordon declares that "the great sorrow of this nation [of the Jews]" is nothing but "a comprehensive and in-depth explanation for the sorrow of the world"

---

[26] In an entirely different philosophical climate, Nietzsche also tried to extract his philosophy of power from a study of the history of the ancient religion of Israel, which he perceived as a religion that confirms man's strong bond to nature. In this spirit he declares in *The Antichrist*, "Originally, especially at the time of the kings, Israel also stood in the right, that is, the natural, relationship to all things. Its Yahweh was the expression of a consciousness of power, of joy in oneself, of hope for oneself: through Him victory and welfare were expected; through Him nature was trusted to give what the people needed above all, rain"; Friedrich Nietzsche, *The Antichrist*, in Nietzsche, *The Portable Nietzsche*, trans. Walter Kaufmann, New York: Penguin, 1977, section 25, p. 594. For discussion see Yirmiyahu Yovel, *Dark Riddle—Hegel, Nietzsche, and the Jews*, University Park: Pennsylvania State University Press, 1998, chap. 3; Israel Eldad, "Nietzsche and the Bible" [Heb.], in Jacob Golomb (ed.), *Nietzsche and Hebrew Culture* [Heb.], Jerusalem: The Hebrew University Magnes Press, 2002, pp. 295–311.

(GWA, I: 80). In this spirit he also declares in "An Open Letter to My Fellow Laborers" (1911),

> We came to the Land of Israel to ask for something, to ask for that which is not ready to hand and there is no paved road leading to it, to ask for what we do not have, not only as Jews but perhaps also as humans. (GWA, I: 62).[27]

IV. The fourth and final stage in the genealogy marks the degeneration and decline of religion, due to the tendency of religious forms and rituals to subjugate essence and content. In addition to the form–essence pair, Gordon employs the static–dynamic and individual–society pairs of concepts to elucidate the process of decline and degeneration of religion. From different directions these pairs of concepts converge with the fundamental metaphysical dichotomy in Gordon's philosophical system. It is the metaphysical dichotomy between contraction and expansion, which in the human realm appears as a dichotomy between cognition and experience. Indeed, as we shall see, the crisis that besets religion when form subjugates essence is an integral part of the crisis that besets man when cognition subjugates experience.

The essence of religion is the reunification of man with nature. This reunification occurs in the experiential realm. For in this realm, as we have seen in the previous chapter, man satisfies the fundamental and metaphysical urge shared by all existing beings, which is to expand the boundary of their being and merge with all that exists.[28] Firmly located in the experiential realm religion is a distinctly private matter indicating the "feeling of a complete unification of the 'self' with the entirety of worldly beingness" (MN, IV.7: 122). "Religion is entirely subjective" (MN, IV.3: 98)—Gordon declares—it is "a

---

[27] Gordon eloquently and aptly describes the self-understanding of the pioneers of the Second Aliyah who identified their existence in the Land of Israel with existence in general. "Being-in-the-Land-of-Israel was, for them," as Neumann put it, "not merely being situated in a specific place. Being-in-the-Land-of-Israel was, for them, to be." See Boaz Neumann, *Land and Desire in Early Zionism*, trans. Haim Watzman, Waltham: Brandeis University Press, 2011, p. x. In this important book Neumann compiled an impressive collection of descriptions of the intimate affinity that the pioneers of the Second Aliyah felt toward the Land of Israel. To illustrate Gordon's philosophical explanation and justification of the pioneers' sentiments, their descriptions are incorporated in this, and in the following chapter, along with reference to their source.

[28] As we saw in the previous chapter, the yearning for reunion with nature overlaps and includes not only Gordon's prevalent identification of the concept of experience with the principle of expansion, but also the identification of the concept of experience with the dialectical synthesis between cognition and experience.

place where the human soul clings to the soul of the world and unifies with it, as if it and the worldly existence were one" (MN, IV.3: 98).

Thus, the religious experience is fully felt only when man is "free from the shackles of others . . . only when he sees himself alone within the worldly creation, or when he participates with it in creation [of the world]" (MN, IV.3: 98). Indeed, in Gordon's quasi-autobiographical account of the religious experience the tiller of the soil is presented as an individual who stands alone, without mediation, on the verge of complete fusion with nature through his toil (MN, I: 32–33). Through religious experience, the individual

> lives with all that lives and into all that lives . . . as if his self is the self of the entire existence; as if all parts of existence, all the visions of nature and life, all that lives and exists, including himself, are nothing but details of one ultimate wholeness, all in perfect accord. The individual lives in its entirety. (MN, IV.3: 98–99)

Although religious experience is not mediated by the social collective, it will not occur if the individual withdraws from human society and alienates himself from the social collective to which he belongs. This is due to the dialectical relationship between the individual and society. "The religious core," Gordon states, "belongs to every individual, not only as an individual but also as a part of the [social] collective" (MN, IV.2: 88). Gordon grants the social collective a status of a "second-order organic entity" (MN, IV.2: 88). The individuals who make up the social collective are bound together in an "organic, and vital relationship that transforms them into one living collective body" (MN, IV.2: 88). The individual and the social collective lean on each other and build each other up, even though they are distinct and different from each other. Therefore, "even if all his life the individual is created by society" (MN, IV.4: 106), he is not "swallowed" up in the collectivism but, rather, emerges from it as having a "complete, broad, deep, and magnificent personality" (MN, IV. 4: 107).

In the previous stage of the genealogy, we saw how the mutual development of cognition and experience, which corresponds to the mutual development of the individual and society, reached its peak. In the religious realm, Gordon argues, this mutual development helped to evolve monotheism from the religious forms that preceded it. However, this reciprocal complementary growth came to an end when for unknown reasons the scope and strength of cognition and society had expanded, without parallel expansion and growth of the individual and his experiential world (MN, IX: 178–180). As a result, human life—which in the state of nature is based on a balance with and mutual dependence between cognition and experience—has been severely impaired. Religion lost all of its existential and experiential content and became nothing more than a collection of rituals, customs, and dogmas whose goal is to ensure social continuity, cohesion, and stability. Religious form (which is a product of the social collective) takes over religious content (which is distinctively individualistic).[29]

Thus, instead of an event in which life erupts and overflows with exaltation before the absolute, religion has become "a static object passed on unchanged from generation to generation, as if religion is nothing but a remnant of wealth from the past and not a living, dynamically regenerating resource that invigorates those who possess it" (MN, IV.5: 113). The social collective subjugates man's religious world, thereby weakening the contact between his soul and the soul of the world.

The social issues "swallowed up the natural issues. The multiplicity of needs and concerns, the negotiation with different people on different matters, not for the purpose of satisfying an unmediated need, but for reaching a distant goal, have been helpful in developing in man," Gordon argues, "an objective cognition." But to an equal extent these factors also "weakened man's subjectivity and the vital connection between man and the living and non-living things, with which he comes in contact. Man's attitude towards his surroundings has become more cerebral, but less vital" (MN, IV.5: 116). Institutionalized religion became hostile toward individuals who were imbued with a deep religious feeling. As a result,

the deep soul that possesses a deep religious feeling, was forced to adapt, to seek compromises with the religious forms which became stagnant and obsolete, or to isolate in its own distinct corner and to be 'torn' away from the nation's soul, in stark contrast to the highest aspiration of religion.[30]

---

[29] See MN, IV.2: 88. The distinction between the form of religion and its essence is prevalent in Simmel's writings. However, Simmel prefers to employ in this context the pair of concepts of "religion" and "religiosity," respectively. See, for example, Georg Simmel, "A Contribution to the Sociology of Religion" [1898], in Simmel, *Essays on Religion*, pp. 101–120. See also Rudi Laermans, "The Ambivalence of Religiosity and Religion: A Reading of Georg Simmel," *Social Compass*, 53: 4 (2006), pp. 479–489. In the next section of this chapter, we will discuss in detail Simmel's influence on Gordon.
[30] MN, IV.2: 89. In his 1912 essay "The Procession of Ideas in Israel" Rav Kook (Rabbi Abraham I. Hacohen Kook; Latvia–Land of Israel, 1865–1935) also laments, like Gordon, the loss of religious vitality. See Avraham Yitzhaq Ha-Cohen Kook, "The Procession of Ideas in Israel," in Kook, *Orot* [Heb.], Jerusalem: Mossad Ha-Rav Kook, 1950, p. 114. For in-depth dissuasion of this essay see

In these circumstances, man lost his most vital and basic talent, "the talent of living," in Gordon's words (MN, XI: 185).

This is the psychological infrastructure from which emerged various forms of secularism,[31] which will be discussed in detail below. In its radical form, secularism's outspoken and uncompromising aim is to abolish religion as nothing more than a "soporific lullaby, a remnant from mankind's childhood age, that, even nowadays, may lull big kids to sleep, although truly its time has passed and it is a *mitzvah* (religious obligation) to eliminate it from the world, like an intoxicating drug that corrupts the soul" (MN, IV.2: 94). But "religion," as Gordon declares defiantly, "will not die, as long as there is a human soul in the world" (MN, IV.2: 94). The religious element in human life—indicating the yearning of the finite for the infinite—is anchored in the structure of reality itself, one of whose organizing principles is the principle of expansion. This principle indicates, as we saw in the previous chapter, the yearning of all existing beings to expand the boundary of their being toward other existing beings in order to merge with existence itself. Therefore, Gordon dismisses the proclamation of the end of religion associated with Nietzsche's well-known image of "the death of God" as wishful and unrealistic:

> Only the stale, rigid concept of God died, but not God; Not the hidden intellect, which you encounter in all your thoughts and feelings, yet cannot perceive, cannot attain . . . The hidden will never die, even if all the thinkers and all the scientists in the world argue that everything is evident and known and clear. (MN, IV.2: 94)

Religiosity, according to Gordon, is a natural element in human life. As such, it cannot be reduced to sociological or psychological manipulation. While it might become blurred, it cannot be canceled or erased. In this context, Gordon famously declared, "The human spirit, the greater its depth, cannot be at peace without religiosity" (MN, IV.2: 94). Therefore, even in the religious darkness that enshrouds our lives, we witness "a quest for religion,

---

Yehudah Mirsky, *Rav Kook: Mystic in a Time of Revolution*, New Haven: Yale University Press, 2014, pp. 77–81. For a comprehensive comparison between Rav Kook and Gordon see Sara Strassberg-Dayan, *Individual, Nation and Mankind: The Conception of Man in the Teachings of A.D. Gordon and Rabbi Abraham I. Hacohen Kook* [Heb.], Tel Aviv: Hakibbutz Hameuchad, 1995.

[31] See Yuval Jobani, "Three Basic Models of Secular Jewish Culture," *Israel Studies*, 13: 3 (2008), pp. 160–169.

a longing for new manifestations of religion" (MN, IV.5: 111).[32] But how will these "new manifestations of religion" allow man to reunite with nature from which he has been torn? And how might we hasten the arrival of what can be called the religion of the future? Let us turn to the next section where we will try to answer these questions.

Religion of Nature or Religion of the Future

"It is widely believed," Gordon states, "that religion's time is over, but in fact and in depth its time has not yet come" (MN, IV.5: 113–114). In this significant statement Gordon predicts that the future will bring a comprehensive and profound religious renewal. Not a return to a lost form of religion but an advance forward, toward a new religious existence that surpasses all that preceded it.

Gordon's call to establish a dialectical relationship between the past and the future of religion resonates with the call for a "Jewish renaissance" and the centrality of the idea of *techiya* (rebirth) in nineteenth-century fin de siècle Jewish culture.[33] Moreover, Gordon's declaration that the future of religion is yet to unfold proves that the four stages of the genealogy of religion, discussed in the previous section, do not provide a full description of the religious phenomenon. The future entails a religious existence in which man's unity with nature will be deeper and more comprehensive than anything previously achieved. This is, so to speak, the "religion of the future" or

---

[32] In this spirit John Dewey (Vermont–New York, 1859–1952) notes in his book *A Common Faith* [1934], "Any activity pursued in behalf of an ideal end against obstacles and in spite of threats of personal loss because of conviction of its general and enduring value is religious in quality"; John Dewey, *A Common Faith*, New Haven: Yale University Press, 1934, p. 34.

[33] The term "Jewish renaissance" became commonplace, among other things, following Buber's influential essay "Jewish Renaissance," published in 1901 in the first issue of the journal *Ost und West*. See Martin Buber, "Jüdische Renaissance," *Ost und West*, 1: 1 (1901), pp. 1–10. As Asher Biemann puts it in his groundbreaking study of the idea of renaissance in modern Judaism, "What Buber expected for the new renaissance of Judaism was akin to what he believed the 'old' renaissance had mastered for its own age: A 'return' that meant radical innovation; a spontaneous 'rebirth' to a 'new life' that promised freedom from decline and inward decay. In this respect, the Jewish Renaissance echoed and expanded the call for *techiya* [rebirth] that had come from the Hebrew Renaissance in eastern Europe; and it echoed no less the development of 'cultural' or 'spiritual' Zionism, as whose cousin—and corrective—it often posed. But it also echoed a broader longing for a 'new renaissance' that was common among European intellectuals at the fin-de-siècle and during the three remarkable decades to follow"; Asher Biemann, *Inventing New Beginnings: On the Idea of Renaissance in Modern Judaism*, Stanford: Stanford University Press, 2009, pp. 2–3. On the idea of renaissance in the world of the Hebrew pioneers see Muki Tsur, *Doing It the Hard Way* [Heb.], Tel Aviv: Am Oved, 1976 , chap. 7. See also Motti Inbari, *The Making of Modern Jewish Identity: Ideological Change and Religious Conversion*, New York: Routledge, 2019.

the "religion of nature," and Gordon is its prophet.[34] Even if Gordon did not use these terms himself, they nevertheless capture well his religious position and highlight how crucial his ideas are to understanding our environmental crisis—and how to overcome it.

One of the best entry points into Gordon's conception of the religion of the future can be found in the following passage from the fourth chapter on MN, in which Gordon states that

> As long as man conceives nature only through the intellect and not through life, as long as he sees nature only as a contractor, whether blind or not, for satisfying his needs, whether material or spiritual, whether at his command or not; whether man approaches nature as a simple slave or as a reigning slave—there is no place for religion in the highest sense. (MN, IV. 5: 114)

The emergence of the religion of nature or the "religion in the highest sense," as it is called here, marks a turning point in man's relation to nature. On the one hand, man should not put himself above nature, which he perceives as a stockpile of objects to be manipulated. On the other hand, he must not put nature above himself, nor should he worship nature or diminish himself. In this vein, Gordon declares in his essay "Our Self-Reflection" (1916),

> We return to nature, but not as slaves and not as masters, nor even as tourists or researchers, viewing from the height of their knowledge the surrounding universe, but as active partners and as loyal brothers: we come as partners with nature, participating in life and creation. More precisely, we come to unite with God in a wholly singular, inseparable union, in the sense that man and nature are one single entity. (GWA, III: 196)

In this pertinent section Gordon rejects not only the notion of placing man above nature, but also the opposite notion of placing nature above man.

Gordon's reservations regarding the first approach, which places nature above man, foreshadows contemporary criticism against radical environmentalism that—in the name of protecting nature—harms man. Some, for example, oppose the adoption of efficiency as the only criterion of international

---

[34] For discussion of Gordon as a prophet see Eliezer Schweid, "The Crazy Man of Spirit: The Prophetic Mission in Gordon's Life and Thought" [Heb.], in Schweid, *Prophets for Their People*, Jerusalem: Hebrew University Magnes Press, 1999, pp. 144–160. See also the discussion in the next chapter.

environmental policy and call to couple it with the moral criteria of distributive justice. Darrel Moellendorf suggested in this context the antipoverty principle according to which the cost of climate change policies should not be imposed on the global poor, of present or future generations, if there are alternative policies that could prevent the poor from assuming those costs.[35] In a similar vein, others oppose the sweeping adoption of the precautionary principle according to which action or policy should be avoided if there is a suspicion that it may cause environmental damage, even if there is no clear scientific proof as to the likelihood of potential harm.[36] The opponents of the precautionary principle argue that the adoption of this draconian principle by international bodies and institutions—such as the United Nations Rio Conference (1992)[37]—thwarts human flourishing. Prosperity and progress, the argument continues, are a product of innovation and trial and error, which are not possible without calculated risk-taking.[38]

The second approach to nature that Gordon opposes is the anthropocentric approach. This approach places man at the center of nature, thus enabling him to manipulate nature. Western culture has a long-standing historical legacy of anthropocentric orientation regarding the natural world due to, among other things, the legitimacy given to it by all monotheistic religions. In fact, the anthropocentric approach can be found already in the first chapter of the Bible, in the story of creation. In his first blessing and commandment of vocation for the first humans, God declares, "Be fertile and increase, fill the earth and master it; and rule the fish of the sea, the birds of the

---

[35] Darrel Moellendorf, *The Moral Challenge of Dangerous Climate Change: Values, Poverty, and Policy*, New York: Cambridge University Press, 2014, p. 22.

[36] According to this principle, to use Sunstein's words, "Regulators should take steps to protect against potential harms, even if causal chains are unclear and even if we do not know that those harms will come to fruition"; Cass Sunstein, *Laws of Fear: Beyond the Precautionary Principle*, Cambridge: Cambridge University Press, 2014, p. 4. See also Yuval Jobani and Nahshon Perez, *Governing the Sacred: Political Toleration in Five Contested Sacred Sites*, Oxford: Oxford University Press, 2020, pp. 148–150.

[37] According to Rio declaration, "In order to protect the environment, the precautionary approach shall be widely applied by states according to their capabilities. Where there are threats of serious or irreversible damage, lack of full scientific certainty shall not be used as a reason for postponing cost-effective measures to prevent environmental degradation," *Rio Declaration on Environment and Development*, Principle 15, 31 I.L.M. 874, 879, (1992). See also Art. 3(3) of the U.N. Climate Change Convention (1992). For a comprehensive discussion of the Rio declaration see Jorge E. Viñuales (ed.), *The Rio Declaration on Environment and Development: A Commentary*, Oxford: Oxford University Press, 2015.

[38] For a detailed discussion of this argument see Roger Scruton, *How to Think Seriously about the Planet: The Case for an Environmental Conservatism*, New York: Oxford University Press, 2014, pp. 104–136.

sky, and all the living things that creep on earth" (Genesis 1:28).[39] With the adoption of the anthropocentric approach man perceives nature as a reserve at his disposal, and nothing more. In the framework of the anthropocentric approach, as Gordon puts it,

> Nature functions as a grocery store that supplies all the material and spiritual needs of life. It functions as a store or warehouse, not a source of life . . . the sown field, the forest, for example, are valued according to the amount of grain they produce . . . or according to their economic value. Livestock are valued for their pragmatic use; the price of the meat, the skin, the wool, the labor power and so on. (MN, IV.4: 105)

Gordon's opposition to the appropriation of nature is intensified by the fact that his opposition is grounded in a comprehensive philosophical system. Gordon is not content with laws and regulations whose limitation of man's devastating impact on the fauna and wildlife is merely a ploy designed to extend man's long-term potential to continue plundering nature:

> Don't they cut down, for example, entire forests, and even rainforests, which are not only the splendor of nature, like noble drawings sketched on nature's face, but also beneficial to both human and plant growth and health? Don't they cut them down, just for the money, or for the most insignificant and trivial reasons? Even the [environmental] regulations which the governments had introduced rely on limited criteria, perhaps less limited but they are definitely not in line with nature in its entirety as something that stands for itself. (MN, XV: 230)

Gordon may be referring here to the reinforcement of environmental laws and regulations in the Russian Empire at the end of the nineteenth century, some of which were initiated by Peter the Great (Pyotr Alekseyevich Romanov; Russia, 1672–1725). The considerations behind this legislation, as

---

[39] As we shall see in detail in the next chapter, in the story of creation as well as in the Bible in general, one may find different and contrasting environmental voices and conflicting perspectives. According to Midrash Ecclesiastes Rabbah, for example, man's control over nature does not bring with it the right to do with nature as he pleases, but an ultimate responsibility toward nature. As the Midrash puts it, "upon creating the first human beings, God guided them around the Garden of Eden, saying; 'Look at my creations! See how beautiful and perfect they are! I created everything for you. Make sure you don't ruin or destroy my world. If you do, there will be no one after you to fix it"; *Midrash Ecclesiastes Rabbah* [Heb., Vilna Edition], Jerusalem: Vagshal 2001, VII: 13, p. 113.

Douglas Weiner showed, were utilitarian rather than ethical-philosophical, and were intended to prevent irreversible damage to the hunting and timber resources of the Russian Empire.[40] Moreover, in the Land of Israel, Gordon witnessed the swift and savage elimination of forests by the Turks during the First World War. To move troops and supplies to the front, as Alon Tal points out, "the Ottoman regime indiscriminately helped itself to any local trees it could harvest, with little regard for property rights or ecological uniqueness. According to the retroactive British forestry reports, sixty percent of the country's economically viable olive trees were used for rail fuel."[41]

Gordon, as we have seen in the previous chapter, argues that the good life or the supreme life is based on a dialectic interplay between what he calls the "tendency to a life of contraction and the tendency to a life of expansion" (MN, VII: 157). Therefore, what he opposes is not the actual use of nature to satisfy human needs (which expresses the principle of contraction) but that man neglects to balance his manipulation of nature with an experiential fusion with it (which expresses the principle of expansion).

The question we need to ask ourselves, Gordon states, is: What has man done to nature,

> since regarding it as his private property? What mark did he leave on nature which became his home and the source of his livelihood, in which he found rest, pleasure, recreation etc.? Did he try to turn nature into an unfailing source of life, rather than an unfailing source of livelihood, or more precisely an unfailing source of wealth? Did he at least do something to protect the flow of life from decreasing or from ceasing due to the limitless expansion of the flow of wealth? Didn't he turn nature into a business, a commerce? Did he incorporate into the economic account of the pennies he eagerly tries to extract from nature, the account of life, the life that his body and soul sucks from nature? . . . What does this nature convey to the human soul, what can its facial expression tell us? . . . Is there here any mindful

[40] See Douglas R. Weiner, *Models of Nature: Ecology, Conservation, and Cultural Revolution in Soviet Russia*, Pittsburgh: University of Pittsburgh Press, 2000, pp. 9–10. See also Philip Rust Pryde, *Conservation in the Soviet Union*, Cambridge: Cambridge University Press, 1972, pp. 9–13.

[41] Alon Tal, *Israel's Woodlands from the Bible to the Present (Yale Agrarian Studies Series)*, New Haven: Yale University Press, 2013, p. 26. On the high symbolic value of the forest and trees in the emergent Hebrew culture of the pre-state Jewish society in the Land of Israel see Yael Zerubavel, "The Forest as a National Icon: Literature, Politics, and the Archeology of Memory," *Israel Studies* 1: 1 (1996), pp. 60–99.

consideration of the plant as a being in itself, of the entire field, and garden, and forest as beings in themselves? (MN, XV: 230)

Man's dependence on nature for housing, food, clothing, livelihood, and even vacation and recreation is not in itself wrong. What Gordon contends with is the fact that man's contact with nature serves only to satisfy his various needs. Cognitive and rational calculations of the profitability of the various attachments with nature block the possibility of experiential communion with nature.

The anthropocentric approach to nature, as Gordon puts it, hides from man the "facial expression" of nature and does not allow him to hear "what this nature speaks" to him.[42] Man's connection with nature within this approach is indirect rather than direct since it is cerebral rather than emotional. Gordon himself documents in one of the only autobiographical reflections in MN his deep spiritual bond with the nature of the Land of Israel. In 1913, Meir Rotenberg (Galicia–Israel, 1887–1951), the secretary of the Judean Workers' Council who was nicknamed "king of the hoe" for his quick and successful acquisition of farming skills, invited a group of sixteen young pioneers to settle the Uriah village in the Judean lowlands. Gordon, who belonged to this group of pioneers, lived in the khan of the village for nearly a year.[43] As he arrived for the first time at the site Gordon felt that the pristine landscape of the Judean Plain gazed openly at him,

> Nature has given me the impression of a new nature, an untended and uncultivated nature that looks at you with innocence and faith. I recall reading

---

[42] In this spirit the French painter Andre Marchand (1907–1997), like many other painters, said that he felt that nature was looking at him: "In a forest, I have felt many times over that it was not I who looked at the forest. Some days I felt that the trees were looking at me, were speaking to me . . . I was there, listening . . . I think that the painter must be penetrated by the universe and not want to penetrate it. . . ." Quoted in Maurice Merleau-Ponty, *The Primacy of Perception: And Other Essays on Phenomenological Psychology, the Philosophy of Art, History and Politics (Studies in Phenomenology and Existential Philosophy)*, ed. James M. Edie, trans. Carleton Dallery, Evanston: Northwestern University Press, 1964, p. 167.

[43] Among the settlers at the site were Noah Naftolski (Russian Empire–Israel, 1883–1974), Yitzhak Tabenkin, Hava Tabenkin (Russian Empire–Land of Israel, 1889–1947), Ben-Zion Israeli (Russian Empire–Israel, 1887–1954), Yosef Salzman (Warsaw–Land of Israel, 1890–1913), and Isaak Feynerman (Russian Empire–Land of Israel, 1863–1925). Yael, Gordon's daughter, described his life in Uriah village as follows: "Dad lived in a small room on the second floor. It was one of the most pleasant periods of his life in the Land of Israel. His friends were good young fellows, and he forged a tight bond with them. Dad lived with them as a father with his sons. Uriah village was a lonely, wonderful corner. Many friends would come to the village from nearby settlements as well as from Jaffa to have a nice chat and enjoy the beauty of the place"; Yael Gordon, "From His Life in Israel," GWT, 234. See also "Uriah Village" [Heb.], author not indicated, *Ha-Tsfira*, January 8, 1913, p. 3

somewhere that in some places where humans are practically absent, animals approach man and look at him innocently without any suspicion
as if in friendship. And I thought then: this desolate nature, so wonderful
and humble in its beauty and heroism, so close to our soul, that secretly
and pleasantly recites poetry from the depth of our soul, that welcomes
us with open arms, that promises us so much and is faithful in fulfilling
its promise—What do we promise it and what can we promise?" (MN,
XV: 233–234)

When man comes into direct and extended contact with nature, he might
feel the gaze of nature and hear the poetry it recites. In this context, Israeli
historian Boaz Neumann (1971–2015) argued that Gordon made the landscape of the Land of Israel an integral part of the territory of his soul.[44]

When agricultural work is not only a source of financial income necessary
for living, but also a source of spiritual growth and fusion with nature, it is
perceived by Gordon, as we will see, as the pinnacle of religious experience.
However, when the only motivation of the pioneers is profit, based on employment of non-Jewish workers who work in place of them, Gordon vehemently opposes their exploitative agenda, while using distinctive religious
terms, such as "desecration of the sacred" or the "desecration of the wilderness." Gordon, for instance, flies into a kind of holy rage when he denounces
the agricultural settlers of the First Aliyah, whom he encountered when he
arrived in the Land of Israel:[45]

We all know what the settlers and the builders of the Yishuv created and
achieved. All those vineyards, orchards, etc., planted and cultivated by
foreigners, all this pretentious "creation" which relied on strangers "to
turn a wilderness into a garden of Eden." What do all these say? Does it

---

[44] Neumann, *Land and Desire*, p. 65.

[45] Some sixty years before Gordon, Thoreau also used religious terms to describe human assault
on nature. "The woodcutters, and the railroad, and I myself," as he puts it, "have profaned Walden,
perhaps the most attractive, if not the most beautiful, of all our lakes"; Thoreau, *Walden*, p. 197. In a
similar vein, he strictly criticizes the American settlers around him who view nature as a commodity
that is to be exploited to the maximum, useful as a resource only: "I respect not his labors, his farm
where every thing has its price; who would carry the landscape, who would carry his God, to market,
if he could get any thing for him; who goes to market for his God as it is; on whose farm nothing
grows free, whose fields bear no crops, whose meadows no flowers, whose trees no fruits, but dollars;
who loves not the beauty of his fruits, whose fruits are not ripe for him till they are turned to dollars";
Thoreau, *Walden*, p. 196. In contrast Thoreau argues that while he lived in his small and modest cabin
on the shore of Walden Pond, "Every morning was a cheerful invitation to make my life of equal simplicity, and I may say innocence, with Nature herself"; Thoreau, *Walden*, p. 88.

not say: money, money, money? Is a musical ear required in order to hear the voice from Heaven condemning this "creation" and saying: You have desecrated the wilderness . . . " (MN, XV: 234)[46]

It is important to note here that Gordon links the exploitation of nature with the exploitation of humans. In fact, both forms of exploitation not only overlap but also reflect the same basic tendency of domination. Through his domination of the other, the man of culture seeks to fill the existential emptiness brought about by his alienation from nature (MN, IX: 184).[47]

Indeed, Gordon witnessed a similar desecration of nature in Europe. Documenting his impressions of his train ride from Trieste to Vienna, he writes,

> The nature of the place is simply unparalleled in its beauty, at least for those who see it for the first time. And what does this nature say to humans? As if it's not enough that everywhere you come across trees pruned according to the fashion [. . .] all along the way your eye constantly encounters large billboards, easily read from the train, advertising all kinds of products that manufacturers manufacture in their factories and that all kinds of grocers sell in their grocery stores. The billboards are usually tacked upon or hung from rocks or trees, detracting the eye—and even more the soul—from the more beautiful and sublime sights. And human beings, all kinds of human beings, some of whom probably have a large soul and intellect, pass this way every day in their thousands and tens of thousands—Yet still, the world keeps on turning, . . . Is this not desecration . . . ? I would say: "desecration of the sacred," had the term itself not been so dismally desecrated nowadays." (MN, XV: 231)

In this passage, Gordon is troubled by two phenomena that express, in his opinion, human alienation from nature within modern societies. The first

---

[46] Here, as in other places in MN (for example, VIII: 163), Gordon echoes the term "musical religiosity" popularized be Max Weber (Germany, 1864–1920) in his 1909 letter to the sociologist Ferdinand Tönnies (Germany, 1855–1936). In this well-known letter Weber wrote, "It is true that I am absolutely unmusical religiously and have no need or ability to erect any psychic edifices of a religious character within me. But a thorough self-examination has told me that I am neither antireligious nor irreligious"; quoted in Marianne Weber, *Max Weber: A Biography*, New Brunswick, N.J.: Transaction, 1988, p. 324.

[47] A thematic discussion of Gordon's critique of domination can be found in his essay "Short Study of Halachic Ruling (Reflections on the Army)" (1918), written at the end of the First World War. See GWA, IV: 149–163.

is the preference for artificial over natural beauty ("trees pruned according to the fashion").[48] The second is the placement of billboards by the side of intercity roads and highways, which separates man from the nature that surrounds him.[49]

Gordon was ahead of his time in foreseeing the environmental danger posed by the road construction project that had commenced in the Yishuv (see Figure 4.2). A few decades after Gordon's death, the Israeli Parliament (Knesset) enacted the billboard law (1966). This law, as was mentioned earlier, was initiated by, among others, the prominent writer and parliamentarian S. Yizhar, who saw himself as a disciple and follower of Gordon.[50] Yizhar used the discussion in the Knesset committee that initiated the billboard law as a platform to present his environmental vision. His dramatic speech at the Knesset on the billboard law is a masterpiece of eloquence, and a notable milestone in the history of environmentalism in Hebrew culture.[51]

[48] Gordon develops his aesthetic theory in chapter 11 of MN ("On Beauty"). In the background of Gordon's assault on the worship of artificial beauty is Tolstoy's critique—whose essay "What Is Art?" Gordon translated into Hebrew—of admirers of artificial beauty like the French poet Charles Baudelaire (Paris, 1821–1867), who preferred "woman's face painted rather than showing its natural color, and metal trees and a theatrical imitation of water rather than real trees and real water"; Leo Tolstoy, *What Is Art?*, trans. Aylmer Maude, Overland Park, Kans.: Digireads Publishing, 2020, p. 65. Like Gordon, the Italian author and political activist Natalia Ginzburg (Italy, 1916–1991) was also troubled by urban ornamental trees. In an essay, "Praise and Complaint of England" (1961), written during her stay in London she notes that "from time to time on the street you find yourself in front of a beautiful tree covered in tender pink or brilliant white blossom, a gracious adornment to the street. But as you look at it you realize that it is there according to some precise plan and not by chance. And the fact that it is not there by chance but according to a precise plan makes its beauty seem sad. In Italy a tree in blossom at the roadside would be a delightful surprise. It would be there by chance . . . " Natalia Ginzburg, "Praise and Complaint of England," in Ginzburg, *The Little Virtues*, trans. Dick Davis, New York: Arcade Publishing, 2016, p. 22.

[49] In various places in Germany the desire to rid the roadways of advertising led to their restriction by law already in the beginning of the twentieth century. See John Alexander Williams, *Turning to Nature in Germany: Hiking, Nudism, and Conservation, 1900–1940*, Stanford: Stanford University Press, 2007, pp. 225–226.

[50] Like Gordon before him, Yizhar belongs to the tradition of enchantment of nature in the Land of Israel. In her comprehensive biography of Yizhar, Nitza Ben-Artzi puts is as follows: "Some see the forest that will be on the bald hills in fifty years, and some see the prophets who walked on the hills two thousand years ago—while Yizhar sees only the praying Stellagama [rough-tailed rock lizard prevalent in the Land of Israel] which no one cares about, and no one understands what Yizhar found in it"; Nitsa Ben-Ari, *S. Yizhar: A Life Story* [Heb.], Tel Aviv: Tel Aviv University, 2013, vol. 1, p. 27. In the spirit of Gordon's remarks regarding the monotheistic nature of the desert (MN, IV.2: 86–87), Yizhar describes in one of his early novellas, "On the Outskirts of the Negev" (1945), how the pioneers who are laying water pipes in the Negev merge with the landscape in which they are working. See S. Yizhar, *On the Outskirts of the Negev* [Heb.], Tel Aviv: Hakibbutz Hameuchad, 1978, pp. 133–134. On Gordon's influence on S. Yizhar see Yuval Jobani and Gideon Katz, "In the Convoy and alongside It: A Study of S. Yizhar's Works on Education and Literature," *Contemporary Jewry*, 36: 2 (2016), p. 204, n. 3; ibid., p. 211, n. 32. See also Dvir Tzur, "Between Hallelujah and Requiem: Toiling of the Land in the Works of A.D. Gordon, S. Yizhar and Elie Shamir" [Heb.], *Alpayim Ve'Od: Rethinking Culture in Israel—A Biannual Journal*, vol. 2 (2019), pp. 175–197.

[51] "Debate of Billboard Law," in *Knesset Protocols*, Jerusalem: Government Print, 1965, vol. 44, pp. 57–58.

Figure 4.2. Members of the Labor Battalion (*Gdud HaAvoda*) during road construction work in Migdal Farm near the Sea of Galilee, 1921. Unknown photographer. Nadav Mann, Bitmuna. From a collection of glass slides in Messiah Church. The Pritzker Family National Photography Collection, The National Library of Israel.

Yizhar, "The knight warrior for protection of the landscape of the country," as he was called by one of the participants in the discussion,[52] declared,

> A damaged object located at a top of a hill damages its entire surroundings from horizon to horizon. . . . One hundred meters is not distant enough, not even two hundred meters. Open and clean as far as the eye can see, beyond the hill ridge. The sides of the road must be completely clean; nothing should damage or pollute the open fields. No billboards, no signs, no artificial objects and even, as far as possible, no utility or telephone poles. . . . Let there be an advertisement-free space, the marketplace boundary should

---

[52] Member of the Knesset Shlomo-Ya'akov Gross (Austro-Hungarian Empire–Israel, 1908–2003) of the Religious Torah Front Party. See "Debate of Billboard Law," p. 59. Gross was a member of a special Knesset committee on environmental issues. On contemporary attitudes toward environment and wastefulness among Ultra-Orthodox Jewish communities see Tanhum Yoreh, "Consumption, Wastefulness, and Simplicity in Ultra-Orthodox Communities," *Studies in Judaism, Humanities, and the Social Sciences*, 2: 2 (2018), pp. 137–152; ibid., "Recycling in Jerusalem: Right or Privilege?," *Local Environment* 19: 4 (2014), pp. 417–432.

be the same as the boundary of the city, it should not go beyond the *eruv* line. . . .[53] In our time there are not many pedestrians; everyone "flies" in their vehicle, and what they see on both sides of the road they see only dimly and hastily. Nevertheless, they conceive something which accumulates from their day-to-day travels. And why should it not be a thing of beauty, peace and openness, a clean space, instead of corrupted things that take possession [of the drivers' mind]?[54]

Yizhar even goes as far as to demand that the subcommittee authorized to permit the placement of noncommercial signs by the side of the roads, such as safety signs, must include "not only representatives of the National Highway Traffic Safety Administration and the Ministry of Agriculture, but also representatives on behalf of the landscape, the historic sites and relics, groups of trees, as well as representatives on behalf of even a single tree or field. . . ."[55]

In the spirit of Gordon's view of the subconscious influence of nature on man (MN, I: 18), Yizhar states that everything in nature "sticks like glue to the passers-by, even as they rush past in a car, even when they are drowsy and inattentive to the scenery. The beauty outdoors sticks like glue, while the opposite, the ugliness outside, sticks like glue even more firmly."[56] In the discussion Member of the Knesset Uri Avneri also highlighted the subconscious influence of nature on man. Avneri argued that billboards by the side of intercity roads and highways should be removed immediately because they "cruelly disturb the unconscious intimacy [of man] with nature."[57]

Gordon, who warns against the mental damage caused by the billboards placed alongside the railway tracks on his way from Trieste to Vienna, is not enthusiastic, to say the least, about what he encounters when he arrives in Vienna. This city, "praised as one of the most beautiful cities in Europe" (MN, XV: 232), well illustrates the psychological turmoil of urban life, or

---

[53] Literarily "mix," the eruv is a legal halakhic device that circumvents the restrictions concerning mobility and carrying things on Shabbat. The eruv involves a series of strings hung around the boundary of the city. Yizhar employs here the distinctive halakhic term *eruv* despite his radical secularism, which is expressed, for example, in his influential essay "The Courage to Be Secular." On Yizhar's "secular radicalism" see S. Yizhar, "The Courage to Be Secular" [Heb.], in Yizhar, *A Call for Education*, Tel Aviv: Sifriat Poalim, 1984, pp. 125–139; See also Jobani and Katz, "In the Convoy and Alongside It." On the eruv see Barry Smith, "On Place and Space: The Ontology of the Eruv," in C. Kanzian (ed.), *Cultures: Conflict—Analysis—Dialogue*, Frankfurt: Ontos Verlag, 2007, pp. 403–416.

[54] "Debate of Billboard Law," p. 37.

[55] "Debate of Billboard Law," p. 58.

[56] Ibid., p. 57.

[57] Ibid., p. 56.

as Gordon puts it, "the effect of the city on the soul, on the soul that is not polished and not constricted in a corset!" (MN, XV: 232). The psychological challenges posed by the dizzying rate of growth of cities in the early twentieth century is a recurring theme in MN.[58] In this context Gordon claims that in Vienna there

> are indeed many wide streets, plenty of trees and greenery, but it is full of tall crates, six to nine stories tall, that resemble tombstones, sometimes re- markably beautiful, rather than lively dwellings. Again, the same skyline of icy rigidness, imposes itself on the streets, the same seething live money and hypnotic clinging to the slogan: "time is money,"[59] the same anxious pursuit after business, wealth, and all kinds of pleasures, or after mere bread, as if life is held in some bowl or cauldron, and everyone hurries to snatch as much as possible before all the others. Again, the same alienation between one another, the same withdrawal from one another and the same formal elegance and decorous civility conveyed in the facial expressions. (MN, XV: 232–233)[60]

[58] Various factors promoted rapid population growth in capital cities in Europe between 1890 and 1914. The population of London, for example, grew from about 5.5 million inhabitants in 1891 to nearly 7 million in 1911; Paris grew from about 3 million inhabitants in 1885 to nearly 4.5 million in 1911, and Berlin from 1.6 million in 1890 to 2.1 million in 1910. Vienna, to which Gordon refers here, had a little over half a million inhabitants in 1850, in 1890 it had nearly 1.4 million inhabitants, while in 1910 it had more than 2 million inhabitants. See Rina Peled and Sharon Gordon (eds.), *Vienna 1900: Blooming on the Edge of an Abyss* [Heb.], Jerusalem: Carmel, 2019, p. 13.

[59] Benjamin Franklin's (Boston–Philadephia, 1706–1790) well-known slogan "Time is Money" appears in his short letter "Tips for a Young Merchant" (1748) in which he writes, "remember that time is money"; Benjamin Franklin, "Advice to a Young Tradesman" (July 21, 1748), *The Papers of Benjamin Franklin—Vol. 3, January 1, 1745, through June 30, 1750*, ed. Leonard W. Labare, New Haven: Yale University Press, 1961, pp. 304–308. In this vein, the historian David Potter called the American nation the "People of Plenty," i.e., a people whose distinctive character has been shaped by economic abundance. See David M. Potter, *People of Plenty: Economic Abundance and the American Character*, Chicago: The University of Chicago Press, 2009 [1954].

[60] Only decades later, in stark contrast to Gordon, for whom Vienna stands as a beacon of urban detachment from nature, Stefan Zweig (Vienna–Brazil, 1881–1942) describes Vienna in his auto- biography *The World of Yesterday: Memoires of a European* as a green city that was in tune with its surrounding nature. Vienna, he argues, was "growing slowly through the centuries, organically de- veloping outward from inner circles, it was sufficiently populous, with its two million, to yield all the luxury and all the diversity of a metropolis, and yet it was not so oversized as to be cut off from nature, like London or New York. The last houses of the city mirrored themselves in the mighty Danube or looked out over the wide plains, or dissolved themselves in gardens and fields, or climbed in gradual rises the last green wooded foothills of the Alps. One hardly sensed where nature began and where the city: one melted into the other without opposition, without contradiction. Within, however, one felt that the city had grown like a tree that adds ring upon ring, and instead of the old fortification walls the Ringstrasse encircled the treasured core with its splendid houses"; Stefan Zweig, *The World of Yesterday: Memoires of a European*, trans. Anthea Bell, Lincoln: University of Nebraska Press, 1964 [1942], pp. 13–14.

Gordon argues that the physical architectural features of the tall urban buildings significantly affect the mental life of their tenants. Beneath the politeness and banalities of social interaction of the tenants of the "tall crates" that look like beautiful tombstones lurks the aggression of total war of all against all. In fact, Gordon's use of the image of the tombstone suggests that people who live in the tall urban buildings are actually dead although they still breathe, eat, and drink.[61]

Gordon's critique of urban life in MN echoes the well-known and influential distinction made by the German sociologist Ferdinand Tönnies (1855–1936) between community (*Gemeinschaft*) and society (*Gesellschaft*). While the "organic" community is bound together by personal ties, shared custom, tradition, and values, individuals who live in a "mechanical" society interact through self-interest, institutions, and commercial contracts.[62] Since *Gesellschaft* is based on economic interest alone it set up for the individuals who live in it a life of alienation that starkly contrasts with the cohesive and natural life in the *Gemeinschaft*.

Moreover, in pointing out the psychological damage caused by the urban lifestyle, Gordon is close to his contemporary German-Jewish sociologist and philosopher Georg Simmel. In his classic and influential essay "The Metropolis and Mental Life" (1903) Simmel argues that the alienation, loneliness, and indifference of urban man are a form of existential defense against the flow of stimuli that otherwise would overwhelm him. In order to

---

[61] Gordon's criticism of the Viennese extravagance and their boundless proclivity to luxury resembles the way in which the pre-Socratic Greek philosopher Empedocles of Akragas (Sicily–Peloponnese, 494–434 BCE) is said to have described the mindset of his fellow citizens: "The Agrigentines live delicately as if tomorrow they would die, but they build their houses well as if they thought they would live forever"; Diogenes Laertius, *Lives of Eminent Philosophers*, trans. Robert Drew Hicks, Cambridge: Harvard University Press, 1925, vol. II, 8.63, p. 377.

[62] Although Ferdinand Tönnies' classic in sociology, *Gemeinschaft und Gesellschaft*, was first published as far back as 1887, it made its fortune only after its 1912 reissue, and especially after World War I. Tönnies was not the first one to employ the dichotomy between *Gemeinschaft* and *Gesellschaft*, and he was mainly influenced by Theodor Mommsen's (Germany, 1817–1903) usage of these terms in his 1870 edition of Justinian's *Digest*. Tönnies expands and deepens this distinction and uses it as a tool for understanding different disciplines of society and culture, such as religion and art. See Jose Harris, "Introduction to Community and Civil Society" in Ferdinand Tönnies, *Community and Civil Society*, ed. Jose Harris, trans. Margaret Hollis and Jose Harris, Cambridge: Cambridge University Press, 2001 [1887], pp. xxi, xxvii–xxviii. See also Peter Gay, *Weimar Culture: The Outsider as Insider*, New York: W. W. Norton & Company, 2001, p. 80. Although Gordon does not refer explicitly to Tönnies, he shared several of his main premises. A thorough comparison between Tönnies's and Gordon's accounts of human nature and society extends beyond the scope of this study. Its essence is in the broad psychological framework they provide for their critique of culture and society. In this context Tönnies argues that the two basic types of social formations, *Gemeinschaft* (community) and *Gesellschaft* (society), are respectively anchored in two fundamental types of human will: the natural and spontaneous will (*Wesenwille*) on the one hand and the calculated and rational will (*Kürwille*) on the other. See Tönnies, *Community and Civil Society*, pp. 95–131.

maintain mental and emotional equilibrium in face of external disturbances, the urban man adopts a detached and cold attitude toward the things, events, and people around him. The intensification of the intellectual and cognitive capacities of urban man had "dried up" his emotional capacities, as well as his ability to maintain meaningful connection not only with others, but also with himself. The urban man "becomes a single cog facing an overwhelming, vast organization of factors and forces which gradually take out of his hands everything connected with progress, spirituality and value."[63] Unlike Gordon, who points out only the flaws in urban life, Simmel also points to the freedom and anonymity enjoyed by those who dwell in the metropolis, and he clearly holds a nonjudgmental attitude toward urban life. In an objective tone—which itself can be seen as a product of urban life—Simmel concludes his essay with the following reflection: "It is our task not to complain or to condone but only to understand."[64]

Gordon's proximity to Simmel is clear and well established. In addition to the issue of urbanity, Gordon is also close to Simmel's distinction discussed earlier between religiosity and religion, that is, to the distinction between the experiential content of the direct contact with the absolute ("religiosity") and its institutionalization and stagnation in the social realm ("religion").[65]

In addition, like Simmel in his monumental book *The Philosophy of Money* (1900), Gordon also acknowledges the absolute domination of money as the organizing principle of modernity. The character of modern social life, as Gordon puts it, is commercial by reason of its nature (MN, XVI: 238). Gordon argues repeatedly that the evils of modern society result from the tendency of individuals to put their financial interests above all other goals and values.[66]

The spirit of Simmel's *Lebensphilosophie* (philosophy of life) also hovers above MN. Life, Simmel argues, is an experiential outburst that constantly struggles with cognitive, religious, and social forms that seek to flatten life into concepts, norms, and rituals. Gordon's philosophy is a philosophy of life in the simplest and most elementary sense; it issues from life and returns to it.[67] In this sense, Gordon provides a solid philosophical foundation for the

[63] Simmel, "The Metropolis and Mental Life," in Donald N. Levine (ed. and trans.), *Georg Simmel on Individuality and Social Forms*, Chicago: The University of Chicago Press, 1971, p. 337; translation slightly changed.
[64] See ibid., p. 339.
[65] Simmel, "A Contribution to the Sociology of Religion."
[66] See, for example, MN, I: 32, IV.4: 105, XV: 230–234, XVII: 237–238.
[67] Gordon's philosophy, as Schweid put it, was "for him an organic continuation of his life. He spent the greater part of his life immersed in daily work in the fields and devoted much of his time

pioneers' identification of the Land of Israel with Life, and their yearning to live in the Land of Israel "Life itself," as Yoseph Aharonovich, Gordon's close friend and the editor of the first edition of his writings, has put it.[68]

Although Simmel is not mentioned by name even once in MN, Gordon's daughter Yael confirmed that he had read Simmel's writings during the time they lived in the Baron Ginzburg's (David Goratsiyevich Günzburg, Russian Empire, 1857–1910) Mogilno estate near Minsk.[69] In any case, Gordon could have been indirectly exposed to Simmel's ideas given their significant presence in the cultural landscape in which he was immersed. Simmel's philosophy of life had received keen attention in Russia. In fact, when Simmel passed away in 1918 it was in Russia that he had the largest number of translations.[70] Moreover, at the beginning of the twentieth century, Simmel's ideas permeated the reviving Hebrew culture through the works of Yosef Haim Brenner and Micha Berdyczewski as well as Eastern European Hebrew literature in general. However, it was Martin Buber, one of Simmel's closest students and a member of his inner circle, who contributed more than anyone else to the reception of Simmel's *Lebensphilosophie* into Hebrew culture.[71]

Gordon argues that the disjunction of urban man from nature has corrupted him and made him miserable. As society advances, men's natural virtues are replaced by artificial desires and false needs. "The intensification of city life," states Gordon, "results in overdevelopment of various inclinations and desires, such as lust for power, wealth, and honor—all of

and spiritual energies to warm and genuine friendships with his fellows"; Eliezer Schweid, *The Individual: The World of AD Gordon* [Heb.], Tel Aviv: Am Oved, 1970, p. 15.

[68] "Our lives in exile are broken today as they have been broken throughout the ages," writes Aharonovich, "and we want to change them not for any external purpose, but for its own sake, for the sake of life itself"; Yoseph Aharonovich, "The Spirit and Matter in Zionism" (1913), in Aharonovich, *Collected Works of Yoseph Aharonovich* [Heb.], Tel Aviv: Am Oved, 1941, vol. 1, pp. 107–108. Eliezer Shochat, who co-edited the second edition of Gordon's writings with Hugo Bergman, writes in a similar spirit, "Life is wide and deep . . . if we ourselves do not contract it"; Shochat, "Letter to His Wife Hannah Meisel Shochat" (August 17, 1923), in Yosef Shapira (ed.), *Eliezer Shochat: About Him, His Path, in His Memory* [Heb.], Tel Aviv: Mifaley Tarbut Vechinuch, 1973, pp. 142–143.

[69] Yael Gordon, "My Father prior to His Arrival to Eretz Israel" [Heb.], T: 31.

[70] David Frisby, "Bibliographical Note on Simmel's Works in Translation," *Theory, Culture & Society*, 8: 3 (1991), p. 236.

[71] On the reception of Simmel into Hebrew culture at the beginning of the twentieth century see Amos Morris-Reich, "Introduction" [Heb.], in Morris-Reich (ed.), *How Is Society Possible and Other Essays by Georg Simmel*, trans. Miryam Kraus, Tel Aviv: Hakibbutz Hameuchad, 2012, pp. 14–18. On Simmel's profound impact on Buber see also Paul Mendes-Floher, *From Mysticism to Dialogue: Martin Buber's Transformation of German Social Thought*, Detroit: Wayne State University Press, 1989.

which are symptoms of a parasitic life. In addition, the satisfaction of sexual desire becomes a goal in itself" (MN, IV.4: 104). Instead of integrating his life with nature due to a deep sense of responsibility toward it, man strives to dominate nature and in turn becomes aggressive toward other people. He moves away from those who by nature are close and dear to him: "Love of one's fellow man, love of family, love of friends, the virtue of compassion—all of these fade away as man becomes more 'progressive,' especially, as social life increasingly concentrates in large cities" (MN, I: 22). In order to control nature, man strives to understand it through rational scientific inquiry that increasingly distances him from it. Therefore, "large cities are always the centers of knowledge and corruption" (MN, I: 22). The parasitic exploitation that characterizes the relationship between people who reside in large cities is couched in the parasitic exploitation on which the very existence of large cities is based. Large cities, Gordon argues, "always exist at the expense of the villages and small towns that they ruin in order to decrease their deficit" (MN, I: 22).[72] Alienation from nature cannot be alleviated by planting trees, flowers, and bushes or by establishing public gardens and parks in large cities, as they themselves are nothing but products of an artificial and alienated urban culture. Summing up his impressions of Vienna, Gordon writes, "the trees and the greenery and nature in general look as if they were given the right to reside here only as a decoration, granted the permission to show themselves to people only when trimmed and embellished according to the current dictates of fashion" (MN, XV: 233). Gordon's uncompromising critique of the green lungs of large cities proves how aptly the subtitle of MN, "*Meditations and Dreams of a Radical*," captures his basic philosophical impulse.

Gordon does not mention the name of the friend who was with him on the train. But he notes that his companion (just like Yehuda Leib Metmann, whose enthusiasm for urbanism was discussed at length earlier) lauded the wonders of urban life and saw it as a means to ensure the prosperity of the Yishuv. Gordon, however, was horrified:

When my friend, who was with me on the train, asked with admiration, "Would you like us to have such cities in the Land of Israel?"—the answer erupted from my heart, without prior thought, erupted by the power of

[72] As noted earlier, Gordon's critique of urban lifestyle is close to the one that can be found in Rousseau, *Emile, or On Education*, p. 468.

Figure 4.3. Casino "Galei-Aviv," Tel Aviv, 1920s. Gordon opposed those who wished to turn Tel Aviv into a kind of Vienna on the shores of the Mediterranean. Unknown photographer. Album of Yechiel Zehavi, Yad Ben-Zvi Photo Archives.

my depressed feeling, which accompanied me all the way and now grew stronger: "No!"—"No!" And there are people with great intellectual abilities and emotional capabilities who claim that beautiful cities produce people with beautiful souls! It may be a beauty of trimmed trees that serve as decoration for cities, but it is not a beauty of nature. (MN, XV: 233)

In fact, the controversy between the proponents and the opponents of urbanism in the days of the Second Aliyah left its mark on two of its greatest enterprises: the establishment of the first Hebrew city, Tel Aviv (1909), which was supposed to be a kind of Vienna on the shores of the Mediterranean on the one hand (see Figure 4.3),[73] and the founding of Degania (1910), the

[73] In his notes following his first visit to the Land of Israel in 1912, historian and Zionist leader Joseph Klausner (1874–1958) described the newly founded city as follows: "Tel Aviv is surrounded by sand, in front and in the back of the city. And when one considers that but three years earlier sand covered the site on which this charming community stands, you begin to become proud of the movement for national revival. . . . Come see the place in the world where Jews are 'carriers of culture'. . . in place of Jaffa's sand dunes they created the community of 'Tel Aviv' with its beautiful broad streets, marble sidewalks, beautiful boulevards, and villas that offer all that one might find in urban residences of the largest European cities. Is this not the most authentic culture that is worthy of its name—which the children of Israel are bringing from Europe to Asia?" Quoted in Ilan Troen,

earliest socialist Zionist farming commune in the Land of Israel, which is also referred to as "the mother of all *kvutzot* and *kibbutzim*," on the other hand.

Life in Nature as a Religious Life: Between "Minor Heresy" and "Great Heresy"

Instead of living above or below nature, man must live "with and within nature" (MN, IV.2: 92). A life of "supreme union with nature and supreme responsibility toward it is a life of true religion" (MN, IV.2: 92). A truly religious life is a life of complete unification with nature, which necessarily leads to moral responsibility toward nature. Rather than a belief in God, it is such deep and holistic unity with and responsibility toward nature that constitutes according to Gordon the essence of a truly religious life (MN, IV.2: 92). Religiousness can be found, according to Gordon, "whenever a profound soul feels a profound, unmediated appreciation of life . . . wherever there is belief in God and even when there is no belief in God."[74]

The split between religiosity as a profound inner experience and the belief in the existence or nonexistence of God allows Gordon to distinguish between two types of heresy, "minor heresy" against which he contended, and "great heresy," which he elevates to the level of true religiosity. We will turn now to explore the different characteristics of these two types of heresy and Gordon's attitude toward them, and we shall begin with the "minor heresy."

In the first chapter of MN, Gordon identifies the dire consequences of what he describes as man's separation from nature (MN, I: 21–28). The emotional and spiritual damage inflicted on man in this traumatic process was far worse than the physical harm, and it led to the "clogging of the channels of Divine Abundance [. . .] in the spheres of ideals and creation" (MN, I: 23–24). All

---

"Tel Aviv: Vienna on the Mediterranean" in Troen, *Imagining Zion: Dreams, Designs, and Realities in a Century of Jewish Settlement*, New Haven: Yale University Press, 2008, p. 91 (translation slightly changed). See also Benjamin Zeev Kedar, *The Changing Land between the Jordan and the Sea: Aerial Photographs from 1917 to the Present* [Heb.], Tel Aviv: Israel Ministry of Defense, 1999, p. 94; Tzafrir Fainholtz, "A Mediterranean Vienna: The Work of Viennese Architects and the Presence of Central European Culture in the Haifa of the 1930s and 1940s," *The Leo Baeck Institute Year Book*, 62 (2017), pp. 197–223. For Gordon's criticism of the newly founded Tel Aviv see his "Little Observation" (1911), GWA, I: 77–78.

[74] Gordon, "Our Self Reflection," GWA, III: 161–162. In this context Lahav suggested reading Gordon as a post-secular theologian who propounds a hybrid theology, rejecting traditional religion on the one hand and atheism on the other. See Hagar Lahav, "Postsecular Jewish Theology: Reading Gordon and Buber," *Israel Studies*, 19: 1 (2014), pp. 189–213.

spheres of culture and society, including the religious sphere, have been neg-
atively impacted by man's detachment from nature.

We live in an age of "idol-shattering," Gordon states, echoing the title of
Nietzsche's influential book *Twilight of the Idols, or, How to Philosophize with
a Hammer* published in 1888. Man's disengagement from nature leads him
"to complete heresy, to a terrible emptiness and to utter despair" (MN, I: 26).
However, Gordon insists that

> it is not heresy itself that it is dangerous, but rather the scant, minor heresy,
> which has no deep roots in the soul of the heretic nor in his mind. The
> minor heresy is sown by every wind, which carries this light seed on its
> wings. It grows, like these desert thorns, where there is no food for superior
> plants. . . . That is why there are so few creators and so many who despair
> and take their own life. The heresy of our time is a product of exhaustion,
> stagnation, and lifelessness. Modern man spent the remnants of his vitality,
> his spiritual power and his "additional soul" (*neshamah yetera*) on nega-
> tion, while for creation nothing was left. (MN, I: 26–28)

From this passage it follows that the minor heresy has four characteristics: (I)
It only destroys and negates beliefs and ways of life without creating or offering alternatives for them. (II) It does not issue from the soul of man or
from his inner being but is externally imposed on him by the alienated zeit-
geist in which he lives. (III) It takes root and thrives in people with a weak
and passive personality. (IV) The minor heresy might lead to a dangerous
depletion of men's vitality, and in some cases even to suicide.

The great heresy also denies the existence of God, but its characteristics
and impact are completely different. "The great, original heresy," declares
Gordon,

> the daughter of the great sorrow and the great seeking thought, is no
> less fertile and creative than the great faith, which is also the daughter
> of the great sorrow and the great seeking thought. In ancient times the
> great heresy gave birth to the wonderful religion of Buddha [Siddhārtha
> Gautama *Buddha*; India, fl. ca. 450 BCE]. In our time, it created the idea of
> the Overhuman. This is the power of the great sorrow, the spouse of the
> great thought, that wherever it is found it creates. The great sorrow does
> not let its owner rest, not even in death. For how might death alleviate great
> sorrow if sorrow remains in the world after death? Is it true that "he will

save himself"[75] escaping thus, giving his soul such a label of shame? Can he escape in that way? Without consent he lives, without consent he bears the great sorrow, for who could bear such a burden, who would have the strength to know and understand how to bear the great sorrow?—Without consent, he seeks to help all who suffer, and he creates. This is perhaps the most terrible sense of the saying: "without consent you live" [Mishnah Avot 4: 22],[76] but also the greatest and the most sublime one. Such great heresy—like great faith—is rare to find in our time. (MN, I: 27)

From this passage it follows that great heresy has four characteristics: (I) It creates and offers alternatives to existing beliefs and ways of life. (II) It requires exceptional imaginative and creative powers that only men of merit possess. (III) It offers a solution to the existential crisis (the "great sorrow") resulting from man's separation from nature and from himself. (IV) It provides psychological and philosophical tools for coping with distressing life challenges that may lead to depression and even suicide.

Here, as elsewhere in MN, Gordon presents Buddha on the one hand and Nietzsche on the other as exemplary personifications of great heresy. Indeed, he holds a profoundly ambivalent attitude toward them. On the one hand, he recoils from Buddha's extreme asceticism as well as from Nietzsche's domineering attitude and worship of power. On the other hand, he is drawn to their comprehensive and life-affirming philosophies, which he sees as first-rate expressions of true religiosity.[77] Their ingrained reluctance to view human life as meaningless or worthless and their appeal to man to transcend himself in order to live a life of meaning and purpose, Gordon argues, "is acknowledgement of God . . . stronger than any conscious acknowledgement" (MN, IV.2: 92).[78]

---

[75] Gordon probably has in mind the verse "He pursues ashes! A deluded mind has led him astray, and he cannot save himself; He never says to himself, the thing in my hand is a fraud!" (Isaiah 44:20).

[76] *Mishnah Avot*, in Shaye J. D. Cohen, Robert Goldenberg, and Hayim Lapin (eds.), *The Oxford Annotated Mishnah*, New York: Oxford University Press, 2022, p. 739.

[77] Gordon discusses the thought of Nietzsche and Buddha in different places in MN. See Golomb, "The Agricultural Philosopher"; Arie Kremerman, *Buddhism in A.D. Gordon's Philosophy* [Heb.], MA thesis, Tel Aviv: Tel Aviv University, 2017.

[78] In his separation between religiosity as lived experience and the belief in the existence of God Gordon is close to Simmel, who asserts that "[Religiosity] will usually lead to the development of articles of faith and to the adoption of a transcendental reality, but it is not necessarily bound indissolubly to man's religious nature and inclination. Just as an erotic person is always erotic in nature, whether or not he has created—or ever will create—an object of love, so too is a religious person always religious, whether or not he believes in a God"; Georg Simmel, "Fundamental Religious Ideas and Modern Science: An Inquiry" (1909), in Simmel, *Essays on Religion*, p. 5.

Buddha, for example,

who denied the existence of God, demanded of himself and of others a deep moral commitment. One might say that this demand proves that he unconsciously, in the great depth of his life, believed in God more than any believer who had not reached such deep moral responsibility. . . . Buddha lived in nature and was nurtured by its supreme abundance in an unmediated way. (MN, IV.3: 100)

Gordon identifies a deeply rooted religious impulse also in Nietzsche, especially, "in those moments when a deep spiritual aspiration for a higher morality and for the purity of the supreme virtues emanates from his words" (MN, IV.2: 92).

Gordon's preference for the great heresy over the minor heresy is philosophical. At the same time, it is anchored in a concrete historical setting that deserves attention. The background for Gordon's claim regarding the link between the minor heresy and the phenomenon of suicide is the high suicide rate among young pioneers in the Land of Israel in the beginning of the twentieth century, which was indicated earlier.[79] It was important for Gordon to deny any direct and simple connection between the alarming rates of suicide and the intense secularization process that occurred in the Yishuv at the time. "It is not heresy itself," Gordon argues, "that is dangerous, but the minor heresy" (MN, I: 26). Depleting the vital energies of the youth, it is the minor heresy and not heresy itself that might explain why in the Second Aliyah period "so many people are overcome by despair and take their own life" (MN, I: 27).

The great heresy, on the other hand, might equip the youth with mental resources and philosophical insights that will empower them and enable them to face the changes and challenges brought about by their immigration to Land of Israel. By associating great sorrow with great creation, Gordon continues the Western existential tradition whose outstanding representative

---

[79] Muki Tsur, who estimates suicide was the cause of death in more than a tenth of the deaths of the young people during the Second Aliyah, notes that the pioneers did not keep the Jewish custom of burying the body of a suicide outside the fence of the cemetery. As an expression of sympathy, the suicide was buried in the same place where people who died a natural death were buried, and on his tombstone it was clearly stated that he took his own life. See Tsur, *Doing It the Hard Way*, pp. 27–44. On the high suicide rate among young pioneers of the Second Aliyah see Gur Alroey, "Pioneers or Lost Souls? The Issue of Suicide in the Second and the Third Aliya" [Heb.], *Contemporary Jewry*, vol. 13 (1999), pp. 209–241.

is Nietzsche, who drew special inspiration from Oliver Cromwell's (England, 1599–1658) maxim "a man never rises higher than when he does not know whither his path can still lead him."[80] The tradition of redemption from the depths of despair is also deeply rooted in the Bible and is fully expressed in the well-known proclamation of the prophet Jeremiah: "It is a time of trouble for Jacob, but he shall be delivered from it" (Jeremiah 30: 7).

The call to turn crisis into opportunity had profound resonance in the Second Aliyah period.[81] An outstanding example of this call can be found in one of Gordon's letters to Brenner, in which he identifies the despairing with the pioneers who march ahead of the camp: "We welcome those who despair!" he writes, "We welcome individuals who do not give up and do not abandon the battle, we welcome the desperate, who harness their despair for building . . . for rekindling the power to awaken the nation, the whole nation; to reflect where they are in the world; to prepare the way for revival and resurrection; to ask for everything an awakened nation can ask—and this is the crux of the matter."[82]

On Gordon's "Religious Secularism"

Gordon's equation between "great heresy" and "great faith" (MN, I: 27) makes it difficult to situate his approach to religion in relation to Jewish secularism, which was developed in the Hebrew culture at the beginning of the twentieth century.[83] Is Gordon a spokesman and representative of Jewish secularism or its antagonist? As we saw earlier, Gordon's critique of religion that occupies the longest chapter in MN lies at the heart of his philosophical project. To carefully assess this critique vis à vis various models of Jewish secularism we have to set aside for a moment our reading of MN and turn to a brief exploration of the philosophical foundations and historical manifestations of Jewish

[80] Friedrich Nietzsche, "Schopenhauer as Educator" (1874), in Nietzsche, *Untimely Meditations (Cambridge Texts in the History of Philosophy)*, trans. R. J. Hollingdale, Cambridge: Cambridge University Press, 1997, p. 129.
[81] Avraham Shapira, *The Kabbalistic and Hasidic Sources of A.D. Gordon's Thought* [Heb.], Tel Aviv: Am Oved, 1996, pp. 46, 89–92.
[82] "Open letter to Y. H. Brenner" (1912), GWA, I: 106.
[83] The literature is vast. See, for example, Moti Zeira, *Rural Collective Settlement and Jewish Culture in Eretz Israel during the 1920s* [Heb.], Jerusalem: Yad Ben-Zvi, 2002; David Knaani, *The Labor Second Aliyah and Its Attitude Toward Religion and Tradition* [Heb.], Tel Aviv: Sifriat Po'alim, 1975; David Biale, *Not in the Heavens: The Tradition of Jewish Secular Thought*, Princeton University Press, 2010; Udi Tsabari, *Secularization, Secularism and Secularity in the Lives and Thought of Y. H. Brenner and A. D. Gordon* [Heb.], PhD thesis, Tel Aviv: Tel Aviv University, 2017.

secularism. In what follows we shall offer a succinct presentation of the prevalent understanding of the secularization process and the secular condition resulting from it. Delineating the secular landscape of Hebrew culture in the first half of the twentieth century will not only shed new light on Gordon's original religious vision but also enable us to extract from it concepts, insights, and inspiration for non-halakhic Jewish renewal.

"Secularization," in its narrow sense, is a Christian *terminus technicus*, denoting the transfer of a person or an object from the religious sphere to the secular sphere (*Saeculum*).[84] Beyond this narrow ecclesiastical-legal sense, Charles Taylor offers in his book *A Secular Age* a significant distinction between three basic and well-established notions of secularization.[85]

The first notion of secularization signifies the retreat of religion from the public sphere to the private sphere.[86] Consequently, the organizing principles and values of different fields of human activity—such as politics, economics, and art—become independent and are no longer subordinate to strict religious dogmas and norms. The state frees itself from the grip of the church and its dogmas, which are replaced by new secular values and institutions. However, citizens of countries that have separated church from state, such as the United States, may continue to believe in God and lead religious lives.[87]

---

[84] For a detailed discussion of the different meanings of the term *saeculum* see José Casanova, *Public Religions in the Modern World*, Chicago: The University of Chicago Press, 1994, pp. 12–17. See also Yehoshua Arieli, "Modern History as Reinstatement of the Saeculum: A Study in the Semantics of History," *Journal of Jewish History*, vol. 8 (1994), pp. 205–228.

[85] Charles Taylor, *A Secular Age*, Cambridge: Harvard University Press, 2007. Taylor's distinction is philosophically oriented, and as such more suitable for a better understanding of Gordon's critique of religion than Somerville's historical distinction between six meanings of the notion of secularization. See John C. Somerville, "Secular Society/Religious Population: Our Tacit Rules for Using the Term 'Secularization,'" *Journal for the Scientific Study of Religion*, vol. 37 (1998), pp. 252–253. See also Barry A. Kosmin, "Contemporary Secularity and Secularism," in Barry A. Kosmin and Ariela Keysar (eds.), *Secularism and Secularity: Contemporary International Perspectives*, Hartford, Conn.: Institute for the Study of Secularism in Society and Culture, 2007, pp. 1–13.

[86] Beginning in the late nineteenth and early twentieth centuries, as Margolin argues, "Western culture showed increased interest in the connection between religion and the inner psychological life of the individual. This interest was sparked by the search for new forms of religious life, as sociologists [. . .] predicted a bleak future for institutional religion in the modern world. By revealing the subjective psychological contents of the religious individual, thinkers such as William James and Rudolf Otto showed that modern man could come into personal contact with religious life, while disregarding its institutionalized and social aspects. These elements of religion were increasingly perceived as external only, devoid of inner psychological meaning, and irrelevant for the modern social outer life that replaces organized religion"; Ron Margolin, *Inner Religion in Jewish Sources: A Phenomenology of Inner Religious Life and Its Manifestation from the Bible to Hasidic Texts*, trans. Edward Levin, Boston: Academic Studies Press, 2021, pp. 8–9.

[87] Secularization, as Yehoshua Arieli puts it, "expresses the quintessence of the modern era to the same degree that the domination of the Church and beliefs over all dimensions of society expressed the essence of the Middle Ages"; Arieli, "Modern History as Reinstatement of the Saeculum," p. 217. In this context Somerville even suggests that "the very creation of religious institutions (e.g., churches) could be considered an instance of secularization, where it separated specifically

The second notion of secularization signifies the collapse of religious beliefs, traditions, and institutions. In Western European countries, for example, religion still maintains itself in the public sphere, but the number of people belonging to religious denominations and/or attending religious services is declining significantly. The third notion of secularization signifies a transition from a social-historical context in which faith in God is central and axiomatic, to a social-historical context in which a religious life is not obvious in and of itself but only one among many options.[88] The latter notion of secularization, which we shall adopt in our discussion, suggests religion's loss of hegemony over human existence. Our era is a "secular era" not because religion has no place in it but because religion occupies an increasingly narrow and restricted place in it.

In Hebrew culture of the first half of the twentieth century this fragmentary character of religion gave rise to different attitudes toward the Jewish religion. Some attempt to abolish it, others attempt to integrate it into secularism, and others still demand to maintain its autonomy and call to conduct an ongoing and intense dialogue with the Jewish religion. These attitudes might be clustered under three models of Jewish secularism, each of which is grounded in a different philosophical understanding of the secularization project: the radical model, the pluralistic model, and the religious model of which Gordon, as we will see, was one of its founding fathers.[89]

The radical model of Jewish secularism goes beyond the three understandings of secularism suggested by Taylor. Its demands are not satisfied by the dissolving of religion's political monopoly (the first notion), nor by the loosening of religion's grip on the individual (the second notion), and not even by the "fragmentary character" of religious existence in the secular age (the third notion). The radical model seeks to abolish religion altogether for, as Israeli philosopher Yirmiyahu Yovel (1935–2018) puts it, "it has exhausted its role as a civilization-generating force, and now it is a hindrance to

---

religious institutions from some original 'primitive fusion'"; Somerville, "Secular Society/Religious Population," p. 250.

[88] Taylor describes the position in which the believer finds himself within what he calls "a secular age" as follows: "I may find it inconceivable that I would abandon my faith, but there are others, including possibly some very close to me, whose way of living I cannot in all honesty just dismiss as depraved, or blind, or unworthy, who have no faith (at least not in God, or the transcendent). Belief in God is no longer axiomatic. There are alternatives"; Taylor, *A Secular Age*, p. 3.

[89] For a detailed discussion on these models see Yuval Jobani, "The Lure of Heresy: A philosophical Typology of Hebrew Secularism in the First Half of the Twentieth Century," *The Journal of Jewish Thought and Philosophy*, 24: 1 (2016), pp. 95–121.

man's moral and rational improvement, producing mainly intolerance, violence, oppression, and holy wars."[90]

Y. H. Brenner, Gordon's young friend and interlocutor, provided an illuminating example of the radical secular outlook in his attempt to break free from the authority of the religious canon—a term whose Greek etymon (kanōn) signifies a ruler or measuring stick. In his essay "In Journals and in Literature," which sparked the debate known as the "Brenner affair" (1910–1911), Brenner declared,

> As for me, even the Old Testament does not have the value that all scream about—"Scripture," "The Book of Books," "The Holy Writ," and so forth. I have been liberated from the hypnosis of the twenty-four books of the Bible for a long, long time. . . . Many secular books of recent times are much closer to me, far greater and deeper in my eyes.[91]

Brenner's call for radical secular individualism refers to, among others, Ahad Ha'am's argument of the inevitable indoctrination of the individual through society. As Ahad Ha'am puts it,

> The social environment produces the hypnotic sleep in him [i.e., the individual] from his earliest years. In the form of education, it imposes on him a load of various commands, which from the outset limit his movement. . . . Language and literature, religion and morality, laws and customs—all these and their like are means through which society puts the private individual to sleep and ceaselessly repeats its commands, until he is unable to evade them.[92]

---

[90] Yirmiyahu Yovel, "General Introduction" [Heb.], in Yirmiyahu Yovel, Yair Tzaban, and David Shaham (eds.), New Jewish Time—Jewish Culture in a Secular Age: An Encyclopedic View [Heb.], Jerusalem: Keter Press, 2007, vol. I., p. xv. The publication of the five volumes of this project, to which over two hundred scholars contributed, is the most comprehensive treatment of Jewish secularism so far. Although Spinoza's bold and outright attack on the theological concept of God is employed by proponents of the radical model of Jewish secularism, his critique of religion does not go hand in hand with their call for a complete elimination of religion. Spinoza's critique of religion was for revision rather than abolition of religion. See Yuval Jobani, "Ethical or Political Religion? On the Contradiction between Two Models of Amended Religion in Spinoza's Theological-Political Treatise," Hebraic Political Studies, 3: 4, 2008, pp. 396–415.

[91] Brenner, "In Journals and in Literature," pp. 482–483. On this essay, which was written in response to the conversion of young Jews to Christianity, see Nurit Govrin, "The Brenner Affair" The Fight for Free Speech [Heb.], Jerusalem: Yad Ben Zvi, 1985. See also Avi Sagi, To Be a Jew: Joseph Chayim Brenner as a Jewish Existentialist, trans. Batya Stein, London: Continuum, 2011, pp. 111–135.

[92] Ahad Ha'am, "Two Domains" [Heb.], in Ha'am, Collected Writings, Tel Aviv: Dvir, 1965, p. 83.

As an existentialist, Brenner presents himself as a defender of individualism and freedom grounded in critical reflection against religious forces and norms. Devoid of any moral or existential significance, the religious canon is marginalized by the radical model of Jewish secularism as nothing but an object of philological or historical interest. In the framework of this model the study of the canonical texts turns into science detached from the scholar's cultural and emotional life. It is conducted alongside a determined rejection of the religious culture that produced these texts. In words attributed to Moritz Steinschneider (Austrian Empire–Berlin, 1816–1907), one of the founding fathers of the *Wissenschaft des Judentums* (Science of Judaism) in the nineteenth century, "The object of *Wissenschaft des Judentums* is to give Judaism a decent burial."[93]

A particularly extreme form of radical Jewish secularism was launched by the Canaanite movement, whose activity peaked during the 1940s in British Mandate Palestine and declined after the founding of the State of Israel in 1948. The fundamental assertion of the movement that "a Hebrew cannot be Jewish, and a Jew cannot be Hebrew"[94] is a good example of the attempt to exclude the Jewish religion from the boundaries of the regenerating Hebrew culture.[95] Yonatan Ratosh (pseudonym of Uriel Halperin; Russian Empire–Israel, 1908–1981), one of founders of the movement, declared in his "Letter to the Hebrew Youth" (1943), "The tie that binds the generations of Judaism cannot be loosened . . . it can only be severed. And you, son of the motherland, can sever it."[96] Ratosh calls to get rid of the Jewish heritage and the diasporic way of life as if they were a "borrowed, ragged, patched, and tight

---

[93] See Gershom Scholem, "Contemplations on Science of Judaism," [Heb.] in Scholem, *Explications and Implications: Writings on Jewish Heritage and Renaissance*, Tel Aviv: Am Oved, 1976, vol. II, p. 393.

[94] Yonathan Ratosh, "Opening Speech in the Committee of Groups' Envoys Assembly (First Session)" [Heb.], in Ratosh, *The Beginning of Days: Hebrew Openings*, Tel Aviv: Hadar Press, 1982, p. 152. Uzzi Ornan, a former member of the Canaanites and the founder of the League against Religious Coercion, elaborates the Canaanites' campaign to abandon altogether the Jewish ethos, and specifically Jewish religion in his *The Claws of Asmodai* [Heb.], Kiryat Tivon: Enam Press, 1999.

[95] For a detailed discussion of the Canaanites movement see James S. Diamond, *Homeland or Holy Land? The "Canaanite" Critique of Israel*, Bloomington: Indiana University Press, 1986; David Ohana, *The Origins of Israeli Mythology: Neither Canaanites nor Crusaders*, trans. David Maisel, New York: Cambridge University Press, 2012; Klaus Hofmann, "Canaanism," *Middle Eastern Studies*, 47: 2 (2011), pp. 273–294.

[96] Yonathan Ratosh, "Letter to the Hebrew Youth" [Heb.], in Ratosh, *The Beginning of Days*, p. 35. The Canaanites' critique of the Jewish ethos was accompanied by a critique of Zionism that was seen, as Klaus Hofmann puts it, "as falling short of its original aim of creating an alternative to the Jewish Diaspora existence. In the eyes of the Canaanites, Zionism is held captive by the Diaspora Judaism which it has purportedly left behind. It is accused of perpetuating the Diaspora existence in new circumstances, building another ghetto in Palestine, yet lacking the religious essence of the Jewish ghetto"; Klaus Hofmann, "Canaanism," *Middle Eastern Studies*, 47: 2 (2011), pp. 276.

article of clothing"⁹⁷; the Jewish world is described by Ratosh as one that "poisons our souls and the souls of our younger brethren." Speaking about "Judaism's rotten teeth," Ratosh stated the need to "burn all that is rotten and heal all that is sick," to guard against "the Jewish worm" that gnaws at the heart, and, once and for all, to get rid of the "leprosy of disaster that has held Judaism by its heel from the very beginning."⁹⁸

Like other Romantic right-wing movements harking back to a legendary ancient past, the Canaanites were taken by the primitivism and paganism of the ancient Israelites, and by doing so they distanced themselves from the main strand of radical secularism that stands vehemently against any traces of religious imagination.⁹⁹ However, in terms of their continued influence on the Israeli public, their alienation from the Jewish religion only deepened and strengthened a profound secular undercurrent that has accompanied Hebrew culture since the *Haskalah* [Jewish Enlightenment].¹⁰⁰

The second model of Jewish secularism is the pluralistic model. This model aims to ensure open discourse between individuals and communities,

⁹⁷ The reference to the Jewish religion as a ragged cloth that should be replaced by a new one might be related to Paul's call to abandon the old and to put on the new self (Ephesians 4:22–24). The modern secular adaptation of this image emphasizes the affinity between the European model of the "New Man" and the Canaanites' ideal of the "New Hebrew." See Rina Peled, *The "New Man" of the Zionist Revolution: Hashomer Hatzair and Its European Roots* [Heb.], Tel Aviv: Am Oved, 2002, p. 19.

⁹⁸ As Dan Laor has argued, the confirmed reports of the nature and scale of the Holocaust that were arriving in Mandatory Palestine at the time his "Letter to the Hebrew Youth" was written (1943) did not deter Ratosh from employing anti-Semitic rhetoric and images. See Dan Laor, "From 'The Sermon' to the Letter to the Hebrew Youth: Notes on the Concept of Negating the Diaspora" [Heb.], in Laor, *The Struggle for Memory: Essays on Literature, Society, and Culture*, Tel Aviv: Am Oved, 2009, pp. 240–241.

⁹⁹ Hugo Bergman, the editor of the second edition of Gordon's works and an astute critic of the Canaanites, went so far as to claim that the members of the movement tried to "return to the times before Abraham, just as the Nazis in Germany—only a few years ago—wanted to rid themselves of the Christian inheritance and turn back to the Germanic civilization of the Teutonic forests"; Samuel Hugo Bergman, "On the Shaping of the Nation in Our State" [Heb.], *Hapoel Hatzair*, April 10, 1949, p. 12. In the same vein, Solomon Avinery dismisses the Canaanites as "a paraphrase of fascism," stating that "German thinkers" likewise "expanded the term 'German' to include anyone who speaks in Teutonic dialect; this is quite similar to the Canaanites' expansion of the term 'Hebrew' to encompass all of the inhabitants of the Land of the Euphrates"; Solomon Avinery, "On the Canaanite Affair" [Heb.], *Hapoel Hatzair*, March 25, 1953. See also Yehoshua Porat, *Weapon and Pen in His Hand: The Life of Uriel Shelah* [Heb.], Tel Aviv: Mahbarot le-sifrut, 1989, pp. 258–259.

¹⁰⁰ See Baruch Kurzweil, "The Essence and Origins of the Young Hebrews Movement (the Canaanites)" [Heb.], in Kurzweil, *Our New Literature—Continuity or Revolution?*, Jerusalem: Schocken Press, 1965, pp. 270–300. On Baruch Kurzweil's (Austro-Hungarian Empire–Israel, 1907–1972) attitude toward the Canaanites' movement see also Laor, *The Struggle for Memory*, p. 295; Moshe Goultschin, *Baruch Kurzweil as a Commentator on Culture* [Heb.], Ramat Gan: Bar Ilan University Press, 2009, pp. 140–144. In the opening of his monograph on the Canaanites, Diamond writes "I do not believe that 'Canaanism' stands or falls on the power, the accuracy, or the credibility of the mythological substructure on which it rests or of its specific historiography. It is not clear to me that these were anything other than intellectual window-dressing. . . . What is left is a coherent and substantial ideology of secular nativism"; James S. Diamond, *Homeland or Holy Land?*, p. 5.

each contributing to Jewish culture according to its religious or secular disposition. Unlike the radical model, it does not attempt to replace religion's monopoly over culture with a secular monopoly. Alternatively, it endorses what Peter Berger labeled as "market situation" in which religion is sold like any other consumer commodity.[101] The pluralist secularists are no less confident in their position than the radical secularists, but they refuse, as a matter of principle, to reject the religious position altogether or to participate in any attempt to secularize nonsecular people for their own good. They recognize virtues even in value systems that do not place as much emphasis on self-criticism and autonomy, precisely because they perceive their own virtue as maintaining an openness to otherness and a fundamental preference of decentralization to centralization of worldviews and ways of life.[102]

One of the first prominent proponents of the pluralistic model of secular Jewish culture was Ahad Ha'am, toward whom Gordon, as we saw in the second chapter, had an ambivalent attitude. Ahad Ha'am's intellectual enterprise was dedicated to finding a theoretical and practical paradigm for mutual recognition and cooperation between secular and religious Jews. Despite his robust secular position according to which the Jewish religion is the offspring of Jewish culture, and not vice versa,[103] Ahad Ha'am tried, as Brinker puts it, "to cultivate sympathy and understanding toward Jewish religion among secularists, just as he saw fit to demand that 'enlightened' observant Jews accept secularists and cooperate with them for the sake of common national ends."[104] The pluralism Ahad Ha'am advocated was not

---

[101] Peter L. Berger, *The Sacred Canopy—Elements of a Sociological Theory of Religion*, New York: Anchor, 1990, p. 138. See also Avi Sagi, "Tolerance and the Possibility of Pluralism in Judaism" [Heb.], *Iyyun: The Jerusalem Philosophical Quarterly*, vol. 44 (1995) pp. 175–200.

[102] For a powerful elaboration of this line of thought see Clifford Geertz, "Anti-Anti-Relativism" in Geertz, *Available Light: Anthropological Reflections on Philosophical Topics*, Princeton: Princeton University Press, 2000, pp. 42–67; Richard A. Shweder, "Geertz's Challenge: Is It Possible to Be a Robust Cultural Pluralist and a Dedicated Political Liberal at the Same Time?," in Austin Sarat (ed.), *Law without Nations*, Stanford: Stanford University Press, 2010, pp. 185–231. See also Tamir's distinction between liberalism anchored in autonomy and liberalism that is derived from theory of rights in Yael Tamir, "Two Concepts of Multiculturalism," *Journal of Philosophy of Education*, 29: 2 (1995), pp. 161–172.

[103] "Religion itself," declared Ahad Ha'am, "is none other than a well-known version of [Jewish] *Cultura*," Ahad Ha'am epistle to Israel Abrahams, in Ahad Ha'am, *Epistles* [Heb.], Tel Aviv: Dvir, 1956, vol. 5, p. 104. See also Arye Rubinstein, "The Concept of Cultura in Ahad Ha'am Thought" [Heb.], *Melilah: Manchester Journal of Jewish Studies*, vols. 3–4 (1950), pp. 289–310.

[104] Menahem Brinker, "Ahad Ha'am" [Heb.], in *New Jewish Time*, vol. 1., p. 49. Contrary to Brinker, Kurzweil ascribed to Ahad Ha'am a paternalistic secular position, presenting his philosophy as one that attributes religion to primitive, outdated stages of human development. In Ahad Ha'am's sympathetic public comments on religion Kurzweil saw nothing more than an intentional concealment of his positivist materialism. See Kurzweil, "Judaism as a Manifestation of the National-Critical Life-Will" [Heb.], in Kurzweil, *Our New Literature*, pp. 212–213.

only sociological but also cultural-existential. He believed that the study of canonical religious texts has a distinctive existential meaning, that of the discovery of one's personal identity.[105] However, Ahad Ha'am's conduct during the "Brenner affair" shows that his pluralism was not broad enough to contain, as a legitimate possibility, Brenner's provocative and radical concept of secularization.[106]

The third model of Jewish secularism is well captured by the paradoxical label "the religious model of Jewish secularity." This model aims to offer a secular substitute for religion without entirely excluding the religious impulse, as the radical model does, but by diverting it from religious objects to secular ones. It harnesses myths, rites, and states of mind that are originally entirely religious, to achieve distinctly secular goals, such as nationhood, homeland, and state.[107]

In Simmel's terms, which were elaborated by his close student Martin Buber, this model was founded on the exchange of religion with religiosity whose objects are secular.[108] As opposed to the previous two models, according to the religious model secularization does not mean the eradication of the religious impulse but, rather, its diversion from the transcendent realm to the immanent realm. This model rejects the laws and dogmas of the historical religions out of a denial of the traditional revelation, and disappointment with the religious establishment.[109] Nevertheless, it endorses the

---

[105] As Rina Hevlin has demonstrated, Ahad Ha'am held—in the spirit of Gadamer's "fusion of horizons,"—that the identity of the interpreter is shaped through the continuous process of encounter with canonical texts. See Rina Hevlin, *A Double Commitment: Jewish Identity between Tradition and Secularity in Ahad Ha'am's Thought* [Heb.], Tel Aviv: Hakibbutz Hameuchad, 2001, pp. 46–74. See also Zvi Zameret, "Ahad Ha'am and the Shaping of Secular Education" [Heb.], *Iyunim Bitkumat Israel*, vol. 16 (2006), pp. 171–194.

[106] In "Slavery in Freedom" (1891) Ahad Ha'am advocates complete freedom of speech and evaluation of the Jewish tradition, maintaining that a people are not a spiritual or philosophical movement but, rather, more resemble a family whose close interrelations do not depend on uniformity of opinions. In contrast, in his essays of the late 1890s, he demands of individuals loyalty to the family spirit, arguing that separation from the family spirit would ultimately lead to a separation from the family itself. See Menachem Brinker, *Up to the Tiberian Alley*, pp. 159–164.

[107] Severe criticism is leveled at the claim that the modern state and the nation state are secular projects. Various thinkers argue that the state did not free us from the grip of religious realm but only translated it into the modern world. See, for example, Peter Scott and William T. Cavanaugh (eds.), *The Blackwell Companion to Political Theology*, Oxford: Blackwell Publishing, 2004; Haim O. Rechnitzer, *Prophecy and the Perfect Political Order: The Political Theology of Leo Strauss* [Heb.], Jerusalem: Bialik Institute, 2012; Yotam Hotam, *Modern Gnosis and Zionism: The Crisis of Culture, Life Philosophy and Jewish National Thought*, London: Routledge, 2013.

[108] Simmel, "A Contribution to the Sociology of Religion" (1898); Martin Buber, "Jewish Religiosity" (1913), in Buber, *Martin Buber: Selected Writings on Judaism and Jewish Affairs* [Heb.], Jerusalem: The Zionist Library, 1984, vol. 1, pp. 70–79. See also Ratzabi, *Anarchy in "Zion,"* pp. 89–94.

[109] In this vein, Gordon scarcely mentioned or visited the Western Wall, despite the central significance it holds in the consciousness of Orthodox Jews. For Gordon the Western Wall symbolized only

religious impulse—which expresses the finite's yearning for the infinite or for the absolute—as a natural impulse that cannot be reduced to sociological or psychological manipulations.

Gordon, who famously declared that "The human spirit cannot—and the greater its depth, the less it can—be at peace without religion" (MN, IV.5: 111), was one of the most sensitive and sophisticated pioneers of the religious model of Jewish secularism. As will emerge from the analysis of the "Return to Nature" speech, to which we will turn in the next chapter, although Gordon broke off the shackles of the halakha, he nevertheless endeavored to continue nourishing Jewish religiosity with the unique meaning he attributed to man's return to nature. Gordon argued that contact with the Divine cannot be achieved through adherence to the rigid and ritualistic forms of institutional religion but only through sensitive attention to the varied and renewed needs of life. Religion must constantly change and be renewed like life itself.[110] "In order to provide the basis for supreme human life, to guarantee the intensification, renewal, and flow of life," Gordon states, "religion cannot be a matter of routine and habit, it cannot be dependent on beliefs, opinions, and laws passed down from generation to generation" (MN, IV.7: 122). Gordon's "religion of nature" or "religion of the future" is not subjected to any religious institution or creed. Its "single creed," as he aptly puts it, is the "feeling of total unification of the human 'Self' with the entire worldly existence" (MN, IV.7: 122). The full meaning of this "single creed," as well as of the life according to it, will be the focus of the next chapter.

---

destruction and exile. See MN XV: 234–235. See also Yuval Jobani and Nahshon Perez, *Women of the Wall: Navigating Religion in the Public Sphere*, New York: Oxford University Press, 2017.

[110] In her book *A New Life* Einat Ramon explores Gordon's double attitude toward the halakha. On the one hand, Gordon sharply attacked the institutional nature of halakha, presenting the blind following of religious jurists as a form of idolatry and superstition, but on the other hand he waged a stubborn struggle for the preservation of meta-halakhic principles, such as "sanctity" and "family purity." See Einat Ramon, *A New Life: Religion, Motherhood and Supreme Love in the Works of Aharon David Gordon* [Heb.], Jerusalem: Carmel, 2007, pp. 221–223. In addition, Gordon did not put on phylacteries, which are made of cow's leather, nor did he recite the daily prayers in their full liturgical form (Ramon, pp. 220–221). Gordon seems to have objected in principle to halakhic ruling because it necessarily applies general principles to particular cases and as such may harm some members of the society. Unlike Maimonides, who gave precedence to the whole over the individual, Gordon was not willing to sacrifice the individual on the altar of the collective. See Moses Maimonides, *The Guide of the Perplexed*, trans. Shlomo Pines, Chicago: The University of Chicago Press, 1963, 3: 34, p. 534. On Maimonides' concept of law see Menachem Lorberbaum, *Politics and the Limits of Law: Secularizing the Political in Medieval Jewish Thought*, Stanford: Stanford University Press, 2002, pp. 35–40.

5

The "Return to Nature" Speech

Gordon as an Environmental Prophet

Introduction: Gordon, the Prophet, and the Mad Spiritual Man

Less than a year after the publication of the first chapter of MN, on April 10, 1911, the Jewish-French philosopher Henri Bergson delivered a lecture entitled "Philosophical Intuition" at the International Congress of Philosophy in Bologna. In his opening remarks, Bergson argued that every great philosopher keeps circling around a single fundamental intuition in his philosophical system, without being able to express it accurately and fully.[1] Bergson's statement well applies to Gordon's spiral writing style. For, as we saw earlier, he iteratively examines a particular topic, exploring its various aspects and contexts, each time repeating his thoughts while aiming to illuminate them from a new angle.

A statement by the poet and writer Jacob Fichman (Russian Empire–Israel, 1881–1958) comes to mind here with peculiar aptness, for he said that Gordon,

> would restate the crux of his main idea, formulate and reformulate it, thus articulating and expanding his thought, developing it from one fundamental element into a comprehensive worldview. At every encounter with his idea of life, he sprinkled more sparks and illuminated more areas . . . the most elementary of elements cast upon him from time to time a fresh intoxication, each time demanding a "new enlightenment." He doubted that anyone, not even his nearest, had managed to gain full grasp of his idea of life. In every interaction with his friends, at every meeting and in every

---

[1] Henri Bergson, "Philosophical Intuition," in Bergson, *Key Writings*, K. Pearson and J. Mullarkey (eds.), Melissa McMahon (trans.), London: Bloomsbury, 2014, pp. 285–302.

The First Jewish Environmentalist. Yuval Jobani, Oxford University Press. © Oxford University Press 2024. DOI: 10.1093/oso/9780197617977.003.0005

conversation he continued to clarify and shed new light on his thought which he never deemed fully elaborated, or understood.[2]

Among the many times Gordon revolved around his idea of life—if to use Bergson's metaphor, which is echoed in Fichman's statement—none is more remarkable than the passage from MN that can be titled, in accordance with its content, the "Return to Nature" Speech, which will be the focus of this chapter.

The "Return to Nature" speech ends the first chapter of MN, which was published anonymously as an article in *Hapoel Hatzair* journal on May 10, 1910, under the title "Man and Nature: Meditations and Dreams of a Radical." Except for the second chapter of MN, "Eternity and the Moment" (1913),[3] in which Gordon critiques Nietzsche's notion of eternal recurrence, the first chapter is the only chapter in MN completed and edited by Gordon himself and published during his lifetime. The first chapter of MN is important, for it outlines the entire book and introduces one of its main arguments. According to this argument, human life is invigorated by dialectic interplay between egoism and altruism, as well as between our tendency to detach ourselves from nature in order to understand it and our tendency to experience nature in order to unite with it. Supreme life, therefore, merges between a "life of contraction" and a "life of expansion," to use the precise terminology that Gordon systematically develops later in MN.

A close reading of the first chapter of MN reveals that it consists of two divisions that differ in the style of writing and the rhetorical tools employed by Gordon to clarify and extend his call for humanity to reorient itself toward nature. In the first division of the chapter (pp. 15–18) Gordon appeals to the reader's cerebral faculties by deploying a series of concepts and arguments, such as the distinction between "minor heresy" and "great heresy," which was discussed in the previous chapter. In contrast, his "Return to Nature" speech in the second division of the chapter (pp. 28–34) contains a lyrical description of a personal experience that aims to capture the reader's imagination and appeals to his emotional, inner world. Interestingly, the two main concepts of Gordon's philosophical system—cognition and

---

[2] Fichman, "Introduction to the Volume of Gordon's Letters and Notes" [Heb.], GWB, III: 9, slightly adapted from the original. I do not share Fichman's view that Gordon's idea of work was the crux of his philosophy. For, as was demonstrated earlier, this idea is not an opening premise but only a derivative of Gordon's dialectical concept of the supreme life as a life of constant movement between the selfish contraction of one's self and its altruistic expansion and opening toward its surroundings.

[3] This chapter was published as an article in the *Hapoel Hatzair* newspaper on October 18, 1913.

experience—correspond to the two writing styles he employs in the first chapter of MN. Indeed, throughout MN Gordon alternates naturally between philosophical reasoning and literary-lyrical writing. Gordon's wish to enhance the lyrical atmosphere in MN is uniquely exemplified in his choice to insert into chapter 14 not just a passage but the entire four stanzas of Mikhail Lermontov's (Russia, 1814–1841) untitled poem depicting a quasi-mystical experience of man unifying with nature.[4]

By integrating cognition and experience, Gordon returns to the original meaning of the term philosophy ("philo-sophia,"), which denotes, since its coining in Ancient Greece, an integration of the emotional and rational, the love and wisdom embodied in the term. For Gordon—as for Socrates (Athens, 469–399 BCE), Plato, Spinoza, and Nietzsche before him—man is also an emotional being, and not merely a rational being. Therefore, in order to stir him into action, one must address not only his cognition but also his emotions and imagination.[5]

In the second division of the chapter Gordon presents his philosophy in a literary, lyrical disguise by delivering his "Return to Nature" speech. In this speech Gordon weaves—more than in any other part of MN—fragments of biblical verses, idiomatic phrases, paraphrases, and metaphors from the classical Jewish corpus of the Bible, Talmud, Midrashic literature, and Kabbala. This richness of language lends a distinctly prophetic character to Gordon's speech as well as the validity of religious admonition.

As he lay on his deathbed twelve years after writing his "Return to Nature" speech, Gordon objected to the attempt to associate him with the Russian Orthodox Christian tradition of *Iurodstvo* (holy fool), in which saints feign madness and challenge social conventions in order to provide spiritual guidance yet avoid praise for their vocation.[6] "Among the people of Israel there

---

[4] See MN, XIV: 223–224. See also MN, XV: 227. A writer and painter, Lermontov was one of the most important nineteenth-century Russian poets and one of the central figures in Russian Romanticism. On Lermontov's nature descriptions and their contribution to the consolidation of Russian national identity see Christopher David Ely, *This Meager Nature: Landscape and National Identity in Imperial Russia*, DeKalb: Northern Illinois University Press, 2002, pp. 115–118. Gordon quotes an untitled poem by Lermontov that opens with the words, "When golden corn is waving to and fro"; see Mikhail Lermontov, *Prose and Poetry*, trans. Avrahm Yarmolinsky et al., place of publication not indicated: Rusalka Books, 2020, p. 250.

[5] For a comprehensive discussion of the ways different philosophers have approached this insight see Ran Sigad, *Philo-Sopia: On the Only Truth* [Heb.], Jerusalem: Dvir, 1983.

[6] For a rich exploration of the genesis, nature, and development of the ideal of holy foolishness and its ongoing significance as a religious paradigm in Russian culture see Priscilla Hunt and Svitlana Kobets (eds.), *Holy Foolishness in Russia: New Perspectives*, Bloomington, Ind.: Slavica Publications, 2011; Sergey Ivanov, *Holy Fools in Byzantium and Beyond*, New York: Oxford University Press, 2006; Ewa M. Thompson, *Understanding Russia: The Holy Fool in Russian Culture*, Lanham, Md: University Press of America, 1987.

were and are no holy fools (*Iurodstvo*)," Gordon declares decisively. "Some individuals could however, be typified as 'mad prophets, spiritual men,' but they bear no resemblance to *Iurodstvo*."

The essence of the "mad spiritual man," in its various manifestations "from ancient times to the present day is his inability to accept life as it is. Nor is he able, however, to distract himself from life whether through poetry or singing, through Torah or literature, through art or through his hidden "self" . . . not even is he able to distract himself from life through religion. He seeks life, not distraction from life. He seeks human life or cosmic human life, life in the image of God, infinite life" ("Final Notes," GWA, V: 226–227).

The ultimate goal of the Iurodstvo is personal, Gordon argues, and therefore one should disapprove of it. Through self-humiliation the holy fool seeks to share in the sufferings of Jesus (*Imitatio Christi*).[7] In contrast, the ultimate goal of the "Mad Spiritual Man" in the Jewish tradition, to which Gordon links himself, is to bring about *tikkun olam* (lit. "repair of the world").[8]

The guiding word (*Leitwort*) in Gordon's speech, to use a term associated with Buber,[9] is "son of man" (*ben adam*), which is a characteristic term in the book of Ezekiel. However, while Ezekiel uses the term to demote man

[7] See Priscilla Hunt, "Holy Foolishness as a Key to Russian Culture," in Hunt and Kobets, *Holy Foolishness in Russia*, pp. 3–4; Svitlana Kobets, "The Paradigm of the Hebrew Prophet and the Russian Tradition of Iurodstvo," *Canadian Slavonic Papers* 50: 1–2 (2008), pp. 1–16.

[8] Gordon's remarks seem to disregard the phenomenological and historical affinity between the biblical prophet and the Iurodstvo. As Svitlana Kobets demonstrated, the two figures share a number of intriguing similarities: "Both are believed to be God-chosen who mediate between the sacred and profane realms; both are known to be mentors, clairvoyants, and miracle-workers; both come from various social backgrounds and are represented by both genders. In the same way as the prophet serves his people as a reminder of the Old Testament covenant, the holy fool reminds the congregation of the evangelical message and is seen as a walking, talking, ranting impersonation of scripture. By defying the established order of life and challenging the people's lukewarm faith, the holy fool exposes himself/herself to the wrath and persecution of his/her audiences who, not unlike the Old Testament ones, persistently resist God's will and fail to grasp His message. Just like the biblical prophet, the holy fool utters predictions of calamities and woes and castigates both the common people and the authorities. The vitae further relate that because of his defiance and unsolicited prophecies, the fool for Christ is beaten, rejected, persecuted and marginalized by the infuriated crowds. Quite in line with the prophetic paradigm, the Iurodivyi's safety, indeed his life, is constantly endangered, providing the hagiographies with the topos of the holy fool's martyrdom, which closely parallels that of the prophet"; Svitlana Kobets, "The Paradigm of the Hebrew Prophet," pp. 1–2. On Gordon's attitude to the Iurodstvo see also Eliezer Schweid, "The Crazy Man of Spirit: The Prophetic Mission in Gordon's Life and Thought," in Schweid, *Prophets for Their People* [Heb.], Jerusalem: Hebrew University Magnes Press, 1999, pp. 144–160. See also Menachem Brinker, *Modern Hebrew Literature as European Literature* [Heb.], Jerusalem: Carmel, 2016, p. 200.

[9] Martin Buber, who popularized the term *Leitwort* ("guiding word" or "lead-word"), defined it as follows: "By Leitwort I understand a word or word root that is meaningfully repeated within a text or sequence of texts or complex of texts; those who attend to these repetitions will find a meaning of the text revealed or clarified, or at any rate made more emphatic"; Martin Buber, "Leitwort Style in Pentateuchal Narrative," in Martin Buber and Franz Rosenzweig, *Scripture and Translation*, trans. Lawrence Rosenwald, Bloomington: Indiana University Press, 1994 [1936], p. 114.

to the level of a mere mortal and to distance him from the angels, and other higher beings that appear in some of his visions,[10] Gordon endows the term with a clearly humanistic meaning. In Gordon's speech the term *ben adam* is used to emphasize the dignity and value of humans as agents of historical and environmental change.[11] Moreover, while Ezekiel's prophecies of rebuke revolve around the destruction of the "House of the Lord" (Ezekiel 8:14), Gordon warns against the destruction of nature, which he calls "the glorious foundation of the universe" (MN, I: 30).[12] In this context, Gordon inserts into his speech the beginning of a verse from the farewell speech of Moses in the book of Deuteronomy: "Know therefore this day and keep in mind" (Deuteronomy 4:39), while adding to it an ending of his own, "for you were lost thus far until you have returned" (MN, I: 31). The return to God is replaced by Gordon with the return to nature. Another example of many is the "divine voice" (*bat koll*)[13] calling out toward the end of the speech: "Work, sons of man (*bene adam*), all of you, work!" (MN, I: 33). These words can be taken as divine confirmation of Gordon's call to transfer the worship of God, in its broadest sense, from the Temple to the open field, which is man's ultimate place in cosmos (MN, I: 32).

Like other pioneers of his day, Gordon saw in exile a "non-place" or a utopian space—in the literal meaning of the term "*ou-topos*" a nonexistent place—since it does not enable Jews "to be" within it.[14] In exile Jews perceived themselves as living beyond time and space. The Jewish people defined themselves, in the words of Benjamin Harshav, as

---

[10] For a review of the various uses and meanings of the term in the Bible see Elia Samuele Artom, "*ben adam*" [Heb.], in *Encyclopaedia Biblica* [Heb.], Jerusalem: Bialik Institute, 1971, vol. I, pp. 108–109.

[11] The term "*ben adam*" takes on new content also in Bialik's influential poem "City of Slaughter," which was written in response to the Kishinev pogrom of 1903 and was published a few years before MN. For discussion see Ariel Hirschfeld, *The Tuned Harp: The Language of Emotions in H. N. Bialik's Poetry* [Heb.], Tel-Aviv: Am Oved, 2011, p. 267.

[12] Like Gordon, Thoreau also served as a kind of arbiter at the gate for the American settlers in the nineteenth century. Thoreau, as his biographer Laura Dassow Walls put it, "was the town gadfly and keeper of the public's conscience, his every act was a sermon, and his every encounter—even a casual meeting on the road—was a challenge to explain, to justify, to proselytize"; Laura Dassow Walls, *Henry David Thoreau: A Life*, Chicago: The University of Chicago Press, 2017, p. 19. On Thoreau's affinity to Ezekiel see Stanley Cavell, *The Senses of Walden: An Expanded Edition*, Chicago: The University of Chicago Press, 1992, pp. 17–18.

[13] Literally echo or reverberating sound, in Rabbinic literature the term *bat kol* occasionally signifies a divine voice, a substitute for prophecy.

[14] On exile as "a non-place" in the imagination of the pioneers see Boaz Neumann, *Land and Desire in Early Zionism*, trans. Haim Watzman, Waltham: Brandeis University Press, 2011, pp. 75–76.

an "eternal people" (*am olam*) bound by a complex network of timeless and interdependent codes of law, belief, legend, and behavior. But *olam* means both "eternity" and "the universe." Hence, *am olam*, "the eternal people," also means "the world people," that is, a people living in all time and in all space actually, outside of any specific time and space, any concrete history and geography.[15]

The return to the Land of Israel is perceived by Gordon as a return to "one's proper place," in the concrete, physical, earthly sense of the term. It is a return from the exilic meaning of the term "the place" (*HaMakom*), which as one of God's names marked for Jews in exile a transcendent, spiritual, and abstract entity. But the circle is not complete with the return from the transcendent meaning of "the place" to its earthly meaning. Gordon's passion for "the place" in its earthly meaning is no greater than his caution against being devoured by it. A return to "the place" in its earthly meaning is necessary but in itself is nothing but a ladder that allows for a renewed, correct, and complete ascent, to "the place," in its transcendent sense. In this spirit Gordon describes in "A letter that was not sent in its time to my friend in the Diaspora" (1912) his impressions during his travels in the Galilee:

> Then I remembered, that in these places, in this valley to the south, Elijah went up by a whirlwind into heaven (2 Kings 2: 11) . . . and I also remembered that "a stairway was set on the ground and its top reached to the sky" (Genesis 28: 12). What do we ask for, if not a place for the ladder? . . . (GWA, IV: 248)[16]

In the "Return to Nature" speech Gordon moves as if in a continuous pendulum motion alternating between his enthusiasm for the existential horizon that the union with nature opens up for man and his recoiling from the narrow cage in which the human soul is imprisoned in modernity, detached and alienated from nature and itself. In this vein he declares at the opening of his speech,

[15] Benjamin Harshav, *The Meaning of Yiddish*, Berkeley: University of California Press, 1990, p. 11.
[16] Gurevitch argues that Gordon's thought summarizes the dialectic interplay between the earthly and the transcendent meaning of the Hebrew term *HaMakom* (the place) in the Jewish and Israeli culture as a whole; Zali Gurevitch, *On Israeli and Jewish Place* [Heb.], Tel Aviv: Am Oved, 2007, pp. 43–44. On how Jacob's ladder was captured in the imagination of the pioneers of the Second Aliyah see also Shimon Kushnir, *Men of Nebo* [Heb.], Tel Aviv: Am Oved, 2004, p. 67.

A rich world lies before us, wide vistas, great depths, infinite, boundless, unquenchable light. Plunge, O Son of Man, into the depths of this vast ocean! Open the chambers of your heart to these currents of light and of life. Live! Live with every atom of your being! Live and you will see that there is yet room for love, for faith, for idealism, for creation! And perhaps, who knows, there may yet be worlds still undreamed of! (MN, I: 29; GSE 181)[17]

Directly after this section, in a sharp turn, Gordon moves on to describe how modern man quells the lament in the searching soul, thereby silencing the voice "that beats like the wings of a bird in its narrow cage, and calls: 'Live Nature!'" (MN, I: 29; GSE 181).

But how, Gordon immediately asks, can man return to nature and unite with it? Gordon is unable to answer this question directly as it pertains to the liminal, and therefore elusive, religious realm where man and nature merge. Thus, rather than directly answering the question, Gordon keeps circling around it, to borrow again Bergson's metaphor, which echoes in Fichman's statement: "With each touch of his idea of life, he [Gordon] sprinkled more sparks and illuminated more areas."[18] Indeed, while circling around the idea of his life he proposed several significant means by which man may return to nature and live within it.

(I) Gordon associates the return to nature with the return "to childhood and to a life of childhood" (MN, I: 29).[19] By doing so Gordon adopts here in his own way the so-called Cradle Argument that was prevalent among the schools of Hellenistic philosophy, especially the Stoics, the Cynics, and the Epicureans who used the behavior of unsocialized young children or babies to establish what is natural. Diogenes the Cynic (Sinope–Corinth, c. 412–c. 320 BCE), who made a virtue of poverty, provided an illuminating example of a straightforward adaptation of the Cradle Argument. In one of the anecdotes of his life the Greek philosopher and biographer Diogenes Laertius (fl. third century CE) vividly describes how "one day, observing a child drinking out of

---

[17] Here and in the following quotes from Gordon's writings, mostly from the first chapter of MN, I used Frances Burnce's translation (GSE) with slight alterations to provide the most straightforward reading possible.

[18] Fichman, "Introduction," p. 9.

[19] Yoseph Aharonovich, editor of the first edition of Gordon's writings (GWA), argued that the pioneers experienced a second childhood through their toil in nature. As he puts it, "childhood was then thrown at us, and how pleasant this childhood was for us, human products of the ghetto deprived of nature"; Aharonovich, "Letter from Yoseph Aharonovich to a Friend" (1910), in Yoseph Aharonovich, *Collected Works of Yoseph Aharonovich* [Heb.], Tel Aviv: Am-Oved, 1941, vol. 1, p. 212.

his hands, he [Diogenes the Cynic] cast away the cup from his wallet with the words, 'A child has beaten me in plainness of living.' "[20]

Gordon does not conduct in MN a thematic analysis of childhood. However, by joining together various claims scattered throughout the book one can conclude that according to Gordon the more we let ourselves reconnect with the child we were, the more we reconnect with nature.[21] The reason for this is that the childhood of each of us is a remnant of the "childhood of mankind" (MN, IV.5: 115),[22] a time when human beings were happy, as they were deeply and fully united with nature.[23] At the beginning of our lives, as well as the life of humanity as a whole, as we saw earlier, the cognitive skill that distinguishes and distances our Self from its surroundings has not yet evolved. According to Gordon, the child's melding with everything around him is expressed, among other things, by the fact that he still does not know "how to say 'I' and refers to himself by his first name, as if he . . . and everyone else . . . are present with him in one place, except that he is closer to himself" (MN, IV.1: 74).

---

[20] Diogenes Laertius, *Lives of Eminent Philosophers*, vol. II, p. 39. For a general survey of the ideal of a life according to nature in Hellenistic philosophy see Jacques Schlanger, *Sur la Bonne Vie— Conversations avec Épicure, Épictète et d'autres Amis*, Paris: Presses Universitaires de France, 2000, pp. 19–48. On the cradle argument see Jacques Brunschwig, "The Cradle Argument in Epicureanism and Stoicism," in Malcolm Schofield and Gisela Striker (eds.), *The Norms of Nature: Studies in Hellenistic Ethics*, Cambridge: Cambridge University Press, 2007, pp. 113–144; Brunschwig, "Cradle Arguments," in Lawrence C. Becker and Charlotte B. Becker (eds.), *Encyclopedia of Ethics*, New York: Routledge, 2001, vol. 1, pp. 355–357. See also John Glucker, "Introduction to Cicero's *On the Ends of Good and Evil*" [Heb.], in Marcus Tullius Cicero, *On the Ends of Good and Evil*, trans. Aviva Katzir, ed. John Glucker, Ramat-Gan: Bar-Ilan University, 1997, pp. 29–35.

[21] Along a similar line of thought Nietzsche declares in *Beyond Good and Evil*, "A man's maturity— consists in having reacquired the seriousness one had as a child, at play"; Friedrich Nietzsche, *Beyond Good and Evil*, trans. Walter Kaufmann, New York: Vintage Books, 1966, §94, p. 83 (translation slightly altered). As a child Nietzsche's friends tauntingly dubbed him "the little pastor" partly because he remained serious even when he took part in games. See Rüdiger Safranski, *Nietzsche: A Philosophical Biography*, trans. Shelley Frisch, New York: W. W. Norton & Company, 2003, p. 30.

[22] Elaborating on this assertion, Nobert Elias states that "the specific psychological process of 'growing up' in Western societies, which frequency occupies the minds of psychologists and pedagogues today, is nothing other than the individual civilizing process to which each young person, as a result of the social civilizing process over many centuries, is automatically subjected from earliest childhood to a greater or lesser degree and with greater or lesser success. The psychogenesis of the adult make-up in civilized society cannot, therefore, be understood if considered independently of the sociogenesis of our 'civilization.' . . . Individuals, in their short history, pass once more through some of the processes that their society has traversed in its long history"; Nobert Elias, *The Civilizing Process: Sociogenetic and Psychogenetic Investigations*, trans. Edmund Jephcott, eds. Eric Dunning, Johan Goudsblom, and Stephen Mennell, Malden, Mass.: Blackwell, 2000 [1939], p. xi.

[23] The Romantic identification of childhood with absolute happiness can also be found in Tolstoy's well-known novella *The Death of Ivan Ilyich* (1886), in which human life is summarized as follows: "There was only one bright spot back at the beginning of life; after that things grew blacker and blacker, moved faster and faster"; Leo Tolstoy, *The Death of Ivan Ilyich*, trans. Lynn Solotaroff, New York: Random House, 2004, p. 105.

In this context Gordon takes children's natural aversion to etiquette as con-clusive proof of its artificiality and unnaturalness. Politeness, as he puts it, is nothing but "a falsification of all human emotions, and especially a falsifica-tion of the emotion of honor which it allegedly represents" (MN, XVI: 240). Due to politeness, "a perpetual lie fills all life, puts an imperceptible element of a lie into the core of life, into the core of the soul" (MN, XVI: 240). In order to realize how artificial and false common politeness is, Gordon suggests observing how puzzled and frustrated a child is when told, for the first time, that he is not allowed to address adults in first person—as a *you*, but only in the third person, as *he* or *sir*. "Look into the soul [of this child]," Gordon writes, "and if you have eyes to see—you will see [what I mean]" (MN, XVI: 240). The child's perspective allows us a critical look at how unnatural, corrupt, and alienated our lifestyle had become, and it offers us inspiration for its correction and improvement.[24]

(II) The return to nature spurs a revolution in all areas of life; it obliges man to begin his life anew in the fullest and most radical sense. "You must renew all things," Gordon declares, "your food and your drink, your attire and your home, your manner of work and your mode of study—everything" (MN, I: 30; GSE 248).[25] The return to nature does not entail a complete rejec-tion of culture but, rather, its restructure and adaptation to life according to nature. "When you return to nature," as Gordon puts it, "you shall not return bare. You shall return to nature like a man, who has traveled the whole earth only to return to his place of origin—experienced, firm, educated, and rich with sights and insights, spiritual assets, and material assets. All that has a place in nature will return with you" (MN, I: 30; GSE 248).

In his call to return to nature, as we saw in detail earlier, Gordon deploys heavy rhetoric that may obscure his philosophical position. The idyllic descriptions of the natural state may create the misconception that—under

---

[24] In a similar vein Rousseau notes that the first time a savage or a child drinks wine he grimaces and throw it away since it is not a natural drink. We get accustomed to the strong artificial flavor of the wine, Rousseau argues, only through process of cultural socialization. See Jean-Jacques Rousseau, *Emile, or On Education*, trans. Allan Bloom, New York: Basic Books, 1979, p. 151.

[25] The author Rabbi Binyamin gave poignant expression to the fascination of the youth of the Second Aliyah with the experience of "a new beginning." When he arrived at the Sea of Galilee in the summer of 1908 ten days later than the first settlers, he was filled with envy: "for I had already found everything 'ready and willing' in front of me: a bench to sit on and a table on which to eat and write; I had everything I needed. But [when my friends arrived] they found nothing ready for them, nothing in the strongest sense of the word. And yet they were not at all sad or desolate. On the con-trary, I guess some of them were happy . . . "; Yehoshua Redler-Feldmann, "Around" [Heb., 1908], in Redler-Feldmann, *On the Boundary: Notes and Articles*, Vienna: publisher not indicated, 1922, p. 205.

the influence of the primitivist movement that had gathered momentum in the nineteenth-century fin de siècle—Gordon shuns culture and calls to adopt the lifestyle of "primitive savages" uncorrupted by civilization.[26] But Gordon never claims in MN or elsewhere in his writings that a simple, straightforward return to nature would be desirable, or even possible. On the contrary, he openly and directly opposes it:

> Man cannot go back and cannot give up what he has conquered and what he has acquired, even if this conquest and appropriation is in the realm of cognition and not in the realm of life. Cognition is also part of life, or more precisely, one of its foundations. (MN, VIII: 165–166)[27]

At the same time, in perceiving the relationship between the cultural and the primitive as dialectical, Gordon's approach can be seen to agree with the term "Jewish primitivism" recently coined by Samuel Spinner. According to Spinner, "Jewish primitivism" denotes the fascination of Jewish writers and artists—who sought to blur the border between savage and civilized—with the identification of the Jew with the primitive at the turn of the twentieth century.[28]

[26] "Primitivism in European modernism," as Samuel Spinner puts it, "was the belief that a better way of making art and a better way of living were to be found among those people considered by Europeans to lack civilization. Before humans were corrupted by modernity—so the line of thinking goes—indeed, before they were corrupted by any civilization at all—they were truly free, truly creative, and truly alive. For civilized (read: white, Christian, European) peoples, this time of freedom, creativity, and vitality ended before recorded history. At the turn of the twentieth century, however, many European ethnographers and artists believed that such a state could still be found among 'primitive savages' who lived in a permanent state of prehistory"; Samuel J. Spinner, *Jewish Primitivism*, Stanford: Stanford University Press, 2021, p. 5. For historical and philosophical contextualization of primitivism and a survey of its wide-ranging impact on early twentieth-century arts and sciences see also Elazar Barkan, *Primitivism: Ideology and Desire in Modern Culture* [Heb.], Jerusalem: Ministry of Defense Press, 2001.

[27] In a similar vein, Rousseau's rhetoric in his *Discourse on the Origin and Basis of Inequality among Men* (1755) also exposed him to simplistic interpretations, such as the one in the famous letter Voltaire wrote to him immediately after reading his book: "I have received, sir, your new book against the human race, and I thank you. No one has employed so much intelligence to turn us men into beasts. One starts wanting to walk on all fours after reading your book. However, in more than sixty years I have lost the habit"; François-Marie Arouet de Voltaire, *Voltaire's Correspondence*, ed. Theodore Besterman, Geneva: Institut de Musee Voltaire, 1953–1966, vol. 27, p. 230. See also Arthur O. Lovejoy, "The Supposed Primitivism of Rousseau's Discourse on Inequality," *Modern Philology*, 21: 2 (1923), pp. 165–186.

[28] "In imagining European Jews as primitive savages," as Spinner puts it, "European Jewish writers and artists used Jewish primitivism to undermine the idea of ineradicable difference by blurring the border between savage and civilized. Jews turned the ethnographic lens on themselves not so much to salvage or study the premodern vestiges of their own culture and certainly not to denigrate themselves, but instead of critiquing the distinction, so starkly drawn in modern ethnography and aesthetic primitivism, between subject and object"; Spinner, *Jewish Primitivism*, p. 2. Spinner describes the contrast between European primitivism and Jewish primitivism as follows: "unlike European

Unlike Diogenes in the barrel, Gordon does not fully or in principle object to the very act of human habitation in houses and buildings. But he calls
to refrain as much as possible from building houses that might separate the
souls of those who live in them from the "universal expanse" and "universal
life" (MN, I: 30; GSE 248).[29]

Echoing verses from the *Shema* Gordon writes,

> when you build a home for yourself, you will set your heart not on
> multiplying therein rooms and rooms with rooms—but on this you will set
> your heart: that there be in your home nothing that will act as a barrier be-
> tween you and the universal expanse, between you and universal life. Then
> when you sit within your home, when you lie down, and when you rise—at
> every moment and every hour—your entire being will be surrounded by
> that expanse, by that life. So, too, will you build the homes of work and of
> labor; so, too, the homes of learning and of wisdom. You will allow space
> between one house and another—a generous amount of space—so that
> the house shall not rob or deprive another house of its share in this world.
> You will learn from nature the laws of construction and creation; you will
> learn to build as nature does in all that you will build and in all that you will
> create. (MN, I: 30; GSE 248)[30]

primitivism more broadly, which sought to replace the European subject with the primitive object,
Jewish primitivism was the struggle to be both at once European and foreign, subject and object,
savage and civilized"; Spinner, *Jewish Primitivism*, p. 4.

[29] In the same spirit Thoreau declares, "It would be well perhaps if we were to spend more of our
days and nights without any obstruction between us and the celestial bodies, if the poet did not
speak so much from under a roof, or the saint dwell there so long. Birds do not sing in caves, nor do
doves cherish their innocence in dovecots"; Henry David Thoreau, *Walden*, Princeton: Princeton
University Press, 1971, p. 28. "Our houses," Thoreau writes in another passage of *Walden*, "are such
unwieldy property that we are often imprisoned rather than housed in them"; Thoreau, *Walden*, p. 34.
Thoreau himself carefully plans the tiny and modest cabin he builds for himself on the shores of Lake
Walden in order to realize in his life in it his ideal of natural living. In this sense through the construction of his cabin Thoreau also builds his Self. As Walls puts it, "Others have called the shelter on
Walden's shores a cabin, hut, or shanty, but Thoreau almost always called it a house, insisting on the
solidity and dignity he worked so hard to attain. . . . Had he built only a 'poet's lodge' for 'the good
hours,' his move would have troubled no one; lots of people did that. But spending all his hours there
made him a pioneer not a Western one, but an inward one. . . . Outbuildings or vacation retreats only
exercised a self already established. Thoreau wanted a house to embody a new self, so that building
that house meant building that self, literally from the ground up" Walls, *Thoreau: A Life*, p. 190.
[30] In the spirit of Gordon's call Abraham Itai (Russian Empire—Israel, 1909–1983), a member of
Kibbutz Kfar Giladi, called "to bring nature into the apartment . . . .The apartment of the member of
the Kibbutz—the room, the balcony and its garden, should create a holistic site in which the family
can gather after a day of toil. We should not adopt the urban concept of a life largely confined behind
walls. We have to plan the balcony and the garden plot in front of it as a living space. Grooming the
garden and lawn next to the balcony and caring for the flowers helps to create a desirable living setting for the family's shared rest hours. The handling of these matters by masses of Kibbutz's members

Work in Nature and Its Sanctity

Out of all the different and varied aspects of the life of man who returns to nature—diet, clothing, residence, etc.—Gordon chooses to place at the center of his speech the transformation that the return to nature brings about in man's work. Gordon disapproves of artificial separation between life and work. He also disapproves of the perception of work as a preparatory activity for life or as a means designed to enable life. Contrary to this view, Gordon calls for making work an activity that gives expression and momentum to human life.

Ordinary life, the one that Gordon opposes, is presented by him as "a torn life. Life that is torn into two parts: one very small part of life, and one very big part of non-life: of work, of pain, of nuisance" (MN, I: 31). The "large part of non-life" is also called by Gordon "Shabbat Eve," and "the very small part of life" is called "Shabbat." These labels echo the well-known statement of the Babylonian Talmud, "One who takes pains on Shabbat eve will eat on Shabbat" (BT, Avoda Zara 3a).[31] According to Gordon, this dichotomy between work and life is contrary to nature. For, "nature lives within the preparation for life, within the creation of life" (MN, I: 31); that is, in nature itself there is no distinction between activities designed to enable life and life itself.

The life of every creature in nature includes everything that enables and prepares it. Animals are equipped with all the skills required for survival in the wild, such as orientation and locomotion, feeding and foraging, and so on. Therefore, Gordon argues, those who disconnect work from life and self-realization act not only against nature, but also against themselves and against others. As he puts it, "Your life hung suspended: either in the past, or in the future. You knew no present. When you saw that your life was mean and impoverished, you conceived a passion for adding to yourself the life of others" (MN, I: 31).

and their children in their leisure is one of the expressions of the new life-values that are emerging within us"; quoted in Muki Tsur and Yuval Danieli (eds.), *Mestechkin Builds Israel—Architecture in the Kibbutz* [Heb.], Tel Aviv: Hakibbutz Hameuchad, 2008, p. 118. See also Eyal Amir, "Ideology and Planning of the Kibbutz Dwelling" [Heb.], *Cathedra: For the History of Eretz Israel and Its Yishuv*, no. 95 (2000), pp. 119–140; Freddy Kahana, *Neither Town nor Village: The Architecture of the Kibbutz 1910–1990* [Heb.], Ramat Efal: Yad Tabenkin, 2011; Shmuel Burmil and Ruth Enis, *The Changing Landscape of a Utopia: The Landscape and Gardens of the Kibbutz: Past and Present*, Worms: Wernersche Verlagsgesellschaft, 2011.

[31] In its original context the meaning of this statement is metaphorical. Those who observe Torah and *mitzvot* (religious commandments) in this world ("eve of *Shabbat*") will be rewarded ("will eat") in the next world ("*Shabbat*").

Gordon's claim here regarding the ordinary life, against which he asserts his criticism, is twofold: (i) Only brief, rare fragments of life convey a sense of meaning. The present moment in a person's life is almost always hollow and lacks existential significance. All that is left for man to do in order to relieve himself from the feeling of emptiness is to alternate longing for a better future with an indulgence in memories of meaningful moments from the past that have passed and will never return. It is as if the present moment holds no value or purpose. (ii) In his second claim Gordon moves from the existential realm to the moral realm. In order to fill the emptiness that has opened up in his life man tries to take over and possess others. Abuse and exploitation of others, he argues, serve as an artificial substitute for meaningful action in the world. At this point, Gordon does not shy away from harshly criticizing a broad stratum of the Jewish people that he claims has adopted a parasitic lifestyle:

> You robbed, and you plundered, and you did violence wherever you ex-
> pected to find life, as far as your hand could reach. You sucked, you drank,
> you sapped the blood of your brother if he did not succeed in sucking your
> blood. The life of a leech was a symbol of greatness, of might, and glory to
> you; wealth a symbol of happiness; the rule of man over man, the symbol of
> heroism and of glory. (MN, I: 31)

It is possible that the semi-antisemitic rhetoric and images that Gordon employs in this passage led Shochat and Bergman to omit it from their edition of MN, which was published less than a decade after the Holocaust. This omission is particularly problematic not only because the omitted passage is from the first and most significant chapter of MN, but also because it was edited by Gordon himself, who even brought it to print during his lifetime— unlike the bulk of MN of which we have only unfinished drafts.[32]

---

[32] Similar arguments can be found in Gordon's opening address to the Prague conference in 1920 that merged socialist-Zionist groups from Palestine and the diaspora to form the Zionist Labor Party. In this well-known address, which left a lasting impression on many of the conferees—among whom were Samuel Hugo Bergman himself—Gordon declared, "We must turn a people of peddlers, shopkeepers, pimps, speculators who charge high prices, into a living people, a working and productive people. Yet what do we do? What do all those who come to do, do? Everything but that; not the true work of renewal, not the work of renewing the people. We have all manner of Zionist officials, who do things and get others to do things; we have all manner of parties and sects, who come to bring redemption to humanity, but the main thing, our selves, the work that we must invest in our very selves, the work of revolution within the soul of each individual among us and in the soul and life of the people, we forget or fail to see. We fail to see that our return to life is a new creation, a creation of something that has never before existed, of a new human being, of a new life, the creation of a new people. We come to create a human people"; "Opening Address to the Prague Conference

In one of his first articles, "A Little Observation" (1911), Gordon accuses the pioneers of the First Aliyah of "filling their pockets with foreign laborers' money" and by doing so turning "our people from a parasitic people out of necessity into parasitic people by choice."[33] These pioneers, according to Gordon, bring about the continuation of the exilic lifestyle in the Land of Israel.[34] The parasitic lifestyle that Gordon disapproves of is not the cause of man's existential crisis but only one of its products. Therefore, the adoption of a moral way of life in which man refrains from harming and exploiting others, in and of itself, is not enough to restore life's meaning, which was lost as man moved away and disengaged from nature. In this context Gordon declares,

> Your prophets, too, who urged you to reform your world, to regenerate your life, prophesied falsehood, and folly for you. They did not add anything to the law: "One who takes pains on Shabbat eve will eat on Shabbat." They only taught you to put a bit in your mouth and into the mouth of those who eat with you from the communal kitchen, so that each man may restrain his brother from eating more than his share, more than he prepared on Shabbat eve. But you, O Man, do you not also want life on Sabbat eve, at every moment, at every hour, at every second, and fraction of a second? What will the bit in your mouth give to you or add to you? (MN, I: 31–32; GSE 249)

On the other hand, with the resolution of the existential crisis through a return to nature, man's attitude toward work and hence his attitude toward others will also be corrected. As Gordon put it in his essay "Ideological

---

in 1920," GWA, II: 34–35. Quoted in Michael Walzer, Menachem Lorberbaum, Noam J. Zohar, and Ari Ackerman (eds.), *The Jewish Political Tradition: Membership*, New Haven: Yale University Press, 2006, vol. 2, p. 59; translation slightly modified. In his edition of Gordon's writings, Bregman softened the wording from "pimps, and speculators who charge high prices" to "intermediaries." See GWB, I: 259; the speech appears under the title "A Human People."

[33] "A Little Observation" (1911), GWA, I: 83. Brenner sees Gordon's extreme demand to base the settlement enterprise in the Land of Israel solely on Hebrew work as expression of what he calls "evil-heartedness" of "this old worker"; Yosef Haim Brenner, "The Missing Essence: Notes from Old Notebook" [Heb.], in Brenner, *Yosef Haim Brenner: Complete Works*, ed. Yitzhak Kafkafi, Tel Aviv: Hakibbutz Hameuchad, 1985, vol. 3, p. 587. Gordon himself admits that strictly adhering to the ideal of "Hebrew work" significantly reduces the scope of land acquisition and restricts the ability to hold onto them. "Hebrew labor," as he puts it, "block[s] the road to the redemption of the land"; "Work" (1915), GWA, I: 92.

[34] "A Little Observation" p. 85. For the various characteristics of the phenomenon of "exile in the Homeland," see Israel Bartal, *Exile in Israel: Pre-Zionist Settlement: A Collection of Studies and Essays* [Heb.], Jerusalem: The Zionist Library by the World Zionist Organization, 1994, pp. 15–16.

Foundations for the Management of a Laborers' Settlement" (1921), which he wrote at the end of his life at the request of the founders of Nahalal (see Figure 5.1), the first *moshav* (semi-cooperative agricultural settlement):

> Man returns to nature to the universal creation, the mother of all living beings, after being torn from it. . . . By and large, wherever man sees the motive of life not only bound up with the fruit of his labor, but also in the labor itself there is no need for struggle or for the making of laws against the exploitation of another's labor; for exploitation is in itself abominable. Here there is no need to fight for freedom of the land or for the means of production because exploitation is egregious. In the *Moshav* the freedom of labor is predicated. Here the relationship must, in general, be broader and deeper, more vital, more human. It must be more universal in character than the relationships in present day social life." (GWA, II: 204; GSE 265)

"Above all," Gordon asserts in his "Return to Nature" speech, "you will set your heart to work, to any work, any task amid nature, amid the universal

Figure 5.1. A young pioneer plowing the field in the Nahalal Agricultural School for Girls. In 1921, the founders of Nahalal, a semi-cooperative agricultural settlement, asked Gordon to suggest guiding philosophical principles for the constitution of the settlement. Date and photographer unknown. Nadav Mann, Bitmuna. From the Lancet Collection. The Pritzker Family National Photography Collection, The National Library of Israel.

expanse. So will you work in the field, and so will you work in the house, for so will you build your house" (MN, I: 32; GSE 250). From this assertion it follows univocally that for Gordon the concept of "work in nature" is not identical or limited to agricultural work. "Work in nature" is a broad life principle that can and should be applied to any work, physical, mental, artistic, or other, that is performed anywhere, in the open field, in the factory or at home, in the office or in the studio. "Work in nature" is a life principle that indicates the fusion of human activity and creation with the universal activity and creation that takes place in nature. Adhering to the principle of "work in nature" frames human life with the life of the whole cosmos; thus it renews and refreshes human life and gives it purpose and meaning. This claim, too, is crystallized in Gordon's 1921 essay "Ideological Foundations for the Management of a Laborers' Settlement":

> In the new life man seeks the taste of life and the happiness of life in the activity of his body and spirit, in doing and creating, similar to the plant whose life is sustained without intermediary directly by nature; its roots drawing in the blessing of the earth, its leaves absorbing the wind and light and creating from them living cells. This is the work, the work in all its scope and in all its forms, ranging from the simplest handiwork to the work of the spirit, thought and supreme creation. Man returns to nature . . . to suck from her breast without intermediary, to draw life into the body and soul from the one and first source [of life], in order to merge its limited individual life into its worldly, deepening and ever-expanding life. And the power that draws and merges is work, the activity of the body and the spirit, ascension, and creation.[35]

Like other pioneers of his time, Gordon utilizes in this passage the compelling image of "Mother Earth" prevalent in nineteenth century fin de siècle Russian literature, folklore, and thought.[36] This image is rooted in

[35] GWA, II: 204. "Only after digging for two days" wrote the young pioneer Yosef Weitz (Russian Empire–Israel, 1890–1972), who for much of the twentieth century oversaw forestry in Israel, "did I begin to feel invisible threads intertwining between my soul and the Land and from it back to my soul, tying me to it forever"; a letter from Yosef Weitz to his father (July 25, 1908), in Yosef Weitz, *First Pages* [Heb.], Tel Aviv: Gadish, 1958, p. 134

[36] Eliezer Shochat (Russian Empire–Israel, 1874–1971) also used the image and symbol of Mother Earth. See, for example, "Letter from Eliezer Shochat to his wife Hannah Meisel Shochat" [July 4, 1923], in Eliezer Shochat, *About Him, His Path, in His Memory* [Heb.], Tel Aviv: Mifaley Tarbut Vechinuch, 1973, p. 143. On the image of the suction from the earth of the Land of Israel among the pioneers, see also Neumann, *Land and Desire*, pp. 36–37, 74–77; Eliezer Schweid, *The Individual: The World of AD Gordon* [Heb.], Tel Aviv: Am Oved, 1970, p. 22.

pre-Christian pagan worship of the "Mother Moist Earth" (mat' syra-zemlia) prevalent among the Eastern Slavs. In the Russian imagination, Mother Earth was perceived on the one hand as one who sustains and nourishes all her peasant children, but on the other hand as one who tempts them to give in to her in order to devour them. Well-known representations of this image can be found, for example, in Lev Tolstoy's *How Much Land Does a Man Require?* (1886) and in *Mother Earth* (1924) by Boris Pilnyak (Russia, 1894–1938).[37]

A man's life is revived via his renewed attitude toward work, and vice versa.[38] This mutual renewal, Gordon argues, will stir in man a new emotion and a new pleasure, unfamiliar to him from his previous life where he was distanced from nature. Gordon describes these fulfilling and invigorating spiritual explorations in his characteristic utopian language,

> On that day, O Son of Man, a new spirit will be given to you, and you will experience a new emotion, a new hunger—not a hunger for bread and not a thirst for money, but for work. You will derive pleasure from every task that you undertake, from every deed that you do—a pleasure like that which you derive today from eating and drinking. On that day you will set your

[37] This ambivalence toward the image of "Mother Earth" resonates well with the Jungian mother archetype. The characteristics associated with this archetype, according to Jung, are "maternal solicitude and sympathy; the magic authority of the female; the wisdom and spiritual exaltation that transcends reason; any helpful instinct or impulse; all that is benign, all that cherishes and sustains, that fosters growth and fertility. The place of magic transformation and rebirth, together with the underworld and its inhabitants, are presided over by the mother. On the negative side the mother archetype may connote anything secret, hidden, dark; the abyss, the world of the dead, anything that devours, seduces, and poisons, that is terrifying and inescapable like fate"; Carl Gustav Jung, "Psychological Aspects of the Mother Archetype," in Jung, *The Archetypes and the Collective Unconscious*, trans. R. F. C. Hull, Princeton: Princeton University Press, 1990, p. 82. On the origins and the development of the image of Mother Earth in Russian culture see, among others, Joanna Hubbs, "The Worship of Mother Earth in Russian Culture," in James J. Preston (ed.), *Mother Worship: Theme and Variations*, Chapel Hill: University of North Carolina Press, 1982, pp. 123–144. On the image of Russia itself as a mother see also James Billington, *The Icon and Axe: An Interpretive History of Russian Culture*, New York: Vintage Books, 1970, pp. 19–20.

[38] The sense of a new life that the pioneers gained through the toil of the land is symbolically expressed in the anecdote that opens the autobiography of Tehiya Lieberson, a leading activist for women's rights. Lieberson immigrated to the Land of Israel in the second Aliyah and decided to turn the first day of her agricultural labor in the Land of Israel, which was on the first day of Hanukkah of 1905, into her birthday. "No other day," she writes, "is more fitting to serve as my birthday, and from which to count the years of my mortal life"; Tehiya Lieberson, *The Story of My Life* [Heb.], Tel Aviv: Mifaley Tarbut Vechinuch, 1970, p. 10. Moreover, on immigrating to the Land of Israel, Lieberson had chosen to change her Yiddish name *Chajne* to *Techiya*, which means in Hebrew rebirth. I thank Eylon Weitzman for drawing my attention to this point. In the same vein, Yosef Weitz describes his spiritual mindset of rebirth while toiling in the fields in Rehovot. In a letter he sent to his father in 1908 he writes, "I admire the pangs of labor and the anguish I suffered in conquering it in recent days in every bone and every sinew of my body . . . "; Weitz, *First Pages*, [Heb.], Tel Aviv: Gadish, 1958, p. 134.

heart to make your work more pleasant, more attractive, just as you set your heart today on making your food more pleasing and on paying attention to multiplying the fruit of your labors—your money. (MN, I: 32; GSE 56)

Working in nature achieves a sense of self-realization more profound than any other emotion or physical pleasure. After its emergence this profound self-realization becomes the center of man's life and marginalizes man's pursuit of money, which is perceived by Gordon as a marker and symbol of man's degeneration and detachment from nature. In his essay "Work" (1915), Gordon expresses his conception of work as therapeutic: "We were sick from lack of work (I do not say that we sinned—for we ourselves were not responsible for the situation) and work will heal us" (GWA, I: 98; GSE 56).[39] By endowing religious-spiritual meaning to agricultural work Gordon develops in his own way the ideal of Jewish Agrocentrism, that is, positing the ideal of the toiling of the land at the center of Jewish life and culture. The Agrocentric ideal, as various scholars have shown, had preceded Zionism and continued to exist alongside it. Like other advocates of Jewish Agrocentrism, Gordon aimed at transforming Jews into laborers productively toiling the land with the sweat of their brow rather than resorting to *luftgesheft* [lit. "businesses surviving on air"], such as peddling or commercial speculation.[40]

Despite the significance of working in nature, it must also be subject to the maxim "everything in due measure." In this vein Gordon declares, "You will work enough each day for the satisfaction of your needs, no more and no less" (MN, I: 32; GSE 250). Man must make room in his life for other and no less important activities, as well as express his fusion with nature not

---

[39] "Work" (1915), GWA, I: 98. An anonymous account of one of the pioneers of Degania suggests that the pioneers toil the land from dawn to sunset in an attempt to atone for the sins of past generations of Jews who conducted an unproductive, parasitic life. See *The Paths of Development of Degania: A Story of Fifty Years* [Heb.], editor not indicated, Tel Aviv: Davar, 1961, p. 167. Additional evidence for the existential nature that the pioneers of the Second Aliyah attributed to the toil of the land can also be found in Hannah Katznelson's (Russian Empire–Israel, 1897–1985) assertion, "We would run back to work to find ourselves in it," A letter from Hannah Katznelson to Rachel Katznelson (Russian Empire–Israel, 1885–1975), quoted in Moti Zeira, "Shoshana, Valiant Girl, Where Are You? (18 July, 1918)" [Heb.], *Sdemot: Literary Digest of the Kibbutzim Movement*, vol. 111 (1989), p. 60.

[40] The literature on Jewish Agrocentrism is vast. See, for example, Mordechai Naor, "Working the Land in the Yishuv" [Heb.], *Zmanim: A Historical Quarterly*, vol. 25 (1987), pp. 94–101; Hezi Aminur, *Mixed Farm and Smallholding in Zionist Settlement Thought* [Heb.], Jerusalem: The Zalman Shazar Center, 2016; Jonathan L. Dekel-Chen, *Farming the Red Land: Jewish Agricultural Colonization and Local Soviet Power, 1924–1941*, New Haven: Yale University Press, 2008; Mordechai Zalkin, "Can Jews Become Farmers? Rurality, Peasantry and Cultural Identity in the World of the Rural Jew in Nineteenth-Century Eastern Europe," *Rural History*, 24: 2 (2013), pp. 161–175.

only during working days but also on days of festivity and relaxation (MN, IV.2: 84).

In this context it should be noted that Gordon's call to return to nature inspired communities in rural collective settlements in the Land of Israel during the 1920s to restore and expand Jewish traditions and rituals celebrating nature. These newly established communities sought to renew and invent ecologically related Jewish attitudes, values, rituals, and practices. A well-known, vivid example is the story of the young pioneers of Jezreel Valley who restored and refined the long forgotten "first-fruits" ceremony during the celebration of the festival of Shavuot (see Figure 5.2). In the new arrangement of this ancient ceremony, instead of the priest, a representative of the Jewish National Fund was given the first fruits. In addition to this modification the "procession of first fruits" involved the desecration of the holiday of Shavuot from a halakhic point of view. As such, it provoked fierce

Figure 5.2. Gordon's philosophy of nature inspired young pioneers in rural collective communities in the Land of Israel to restore and refine ancient Jewish rituals, out of a profound sense of dependence on, and responsibility toward, nature. The Festival of Shavuot in Ein Harod, 1920s. Photographer: Yaacov Ben-Dov. Israel Museum, Jerusalem.

opposition from the rabbinical establishment, which saw in this ceremony a threat to the Orthodox Jewish religious tradition.[41]

The invention of tree-planting ceremonies to celebrate Tu Bishvat (New Year of the Trees) is yet another noteworthy manifestation of the young pioneers' yearning to harmoniously integrate with nature out of a deep sense of belonging to it. In this vein, in 1920 the literary scholar and historian Joseph Klausner declared,

> We are now able to take root in the land, and all the evil winds that blow on us from all sides cannot move us from our place . . . as long as we remain close to nature and maintain our feeling of nature as it is expressed during the holiday of Tu Bishvat.[42]

Important expression of Gordon's reliance on religious concepts and images to emphasize the significance of working in nature can be found in "An Irrational Solution" (1909), an essay published by Gordon shortly before the publication of the first chapter of MN. In this essay, Gordon seeks to offer a deep and comprehensive philosophical basis for the demand of the pioneers of the Second Aliyah to build their settlement literally with their own hands, without relying on the services of local non-Jewish laborers.[43]

---

[41] One Should not identify "invention" with "fabrication"; rather, it should be viewed as creation or an act of "imagination." See Benedict Anderson, *Imagined Communities: Reflections on the Origin and Spread of Nationalism*, New York: Verso Books, 2006, p. 6. For a survey of invented religious traditions, see James R. Lewis and Olav Hammer (eds.), *The Invention of Sacred Tradition*, Cambridge: Cambridge University Press, 2017. On the controversy surrounding the celebrations of the festival of Shavuot in the Jezreel Valley during 1920 see Moti Zeira, *Rural Collective Settlement and Jewish Culture in Eretz Yisrael during the 1920s* [Heb.], Jerusalem: Yad Ben-Zvi, 2002, pp. 167–184.

[42] Joseph Klausner, "The Creation of Life (On the Holiday of Tu Beshvat)" [Heb.], *Haaretz*, February 4, 1920, p. 3. See also Moti Zeira, *Rural Collective Settlement*, pp. 228–233; Hizky Shoham, *Israel Celebrates: Jewish Holidays and Civic Culture in Israel*, trans. Lenn Scharm and Diana File, Leiden and Boston: Brill, 2017, pp. 64–116. In the Bible, the religious holidays of the people of Israel are linked to the natural cycle of the agricultural year. Passover is observed at the time of the barley harvest, Shavuot is observed at the time of wheat harvest, and the first fruits and Sukkot mark the end of harvest time and thus of the agricultural year in the Land of Israel. The ceremonies of these holidays are also strongly connected to nature in general and to the toil of the land in particular: the wave sheaf offering in Passover, the "first-fruits" ceremony in Shavuot, and the four species in Sukkot. See Shemuel Yeivin, "Work of the Land" [Heb.], *Encyclopaedia Biblica*, Jerusalem: Bialik Institute, 1971, vol. VI, pp. 36–37.

[43] Like Gordon, the Russian-born Zionist leader Menahem Ussishkin (Russian Empire–Land of Israel, 1863–1941) was also influenced by the populist movement. In his pamphlet "Our Program," which he wrote following his trip to the Land of Israel in the summer of 1903, he declared that "It is essential to create a worldwide Jewish workers' artel drawn from young, unmarried youth healthy in body and mind. It will be the duty of every member of this artel to go for three years to the Land of Israel and to undertake military service to the Jewish people not with sword and rifle but with spade and plow. These thousands of youngsters will have to come to the Jewish colonies and offer themselves as hired laborers on the same terms as the Arab, to live an unprecedentedly hard life. . . . After he has completed his three years' service such a worker can, if he wishes, settle in the country in the

In this context he declares "If they [the Israelites] are virtuous, their work is performed by themselves."[44] In this declaration Gordon alludes to the well-known Talmudic saying, "when Israel performs God's will, their work is performed by others"[45] from the *sugya*[46] of Tractate Berakhot (35b) dedicated to the examination of the relationship between toil of the land and Torah study. In order to understand Gordon's subversive use of the phrase "their work is performed by themselves" it is important to keep in mind the original context in which it appears.

Gordon responds to the *sugya* of Tractate Berakhot that seeks to reconcile two apparently contradictory demands: (I) the demand for total commitment to Torah study—derived from the verse "Let not this Book of the Teaching cease from your lips, but recite it day and night" (Joshua 1:8), and (II) the demand for devotion to the toil of the land,—derived from the verse "You shall gather in your new grain and wine and oil" (Deuteronomy 11:14). The answer to this contradiction is controversial. Rabbi Yishmael (Palestine, 70–135 CE), one of the luminaries of the third generation of the Tannaim, argues that one should adopt "the way of the world" (BT Berakhot 35b), that is, to devote to agricultural work the time required for it, in order to ensure the economic conditions that will enable the study of the Torah in the remaining time. In contrast, Rabbi Shimon Bar Yochai (Palestine, 70–163 CE) presents a more radical position. In his opening remarks he poses the following rhetorical question:

hope of obtaining a lease on a plot of land from the Jewish Colonization Association or else he can join a cooperative settlement (if he brings the requisite means from home). ... If at the beginning of the 80s, we found dozens of Bilu, I sincerely believe that today we can find thousands like them. The young generation is awake, is thirsting for self-sacrifice. But it must be ... shown the way;" Menahem M. Ussishkin, *Our Program* [Heb.], New York: Federation of American Zionists, 1905, pp. 27–28, quoted in Jonathan Frankel, *Prophecy and Politics: Socialism, Nationalism and the Russian Jews, 1862–1917*, Cambridge: Cambridge University Press, 1984, p. 337 (translation slightly modified).

[44] Yitzhak Elazari-Volcani (Russian Empire–Israel, 1880–1955), one of the founders of modern agriculture in the Land of Israel, emphasized the distinct existential character that the pioneers of the Second Aliyah attached to their work. He argued that unlike pioneers in other countries, the Zionist pioneers perceived their work as a vocation, and not just employment for financial reward—important as that aspect of their work is. See Yitzhak Elazari-Volcani (I. Vilkanski), *The Communist Settlements in the Jewish Colonization in Palestine*, Tel Aviv: Palestine Economic Society, 1927, p. 11. Elazari-Volcani belonged to the circle of German scientists, known as Botanical Zionism, led by the botanist Otto Warburg (Germany–Land of Israel, 1859–1938). On the Botanical Zionism see Dana Von Suffrin, "The Possibility of a Productive Palestine: Otto Warburg and Botanical Zionism," *Israel Studies* 26: 2 (2021), pp. 173–187.

[45] Here and in what follows the translations of the Talmud are from the Steinsaltz edition of the Talmud Bavli. See Adin Steinsaltz, *Koren Talmud Bavli Noé*, Berakhot, Jerusalem: Koren Publishers, 2014, vol. 1.

[46] *Sugya* is an extended discussion of a particular topic in the Talmudic literature.

Is it possible that a person plows in the plowing season and sows in the sowing season and harvests in the harvest season and threshes in the threshing season and winnows in the windy season, as grain is separated from the chaff by means of the wind, and is constantly busy; what will become of Torah? (BT Berakhot 35b)

Toil of the land is demanding, time consuming, and Sisyphean. As such, it does not leave one the time or mental space needed for Torah study. Therefore, Rabbi Shimon Bar Yochai argues that one should devote all his time and effort to the study of the Torah, while believing that

when Israel performs God's will, their work is performed by others, as it is stated: "Strangers shall stand and pasture your flocks" (Isaiah 61:5). When Israel does not perform God's will, their work is performed by themselves, as it is stated: "And you shall gather your new grain" (Deuteronomy 11:14). Moreover, others' work will be performed by them [the Israelites], as it is stated: "You shall have to serve ... the enemies whom the LORD will let loose against you." (Deuteronomy 28:48) (BT Berakhot 35b)[47]

Gordon, therefore, uses the phrase "their work is performed by themselves"[48] while completely reversing its original Talmudic meaning. For Rabbi Shimon Bar Yochai it signifies a crisis and a distancing from God, but for Gordon the phrase "their work is performed by themselves" has a positive meaning of man's reconnection to God. Whereas in the Diaspora Jews were dependent on the benevolence of their hosts, upon their return to their homeland they could live independently. The most obvious expression of their independence, according to Gordon, is that "their work is performed by themselves." Gordon seeks to turn the return of the Jews to their homeland from a historical event to a religious event, while using the term "religious," like the early Christian theologian Augustine of Hippo (Roman Empire, 354–430 CE), in the sense of reconnecting something that has been separated and disintegrated.[49]

---

[47] Based on this line of argument, in the exilic communities, Torah scholars were generally exempt from guard duty, and Ultra-Orthodox communities in Israel have claimed the same exemption for themselves from military conscription. See Yuval Jobani and Nahshon Perez, "Toleration and Illiberal Groups in Context: Israel's Ultra-Orthodox Society of Learners," *Journal of Political Ideologies*, 19: 1, 2014, pp. 78–98.

[48] "An Irrational Solution" (1909), GWA, I: 18.

[49] See Augustine, *The Retractions*, trans. Mary Inez Bogan, Washington, D.C.: Catholic University of America Press, 1968, 12: 9, pp. 56–57; Sarah F. Hoyt, "The Etymology of Religion," *Journal of*

Work in nature is presented by Gordon not only as the center of man's life but also as its highest culmination. For it may summon rare moments of distinct religious experience such as that documented in the semiautobiographical lofty description of the spiritual mindset of the tiller of the land toward the end of the "Return to Nature" speech:

> Then when you perform your work, the expanse of the universe will be to you a vast workshop, and you and Nature the workers. One heart and one spirit will animate both of you. On that day you will say: "Beautiful is the face of Nature, but even more beautiful is the spirit of its life, of its work." When you pause a moment to straighten your body, to breathe, you will inhale not only air for breathing, but you will feel that you are drawing in something else, something subtle which you do not know, but which will fructify your sentiment and your mind, and will enliven and enlighten your spirit. You will certainly have moments in which you feel your whole being melting into the infinite. Then you will grow silent. Not only speech but also poetry and even thought will be sacrilegious to you. You will know the secret, the holiness of silence. You will sense that which cannot be expressed except by work; you will labor with all your strength, mightily, joyously. And you will hear a "Divine voice" (*bat koll*) arising from your work and saying: "Work, sons of man (*bene adam*), all of you, work!" Know therefore this day and keep in mind that there is in work such a spiritual wealth of which you can see but the barest fringe; nor will all of this wealth be seen except by those who will look at it from all angles. After the Divine voice, Nature answers, "Amen!" as though to say: "Work, sons of man, let not your work be insignificant in your eyes. I will give you work! You will make perfect what I have left imperfect in order that I may make perfect what you have left imperfect . . . " (MN, I: 32–33; GSE 250–251)

In the Romantic movement, turning to the aesthetic aspects of nature was commonly perceived as a way of empowering the turning of man into himself. According to this view, man's contact with the purity, freshness, and uniqueness of nature purifies his soul, recharges his spiritual powers, refreshes and revives his life energies, and reminds him that like any creature,

the American Oriental Society, vol. 32 (1912), pp. 126–129. On Simmel's use of the term "religion" see Horst Jurgen Helle, "Introduction to Simmel's Essays on Religion," in Georg Simmel, *Essays on Religion*, Horst Jürgen Helle and Ludwig Nieder (trans. and eds.), New Haven: Yale University Press, 1997, p. xii.

plant, or stone in nature he is also singular and unique. This existential adoration of the beauty of nature culminates in a religious union with it. In this spirit the American transcendentalist Henry David Thoreau, for example, presents the very act of walking within nature as an activity by which man merges with nature. In *Walden* Thoreau declares, "This is a delicious evening, when the whole body is one sense, and imbibes delight through every pore. I go and come with a strange liberty in Nature, a part of herself."[50]

Thoreau, however, does not view work as having intrinsic value and calls therefore on man to make a virtue out of simplicity in order to allow himself to devote as little time as possible to his work. In this context he writes,

> I did not use tea, nor coffee, nor butter, nor milk, nor fresh meat, and so did not have to work to get them; again, as I did not work hard, I did not have to eat hard, and it cost me but a trifle for my food;[51] Men labor under a mistake. The better part of the man is soon ploughed into the soil for compost. . . . Actually, the laboring man has not leisure for a true integrity day by day; he cannot afford to sustain the manliest relations to men; his labor would be depreciated in the market.[52]

Thoreau takes pride even in that "for more than five years I maintained myself thus solely by the labor of my hands, and I found, that by working about six weeks in a year, I could meet all the expenses of living."[53]

Thoreau admits that nature may also be "carried out" in people who work in nature—as he puts it[54]—however, this fusion with nature is brought about not through labor, but by being purely present in nature.

> Fishermen, hunters, woodchoppers, and others, spending their lives in the fields and woods, in a peculiar sense a part of Nature themselves, are often in a more favorable mood for observing her, in the intervals of their pursuits, than philosophers or poets even, who approach her with expectation. She is not afraid to exhibit herself to them.[55]

---

[50] Thoreau, *Walden*, p. 129.
[51] Ibid., p. 205.
[52] Ibid., pp. 5–6.
[53] Ibid., p. 69.
[54] Ibid., pp. 283–284.
[55] Ibid., p. 210.

Buber formulates the main difference, in his opinion, between Gordon on the one hand and Thoreau and the American poet Walt Whitman (New York–New Jersey, 1819–1892) on the other hand, as follows:

When I read in Thoreau that the chief thing is to see man as an inhabitant, or as an integral part of Nature, rather than a member of society, I seem to hear the voice of Gordon. But for these Americans Nature is nevertheless still fundamentally the landscape, it is not so really and truly the Cosmos as for Gordon. In their words I see the trees more clearly than the stars. In Gordon's I see the stars, even when he is only speaking of the trees. Talk about a "cosmic consciousness" is no rare thing in American literature, but it sounds to me like an abstraction which is more likely to lead one away from Gordon's simple and practical formulation of the question. And when I think of Whitman or Thoreau, I see them wandering, gloriously wandering, but I do not see them hoeing and weeding like Gordon. In saying this I am not forgetting of course that Thoreau did toil on his farm for all he is worth. But when he does so he does not yet really know what he is doing. Gordon, on the other hand, does know what he is doing. He knows that his work enables man to participate in the life of the Cosmos.[56]

Both Rousseau and Thoreau described themselves alone in a boat that they rowed to the middle of a lake when the water was calm.[57] Thus secluded in the boat, they used to lie back and stretch themselves to their full length, their eyes turned toward the sky, letting themselves drift slowly as the water moved them, sometimes for several hours, experiencing unification with nature. Among the pioneers of the Second Aliyah, it was customary to lie on the ground and to gaze at the sky as a token of melding with the landscape of the Land of Israel. "Through both direct contact with the soil and this panoramic gaze," as Neumann puts it, the pioneers "arrive at the moment when they feel themselves, with their entire beings and in a most concrete way, an integral, organic part of the Land of Israel."[58]

Although Gordon is well aware of the attempt to turn the aesthetic experience of man's presence in nature into a religious experience, he prefers

---

[56] Martin Buber, "A Man Who Realizes the Idea of Zion (On A. D. Gordon)," in Buber, *On Zion: The History of an Idea*, trans. Stanley Godman, London: East and West Library, 1973, p. 156.

[57] Jean-Jacques Rousseau, *Reveries of the Solitary Walker*, trans. Peter France, London: Penguin, 1980, p. 85; Thoreau, *Walden*, p. 191.

[58] Neumann, *Land and Desire*, p. 68.

working in nature, rather than the wandering, hiking, or the mere presence in nature as the ultimate momentum to melding with it; "On that day you will say: Beautiful is the face of Nature, but even more beautiful is the spirit of its life, of its work" (MN, I: 32, GSE 250).[59] But in what way—the reader may justifiably ask—is work preferable to other modes and means of contact, interaction, and unification with nature?

Here, of course, one cannot ignore the historical context in which Gordon and his readers lived. The pioneers of the Second Aliyah (1904–1914), to whom Gordon belonged, glorified the toil of the land, which they associated with the redemption of the individual and the nation.[60] Nevertheless, even though there is no doubt that Gordon's philosophy expresses the spirit of its time and place, it is not possible to reduce his philosophy to the idealization of the toil of land that prevailed in the Zionist vision and imagination in the early twentieth century. The ultimate basis for Gordon's perception of work in nature as the ideal mode of melding with nature is philosophical rather than historical. As such, Gordon's concept of work in nature—as we

---

[59] An example of the attempt to turn the aesthetic experience of man's presence in nature into a religious experience can be found in the travel journal of Absalom Feinberg (Land of Israel–Egypt, 1889–1917), one of the founders of the Nili espionage network who worked at the agricultural research station in Atlit. Gazing at the melting snows on Mount Hermon, Feinberg writes, "an urge awakened in me to race [the burbling streams], to unite with them, to be melting snow, bounding water, golden rays of sun, grasses trembling with the passion of love"; Absalom Feinberg, *Travel Journal* [Heb.] (February 12, 1912), in Feinberg, *Absalom: Papers and Letters of the Late Absalom Feinberg* [Heb.], Jerusalem: Shikmona, 1975, p. 208. In the rabbinic literature, there were those who sought to warn man against addiction to the aesthetic experiences that he has when he is outdoors interacting with the natural environment. Particularly well known in this context is the warning of Rabbi Jacob ben Korshai, a sage from the Land of Israel who lived in the latter half of the second century: "One who is going along repeating traditions, and he breaks off his repetition, exclaiming: 'How lovely is this tree! How lovely is this furrow!' Scripture regards him as if he brings disaster upon himself"; *Mishnah Avot*, in Shaye J. D. Cohen, Robert Goldenberg, and Hayim Lapin (eds.), *The Oxford Annotated Mishnah*, New York: Oxford University Press, 2022, 3: 7, p. 728.

[60] Yoseph Aharonovich, the editor of the first edition of Gordon's writings, documented the experience of redemption through toil of the land, common among the pioneers of the Second Aliyah. In one of his letters, he writes that "At times [during agricultural labor] you raise your eyes to the wide spaces visible among the trees and look at the majesty of eternity around you . . . you negate yourself before the infinite"; Yoseph Aharonovich, "Letter from Yoseph Aharonovich to a Friend" (1910), in Yoseph Aharonovich, *Collected Works of Yoseph Aharonovich* [Heb.], Tel Aviv: Am Oved, 1941, vol. 1, p. 211. In a similar vein, protesting against the severely restricted employment of Hebrew laborers in the drying of Kabara's swamps during the 1920s, Aharon Ben-Barak (Russian Empire–Israel, 1890–1978), a pioneer from Nahalal, declares, "We want to stand in the mud of Kabara to immerse ourself in the water [of the swamp] up to the neck—in order to feel the pangs of creation"; Aharon Ben Barak, "In Kabara's Swamps," *Hapoel Hatzair*, vol. 6, November 13, 1924, p. 15. "In their yearning for the land," as Shapira put it, "came together the psychological needs of the Jewish individual and the political needs of the Zionist movement; the personal urge for revolution was integrated in the urge to solve the problem of the Jewish masses"; Anita Shapira, *The Failed Struggle: Hebrew Work 1929–1939* [Heb.], Tel Aviv: Hakibbutz Hameuchad, 1977, p. 15.

saw earlier—refers to any type of human work (including spiritual work) and is not restricted to agricultural work.

Gordon perceives work as an act of creative renewal. Since nature itself is in a process of infinite creative renewal it is only through work in nature—rather than wandering or hiking in it[61]—that man fully participates in the work of nature. Therefore, man's work in nature in its broadest sense includes spiritual work, since it also allows man to be "one with the universal nature . . . which renews the work of creation every day, continuously!" (MN, I: 29).[62] The tiller of the soil fully expresses the unification of man with nature since—as Gordon puts it in his "Letters from the land of Israel"—he is

> organically woven into the work of the universal Nature. . . . At times he imagines that he, too, is taking root in the soil which he is digging; like all that grows around, he is nurtured by the light of the sun's rays with nourishment from heaven; that he, too, lives a life in common with the tiniest blade of grass, with each flower, each tree; that he lives deeply in the heart of Nature, rising from it all and growing straight up into the expanses of the vast world.[63]

Due to natural regeneration processes wheat will continue to grow even without human intervention. But when man sows and grows wheat he may increase and intensify the renewal and regeneration in nature, given that he strives to integrate and unite with nature through his labor, and not exploit or dominate nature only for his personal benefit. The Hebrew word *haklaut* (agriculture) is a neologism coined by the educator and linguist David Yellin (Jerusalem, 1864–1941) in the final decade of the nineteenth century. The

---

[61] Rachel Yanait-Ben-Zvi (Russian Empire–Israel, 1886–1979), one of the founding mothers of the Second Aliyah, presents the very act of hiking and wandering in the Land of Israel as an activity in which one merges with nature. "Every touch of my bare foot on the soil delights me and awakens latent chords in my body and soul," she writes as she wonders how "to motivate every immigrant to walk the land's length and breadth in order soak into himself its spirit, to give himself over to the wind and sun and to cling to its soil. After all, a person lives only once in this world, so why not permit oneself this wonderful feeling of unmediated contact with nature—this feeling is the real taste of life"; Rachel Yanait-Ben-Zvi, *We Ascend* [Heb.], Tel Aviv: Am Oved, 1959, p. 45.

[62] BT Hagigah 12b. The saying is recited in the morning prayer (*shacharit*): "In His goodness, He renews the work of creation every day, continuously."

[63] "Letters from the Land of Israel: First Letter" (undated), GWA, II: 231–232; GSE, 120–121. In this spirit, Hasia Drori (Russian Empire–Israel, 1899–1976), one of the founders of Kfar Yehezkel and an activist for women's rights, describes her life as a pioneer as a "full life of a woman which regrows in the fields of Jezreel Valley . . . with the planting of each seedling, I felt as if I were also planting myself"; Hasia Drori, "In Kfar Yehezkel "[Heb.], in Yehuda Erez (ed.), *The Book of the Third Aliya*, Tel Aviv: Am Oved, 1964, vol. 2, pp. 514–515.

word stems from the Aramaic word *hakla*, which means field.[64] In Latin, in contrast, the word *Agricultūra*—on which the English word *agriculture* is based—is a portmanteau of two words "field" (ager) and "culture" (cultūra).[65] This intersection of nature and culture, found in the Latin word *Agricultūra*, reflects well Gordon's attempt to turn the toil of the soil into an activity that dialectically incorporates experience (nature) and cognition (culture). Such a dialectical merging of experience and cognition is rare, but when it occurs it allows man to meld with existence in its entirety, which itself is essentially a perpetual dialectical swinging pendulum movement between the principle of expansion (*hitpashtut*) and the principal of contraction (*tzimtzum*). In the human realm this dialectical movement is manifested through constant movement between acts of experience (*havayah*) and cognition (*hakarah*), respectively. As man's finite work is part of nature's infinite work itself, man and nature become full partners in their work (see Figure 5.3). "When you perform your work," declares Gordon, "the expanse of the universe will be to you a vast workshop, and you and Nature the workers. One heart and one spirit will animate both of you" (MN, I: 32, GSE 250).

The protagonist of the "Return to Nature" speech surrenders his body and soul for the sake of tillage in the hope that it will enable an encounter, however brief and fleeting, with the Absolute.[66] In order to emphasize that his addressee is an individual—any individual—Gordon chooses to adopt in his speech the guiding word *ben adam* (son of man), which is a

[64] The word *haklai* (farmer) first appeared in David Yellin's 1896 Hebrew translation of *The Vicar of Wakefield: A Tale, Supposed to Be Written by Himself*, by the Anglo-Irish novelist Oliver Goldsmith (Ireland–London, 1728–1774) first published in 1766. Prior to the acceptance of Yellin's neologism it was customary to use the biblical conjunction *oved adama* (tiller of the soil), which is used to describe Kayin's occupation in Genesis 4:2. In contrast to the Latin word *Agricultūra* the Hebrew word *haklaut* (agriculture) has no connection to the term *culture* (Tarbut). At the same time, the word *tarbut* is also used in an agricultural context, as in the expression *tzimchey tarbut* (cultivated plants). The linguist and lexicographer Yehuda Gur [Grazowski] (Russian Empire–Israel, 1862–1950), for example, refers in 1911 to "Collective Associations for the betterment of cultivation (*tirbut*) of fruit trees." See Yehuda Gur (Grazowski), "In the Big World", in David Levontin (ed.), *Collective Associations in the World and in Our World* [Heb.], Jaffa: England-Palestine Company in Jaffa, 1911, vol. III, p. 9. The book was printed by Atin Press in Jaffa 1910, which also printed Metmann's pamphlet "Life and Nature," which was discussed extensively in the second chapter. On Yellin's contribution to the revival of the Hebrew language see also Ofra Meitlis, *On the Middle Path: David Yellin—A Life Story* [Heb.], Tel Aviv University: The Jaime and Joan Constantiner School of Education, 2015, pp. 87–144. See also Iair Or, *Creating a Style for a Generation: The Beliefs and Ideologies of Hebrew Language Planners* [Heb.], Tel Aviv: Ov, 2016, pp. 260–261.

[65] Glynnis Chantrell (ed.), *The Oxford Dictionary of Word Histories*, New York: Oxford University Press 2002, p. 14.

[66] In an essay published in the journal *HaAdama*, which was edited by Y. H. Brenner, the educator Moshe Karmi (Land of Israel, 1893–1952) describes how God speaks to the pioneers "from the furrow, and from the field that sprouts and rises, and from the ripe golden grain at dawn shortly before sunrise;" Moshe Karmi, "Segment" [Heb.], *HaAdama*, vol. 1 (1919–1920), p. 202.

THE "RETURN TO NATURE" SPEECH

Figure 5.3. Pioneers planting trees, Merhavia, 1920s. Unknown photographer. Nadav Mann, Bitmuna. From the Merhavia Cooperative Collection. The Pritzker Family National Photography Collection, The National Library of Israel.

characteristic term in the book of Ezekiel. But while in the book of Ezekiel the term *ben adam* indicates the prophet (Ezekiel) who is sent by God to deliver his prophecies to "the house of Israel," in the "Return to Nature" speech the addressee of Gordon's own prophecy, so to speak, is *ben adam* rather than "the house of Israel." Using this rhetorical device, Gordon asserts again that for him "religion is entirely subjective" (MN, IV.3: 98).

Even though the religiosity of the individual is distinctly personal, Gordon nevertheless does underline the significance of the social collective to the formation of the individual and the ensuing obligations of the individual to society. Indeed, Gordon aligns here with the ethos of the pioneers, which presupposes the existence of the social collective, the "camp," for which the pioneers aimed to pave the way.[67]

---

[67] The term *halutz* (pioneer) in its Zionist meaning was coined only at the beginning of the second decade of the twentieth century, whereas beforehand the people of the Second Aliyah were called "the young" (*tzeirim*). For a discussion of the origins and development of the term *halutz* see Shmuel Almog, "Pioneering as an Alternative Culture" [Heb.], *Zion: A Quarterly for Research in Jewish History*, 58: 3 (1993), pp. 246–329; Neumann, *Land and Desire*, pp. 3–7. On the dialectical nature of the term see also Zeira, *Rural Collective Settlement*, p. 330. In his "Open Letter to Y.H. Brenner"

Nor does Gordon turn his back on religious customs, language, and images that had crystallized over generations, but, rather, he calls for an ongoing and live dialogue with them,[68] creating what the scholar of nationalism Anthony D. Smith called "poetic spaces" within which religion as well as nature and history gain new meaning.[69] Nevertheless, Gordon asserts that contact with the Absolute is a private matter, unmediated by social or religious structures or institutions. Therefore, the protagonist of the "Return to Nature" speech does not come into contact with the Absolute when praying with a quorum in a synagogue adorned with *tefillin* (phylacteries) and wrapped in *tallit* (prayer shawl). Rather, he is a tiller of the soil who contacts the Absolute in solitude as he rests from his labor in the open field while his body merges with the body of the earth and his soul is attentive to its great silence.

Such religious descriptions refute the arguments against Gordon's conception of work presented by the thinker and educator Akibah Ernst Simon (Berlin–Jerusalem, 1899–1988) in his influential essay "Are We Still Jews?"

(1912) Gordon provides a significant articulation of his understanding of the role of the pioneers in human history. In response to Brenner, who downplayed the power and importance of the few, Gordon declares, "Were not all significant movements of humanity ... conceived by the few? Our national misfortune is not that the masses do not lead or follow us, but that we have not the few; ... we have not those who have 'despaired.' The individual, the one who despairs, does not look for redemption, expects no favors from reality, does not rely on the power of the many. This type of individual is himself a redeemer,—e.g., he himself takes what deadly risks there are. He does not weigh and measure all things, nor does he look to the right or to the left of him. Let what may happen! Since he is desperate, he has but two ways confronting him. Either he must 'free' himself from life or he must free life. This means that he must seek to redeem life; he has no other alternative. ... Give us individuals, give us 'despairing individuals,' the few who do not withdraw from the firing line! Give us those who turn their despair into unified, constructive work!" ("Open Letter to Y.H. Brenner," GWA, I: 105–106; GSE, 18–19). Gordon's letter was written in response to Brenner's essay "Why do the Nations Rage? Letter from the Land of Israel" (1912), in Brenner, *Complete Works*, [Heb.], Yitzhak Kafkafi (ed.), Tel Aviv: Hakibbutz Hameuchad, 1985, vol. 4, pp. 969–990. On the tension between the pioneer's commitment to the social collective and their individualistic aspirations see Eliyahu Rosenow, "On the Figure of the Pioneer in Zionist Thought: Ahad Ha'am's and A.D. Gordon's Concept of Education" [Heb.], in David Nevo (ed.), *The Educational Deed: Study and Research*, Tel Aviv: Tel Aviv University's School of Education, 1977, pp. 35–60.

[68] In one of his last notes, for example, "Considering Our Encounter with Religion (Reflections on Yom Kippur)," which he wrote on his deathbed in Degania, apparently in early 1922, he asks in shock "is this day for us only a heritage from the past, a remnant from antiquity? ... If this day will cease being what it is, and will become an ordinary day like other days, will it not involve a great human and national loss, a decline that will entail no elevation for us, for all of us, sons of this nation?"; "Considering Our Encounter with Religion (Reflections on Yom Kippur)" (date not indicated), GWA, V: 215; GSE, 285. Although Gordon gradually distanced himself from the *halakha* since he arrived in the Land of Israel, he continued fasting and attending synagogue on Yom Kippur as well as observing the Sabbath till the end of his life. See Ramon, *New Life*, p. 221. See also Mordechai Charizman, "In Ein Ganim" [Heb.], in Kushnir, *Reminiscences and Appreciations*, p. 46.

[69] Anthony D. Smith, "The Question of Jewish Identity," in Peter Y. Medding (ed.), *Studies in Contemporary Jewry VIII: A New Jewry? America since the Second World War*, New York: Oxford University Press, 1992, pp. 224–225.

(1951).[70] In his essay, Simon traces what he describes as the collapse of the all-encompassing, original, "Catholic" infrastructure of the Jewish religion. Following this collapse, he argues, the Jewish religion has been squeezed into a narrow "Protestant" pattern in which religion exists and operates along-side other realms of human activity (politics and art, for example), rather than above them. The main factors involved in this decline, in Simon's view, were the growth of Jewish Enlightenment (*haskalah*) on the one hand, and the emergence of Zionist nationalism on the other. Gordon's conception of work as an independent sphere of activity with a unique value in its own right, Simon argues, is clearly a result of the diminishment and decline of the Jewish religion in the modern era.[71]

Gordon, Simon admits, didn't label his view as a "religion of work"; it was the writer Rabbi Binyamin who introduced and popularized the term "religion of work."[72] However, this term, Simon continues, fits well with

---

[70] The essay was first published in the 1951/1952 *Haaertz Almanach* (Luach Haaertz). It was later included in a volume of Simon's essays; Akibah Ernst Simon, *Are We Still Jews? Essays* [Heb.], Tel Aviv: Sifriat Poalim, 1983. The following quotations and references are from this edition. In this essay, as in his other essays, Simon places himself at the intersection between the philosopher and the educator, while his main addressees—as Haim Rechnitzer puts it—are "Jewish educators at the forefront of secularization processes in Jewish society. These educators operate in secular and religious settings that do not adopt a strategy of cultural and sociological withdrawal. They also try to make Judaism, whether they see it as a culture or a religion, an integral part of the student's world. They strive to do so while integrating Jewish values and ethics into the complex framework of multiple cultural options, diverse worldviews, critical thinking and research, and the establishment of secular-humanist culture"; Haim O. Rechnitzer, "Toward a Trans-Liberal Romanticism" [Heb.], in Jonathan Cohen and Elie Holzer (eds.), *Modes of Educational Translation*, Jerusalem: Hebrew University Magnes Press, 2008, p. 93. For discussion of Simon's philosophical and educational position see Avi Sagi, "Are We Still Jews?" [Heb.], in Adi Ophir (ed.), *Fifty to Forty-Eight: Critical Moments in the History of the State of Israel*, Jerusalem: The Van Leer Jerusalem Institute, 1999, pp. 79–88; Carl Frankenstein and Baruch Sarel (eds.), *Akiba Ernst Simon—Educator in Thought and Action* [Heb], Jerusalem: Hebrew University Magnes Press, 1980.

[71] Rabbi Binyamin (pseudonym of Yehoshua Redler-Feldmann), "Rabbi Aharon David Gordon (The 25th Anniversary of His Death)" [Heb.], *HaTzofe*, February 14, 1947, p. 3. See also Yosef Haim Brenner, "Why Do the Nations Rage? Letter from the Land of Israel" (1912), in Brenner, *Complete Works*, [Heb.], Yitzhak Kafkafi (ed.), Tel Aviv: Hakibbutz Hameuchad, 1985, vol. 4, p. 972. In a similar vein in his harsh critique of the Canaanite movement Baruch Kurzweil argued that the exchange of the work of God for the toil of the soil reflects a post-Catholic bourgeois secular phenomenon that penetrated Jewish culture in the Haskalah era. For discussion see Moshe Goultschin, *Baruch Kurzweil as a Commentator of Culture* [Heb.], Ramat Gan: Bar Ilan University Press, 2009, pp. 140–144.

[72] In the account of his journey in the Land of Israel, Joseph Klausner writes that for the pioneers "work was immersed in holiness, and they devote themselves to it with purity and awe, as Jews used to devote themselves in the past to Torah and prayer"; Joseph Klausner, "A World Come into Being (Part III)," *Ha-Shiloah*, vol. 29 (1913), p. 209. Shimon Kushnir argued that it was Noah Naftolski who attributed the idea of "religion of work" to Gordon, who saw it as "a new idol for the House of Israel." See Shimon Kushnir, *Fatherland's Firstborn: A Tale of a Youth in the Days of the Second Aliyah* [Heb.], Tel Aviv: Ayanot, 1968, p. 57; Kushnir, *Men of Nebo*, p. 57; Muki Tsur, *Studies in Kibbutz and Israeli Culture* [Heb.], Jerusalem: Yad Tabenkin, 2007, pp. 67–73. See also Shmuel Almog, "From 'Muscular Jewry' to the 'Religion of Labor,'" *Zionism—Studies in the History of the Zionist Movement and the Jewish Community in Palestine*, vol. 9 (1984), pp. 137–146.

Gordon's attitude to work, which was entirely foreign to the spirit of classical, "Catholic" Judaism. Anyone who attributes to ancient Judaism the obligation to work as an end in itself, declares Simon, "is nothing but wrong ... for such an attitude to work, came into being only with the Reformation. The tremendous innovation of this movement was that it perceived man's occupation (*Beruf*) as his religious-moral mission (*Berufung*)."[73] The attitude of the Jewish religion to work, Simon argues, ranges from reservation and yearning for the creation of the conditions in which it will no longer be needed ("Strangers shall stand and pasture your flocks, Aliens shall be your plowmen and vine-trimmers")[74] to its perception as a necessary tool for the work of God ("If there is no flour there is no Torah").[75] However, even this legitimacy, Simon emphasizes, never turns work from a means to an end in itself as it is done by Gordon.

While Simon's claim that Gordon frees work from any subordination or dependence on any external factor is quite plausible, less plausible is his claim that Gordon detaches work in nature from worshiping the Creator as well as his claim that Gordon's conception of work is a foreign element in the world of Judaism. In contrast to the prevailing reduction of work to economic or national interest, Gordon seeks to turn work, by relying on the creativity at its core, into a distinctly religious activity that allows man to connect with nature and unite with it. Indeed, the biblical infrastructure behind Gordon's conception of work emerges only between the lines of the "Return to Nature" speech, without being referred to directly. This infrastructure, which Simon did not heed, amounts to more than just fragments from biblical verses woven into the "Return to Nature" speech but relates to the biblical sense of work in the story of the Garden of Eden in Genesis (Genesis 2:4–3:24).

The concept of work (*avoda*) in the Bible is a laden concept whose meaning ranges from the narrow meaning of labor or work that requires physical effort ("Judah has gone into exile because of misery and harsh oppression (*avoda*)")[76] to the broader meaning of service or duty, especially in religious worship ("Bringing to the Lord his offering for the work of the Tent of Meeting and for all its service and for the sacral vestments").[77]

[73] Simon, *Are We Still Jews?*, p. 18.
[74] Isaiah 61:5.
[75] Pirkei Avot 3:8.
[76] Lamentations 1:3.
[77] Exodus 35:21.

The introduction to the story of the Garden of Eden, in the second chapter of Genesis, contains an additional version of the creation of man to the one presented in the first chapter. The Bible reads:

> [4] Such is the story of Heaven and Earth when they were created. When the Lord God made earth and heaven—[5] When no shrub of the field was yet on earth and no grasses of the field had yet sprouted, because the Lord God had not sent rain upon the earth and there was no man to till the soil, [6] but a flow would well up from the ground and water the whole surface of the earth—[7] the Lord God formed man from the dust of the earth. He blew into his nostrils the breath of life, and man became a living being. . . . [15] The Lord God took the man and placed him in the garden of Eden, to till it and tend it. (Genesis 2: 4–15)

The first two verses in this passage (4–5) describe nature, immediately after its creation, as incapable of renewing itself. According to these verses "no shrub of the field was yet on earth and no grasses of the field had yet sprouted" (4), not only because "Lord God had not sent rain upon the earth," but also because "there was no man to till the soil" (5). Then, the following verses describe how "a flow would well up from the ground" (6) and water the earth, and how "God formed man" (7) and (metaphorically) planted him in the garden of Eden, in order that he "till it and tend it" (15), to ensure growth and renewal in nature. Only after the development of human cognition, associated in the Bible with the eating from the Tree of Knowledge, work turns from being an activity dedicated to protecting nature and melding with it, to an exploitation of nature and alienation from it. Man is banished from the Garden of Eden for disobeying God and eating from the Tree of Knowledge. Thenceforth the soil would yield nothing but thorns and thistles, and thus man must sweat and toil the land in order to reap bread and earn his living. In consequence, work turns from a symbol of co-operation between man and God into a symbol of a rift between man and God, as well as a symbol of the banishment from the Garden of Eden.

While adhering to the conception of work couched in the story of the Garden of Eden, Gordon develops and enhances this conception by merging its two biblical meanings mentioned earlier: physical toil and the worship of God. The worship of God (*avodat elohim*) described in the Bible tended to involve sacrificial offerings.[78] These rites developed into the worship of the

---

[78] See, for example, Exodus 10:26. The worship of God in the Bible is not limited to spontaneous sacrificial offerings by individuals or to the daily sacrifice service in the Temple but includes all the

tabercle (*avodat Ha'mishkan*),[79] and later into the worship of the Temple (*avodat Ha'mikdash*).[80] In complete contrast to sacrificial offerings, it is the toiling of the land that is Gordon's definitive act of worshiping God. Gordon disapproved of the acts of sacrificial offerings prevalent in the Bible, and he perceived these rites as expressing the decline of the religion of Israel, which had absorbed pagan influences that prioritized religious form over religious content.[81] Therefore, upon the return of the people of Israel to their motherland, they should not seek to renew the worship of God in the temple but, rather, to transfer it to the open fields, where man can be God's partner in the act of creation (MN, I: 30).

The link that Gordon seeks to establish between the toiling of the land in the Land of Israel and the worship of God has a clear biblical basis. Most of the inhabitants of the ancient Land of Israel made their living from agricultural work that relied on rainfall, in contrast to agriculture in Egypt that relied on irrigation:

> For the land that you are about to enter and possess is not like the land of Egypt from which you have come. There the grain you sowed had to be watered by your own labors, like a vegetable garden; but the land you are about to cross into and possess, a land of hills and valleys, soaks up its water from the rains of heaven. (Deuteronomy 11:10–11)

The Bible endows this auspicious agrarian character of the Land of Israel with a distinct religious significance. This land, the next verse immediately states, is "a land which the Lord your God looks after, on which the Lord your God always keeps His eye, from year's beginning to year's end" (Deuteronomy 11:12). The following verses in chapter 11 in Deuteronomy re-emphasize that successful toiling of the land is conditioned upon worshiping God:

---

deeds—and even the mindset—that express the worship of God and the acceptance of His authority. See Yaakov Shalom Licht, "God's Worship" [Heb.], in *Encyclopaedia Biblica*, vol. VI, pp. 37–39.

[79] See, for example, Numbers 4:30.

[80] See, for example, Ezekiel 44:14.

[81] The prophets had almost succeeded in abolishing sacrifices. But, as Gordon points out in the fourth chapter in MN, the Babylonian returnees, influenced by pagan nations, increased the status of the offering of sacrifices to such an extent that, much to Gordon's discomfort, the yearning to restore these practices never ceased (MN, IV.2: 90; GSE 215).

If, then, you obey the commandments that I enjoin upon you this day, loving the Lord your God and serving Him with all your heart and soul, I will grant the rain for your land in season, the early rain and the late. You shall gather in your new grain and wine and oil—I will also provide grass in the fields for your cattle—and thus you shall eat your fill. Take care not to be lured away to serve other gods and bow to them. For the Lord's anger will flare up against you, and He will shut up the skies so that there will be no rain and the ground will not yield its produce; and you will soon perish from the good land that the Lord is assigning to you. (Deuteronomy 11:13–17)

As the last verse states, worshiping God is the necessary condition not only to the successful toiling of the land but also to maintaining hold of it. The Israelites will lose their land, the Bible warns, if they do not worship God. In this spirit, Gordon declares that the outcome of the struggle between Arabs and Jews over the Land of Israel would be determined not by the force of arms or by monetary force, but by the force of physical labor:

The land will be given to those who are able to suffer for it and labor over it— and especially to those who actually suffer and labor over it more. Common sense requires this, justice requires this and so do the circumstances. And here you see yet again the power of work and its role in our revival and our redemption.[82]

The biblical verses quoted above, on which Gordon relies when he argues that the successful toiling of the land and the holding of it are conditioned upon worshiping God, have immense importance in the Jewish tradition. Evidence of the importance of these verses can be found in their inclusion in the reading of the Shema, a canonical text second to no other text in the circle of Jewish life. For generations upon generations, Jews have been inscribing these verses in the *mezuzot* they affixed to the doorposts of their homes, as well as in the *tefillin*, which they placed on their arms and heads. These verses are also recited daily as part of the reading of the Shema in the morning and

[82] "Irrational Solution" (1909), GWA, I: 29. In the spirit of Gordon's words, one of the pioneers from Ben Shemen declared, "As long as the soil has not been drenched wet with our sweat—it will not belong to us!"; Ben Shemani, "Untitled Passage," [June–July 1912], in Eliezer Shochat and Haim Shorer (eds.), *Chapters of Hapoel Hatzair*, Tel Aviv: Tversky, 1935, vol. 1, p. 194. See also the discussion in Neumann, *Land and Desire*, pp. 56–57.

evening Jewish prayer services. Jews also recite these verses with their last
breath as did Rabbi Akiva (Akiva ben Yosef, ca. 50–135 CE), who according
to the legend read the Shema while his flesh was being torn with iron combs
by the Romans.[83]

Gordon's call to return to work in its original meaning as an activity dedicated to protecting nature and melding with it enables man to return, even if
only for a brief moment, to the paradise from which he was expelled. Work in
nature, in its proper, original meaning, enables man to re-establish the part-
nership he had with God and to ensure the continuous renewal of nature as
well as of himself. As we saw earlier, a semiautobiographical account of such
a moment appears toward the end of the "Return to Nature" speech:

> When you pause a moment to straighten your body, to breathe, you will
> inhale not only air for breathing, but you will feel that you are drawing in
> something else, something subtle which you do not know, but which will
> fructify your sentiment and your mind, and will enliven and enlighten your
> spirit. You will certainly have moments in which you feel your whole being
> melting into the infinite. Then you will grow silent. Not only speech but also
> poetry and even thought will be sacrilegious to you. You will know the se-
> cret, the holiness of silence. You will sense that which cannot be expressed
> except by work. (MN, I: 32–33; GSE 250–251)

The religious experience, which is at the heart of this description, is a rare
and extraordinary event even in the lives of the few who attain it. Work in
nature, in the broad sense that Gordon gives it, is a necessary but not sufficient condition for the occurrence of religious experience. Man can prepare
himself for it, but he cannot guarantee its attainment. The religious experience occurs absentmindedly, almost by accident. As the tiller pauses for a
moment to inhale fresh air, as Gordon describes it, he finds himself drawing
in the Absolute itself and attaining an "eternity of the moment" (MN, I: 33).
The image of inhaling air has two layers of meaning. First, although the religious experience occurs rarely—if at all—when it does occur, it seems as
natural and simple as inhaling air. Second, the inhalation of air also expresses
most clearly the continuous and vital dependence of man on the nature
within which he is placed. And as such, inhalation of air reveals the dialectical nature of life: every creature in nature, in order to fortify and protect

---

[83] BT, Berakhot, 61a.

its individual existence, must absorb and assimilate something separate and distinct from it. The alternating expansion and dilation of the respiratory organs is a physiological expression of the constant metaphysical movement between the principle of expansion and the principle of contraction that applies to all existing beings. As we saw earlier, even if experience (which expresses the principle of expansion) is disconnected from cognition and even opposes cognition (which expresses the principle of contraction), it enriches and fertilizes it.

As in the Garden of Eden, work in nature grants man direct contact with the Absolute, without the agency of institutionalized religion, community, or language—without, even, the agency of thought. In his description of the religious experience Gordon borrows fragments from biblical verses, idiomatic phrases, and metaphors from classical Jewish sources. Nevertheless, the religious experience that he describes in his "Return to Nature" speech does not occur during prayer in a *minyan* (quorum), or while fulfilling a *mitzvah* (religious duty), and not even while accepting the yoke of Heaven (*kabbalat ol malchut Shamayim*); thus, it is devoid of any direct connection to the *Halakha* (Jewish legal law) or to religious belief in the traditional and accepted sense.

As we have seen in the previous chapter, in the terms of Tönnies the protagonist of Gordon's "Return to Nature" speech is a member of a *Gemeinschaft* (community) bound together by organic personal ties and customs, rather than a member of a *Gesellschaft* (society) where alienated individuals interact through "mechanical" interests, institutions, and commercial contracts. Just as the protagonist of Gordon's "Return to Nature" speech engages with others in an internal-organic rather than external-rigid way, his engagement with the earth is deeply spiritual, and he does not perceive it to be a mere asset or resource at his disposal.[84] Even though the tiller's work is distinctly communal, the moment of his religious experience in his direct contact with the Absolute is so intense that it takes center stage, thus blurring the communal

---

[84] Gordon's friend, and later the editor of his writings, Eliezer Shochat, wrote in the same vein, "only work can weave for us the threads that will connect us to the land with an inner connection, a true connection. Work will create the same deep mental relationship that exists between the painter and the painting he painted, and not the legal, superficial relationship that exists between the buyer and the painting he bought. All the work that is done in the Land of Israel should be done by us: every tree, anything that grows, every house, every fence. Anything by which man becomes a partner with nature, every line, every sketch in the fabric of our future—everything, everything must be done with our own hands. Our soil must be drenched wet only with our sweat. The clods of our soil must be revived solely by us"; Eliezer Shochat [Poal Galili], "National Creation and Accounts" [Heb.], *Hapoel Hatzair*, December 6, 2010, p. 3.

bond. In Suchovolsky's biographical account of Gordon, discussed at length in the previous chapter, Gordon pays no attention, nor does he hear the fierce quarrel between his fellow pit diggers in the almond tree plantation, since he is "busy with his work of God."[85] While in the sphere of daily life the dialectical relationship of the individual with the community constitutes his being, in the rare moments of religious experience it is his dialectical relationship with the Absolute that defines his essence. The inner-organic relationship with the community is replaced by an inner-organic relationship with the Absolute, and the leap between mere multiplicity (of the community) and infinity (of the Absolute) turns the religious experience into an experience unlike any other experience known to man.

Since the religious experience is personal and independent of the community, it reaffirms the irreducibility of the individual. Thus, the religious element counteracts the social element that threatens to swallow up the individual by blurring and erasing his unique qualities. Gordon accepts the assertion, widely prevalent in socialist circles as well as among the Second Aliyah pioneers, according to which the individual cannot exist or be understood in isolation from the society to which he belongs. But Gordon resolutely qualifies this view by asserting that just as an individual cannot be disassociated from society, neither can he be understood and appraised by it exclusively. The unique qualities of each individual render him incomparable with other individuals. Each individual is a world in its own right; therefore, it is not possible to rank him in comparison with any other individual. The individual is finite, and that is what differentiates him from God, the Infinite. Despite this categorical difference, the uniqueness of the individual is the tangent point between him and God. Indeed, this tangent point is Gordon's interpretation of the biblical assertion according to which "God created man in His image" (Genesis 1:27).[86]

Each individual is unique due to the special way in which the universal life is reflected through him, since "the universal idea cannot be grasped in its entirety, in all its scope and in all its depth, in one drop of life, for in every drop of life it is reflected in another way and from a different point of view" (MN, VI: 155, GSE 251). The religious experience of the tiller of the soil expresses

---

[85] Zvi Suchovolsky, "The Man and the Friend," in Kusnir Mordecai (ed.), *A.D. Gordon: Reminiscences and Appreciations* [Heb.], Tel Aviv: Histadrut HaOvdim 1947, p. 37.

[86] See, for example, MN, IX: 185, V: 138. On the long and complex history of the idea of creation in God's image (*tselem Elohim*) in Classical Judaism see Yair Lorberbaum, *In God's Image: Myth, Theology, and Law in Classical Judaism*, New York: Cambridge University Press, 2015.

his unique angle of perception of existence. As Gordon puts it in the "Return to Nature" speech, "there is in work a spiritual wealth of which you can see but the barest fringe; nor will all of this wealth be seen except by those who will look at it from all sides" (MN, I: 33, GSE 251). The unlimited spectrum created by the varying cognitions and experiences of the individuals reflects the infinite breadth of the natural world. Each and every individual reflects in a unique and singular way, cognitively and experientially, the natural world. And in this sense the finite establishes the infinity of nature—for without it, nature would lack the unique cognitive and experiential reflection of the totality that the individual expresses. The religious experience is inherently ephemeral; it is a fleeting experience even for those who spend a lifetime working in nature. Just as it emerges unexpectedly, it also ends unexpectedly. As soon as it is over, the sacred silence becomes ordinary silence; it loses its intensity, and it reverts to being a vast, hollow silence.

While the sacred moment is no more than fleeting, it does, nevertheless, leave an indelible mark; after the religious experience life does not return to what it was before. Like a flash of lightning illuminating the darkness, the religious experience provides the individual with an existential roadmap, giving him the strength needed to cope with life's challenges and tribulations, and to navigate his way in the quest for a reunion with the Absolute:

> On a day of evil when affliction overtakes you, your suffering will be great, deep, holy. Or in a day of darkness when you stumble a moment and sin, you will find enough strength and enough courage to bear the sin, and enough of the fire of hell to purify you. And you will know the anguish that floods you with a supreme holiness and a supreme love for all who live and suffer; you will not know profanation; you will not know pettiness; you will not know a meaningless life. (MN, I: 33; GSE 251–252)

He who aspires to eternity loses not a single moment of his life in vain. For those who know where they are headed, even deviations from the path become part of the great journey to eternity, which is life itself. "Limpness, shadows, and shortcomings in the virtuous man's path to the higher life"—as Gordon puts it—"do not hinder, and perhaps in a known sense are a driving force."[87]

---

[87] "A Little Observation" (1911), GWA, I: 90.

Man's connection with the Absolute intensifies his connection with his fellow man. He who experiences closeness to something separate from himself, totally unlike himself, is called to echo this closeness also into a moral context of identification with Others. Religious emotion, Gordon claims, is the source of a man's willingness to take care not only of himself, but also of everything around him, as well as everything that will come after him.

The religious emotion is the source of the "emotion of participation in what was, is and will be in all of infinite creation"; it is the source of "sharing the sorrow of all that lives, of all that suffers sorrow," that is, the "feeling of responsibility" toward existence in its entirety (MN, IV.3: 99). The religious emotion, then, is the foundation of the moral emotion. Indeed, "the moral emotion is nothing but the religious emotion itself, the emotion of the supreme unity [leading to] a deep responsibility expressed in life itself" (MN, IV.3: 101). According to Gordon, morality is not obedience to the rules of pure reason articulated by Kant but, rather, a sensitive and concrete manifestation of the deep responsibility toward nature that is rooted in man's experience of unification with the cosmos. Religious emotion is the source of a person's concern for what "will be after his death" (MN, IV.3: 99).

Alongside the care and responsibility toward existence in its entirety, the inherently personal contact with the Absolute teaches man to recognize the importance of maintaining his privacy and solitude. In order to protect his singularity and uniqueness the protagonist of the "Return to Nature" speech avoids becoming too close to others. Gordon describes the right distance from the Other in utopian language:

> On that day, man will not be a burden to his fellow man . . . for there will be enough heaven in the soul of each and every man, and enough earth. . . . There will be enough space for each and every man and enough distance between man and man, that no one should stumble upon the Other. (MN, I: 34)

The religious experience of uniting with existence in its entirety cannot be expressed through words or concepts, for by their very essence they always qualify, and refer to portions of existence and not to existence in its entirety. Words can only say that they cannot say the Absolute. According to Gordon, even while words and concepts are utilized to celebrate the religious experience—the religious experience always remains well beyond words, and even beyond thought: "Any attempt to shed the light of reason on religion ... prevents it from being a religion and turns it into metaphysics or mysticism" (MN, IV.3: 97). Talking about the Absolute can direct us toward it but cannot ensure the very contact with it. For what really matters for Gordon is life in nature itself, rather than writing about it or philosophically analyzing it. Gordon felt uneasy in offering "a philosophical position grounded in a precise scientific method" (MN, VI: 143, n. 4), and he even apologized for innovating the technical philosophical term of *Havayah* (experience) to clarify his thoughts and meditations (MN, VI: 143, n. 4).

According to Gordon, in the Garden of Eden man was completely immersed in nature. The nudity of Adam and Eve in the Garden of Eden, expresses for Gordon "absolute immediacy, life stretching to infinity out of boundless existence" (MN, IX: 182, GSE 202). Only when they were torn from Nature, following the sin of the Tree of Knowledge, Adam and Eve made themselves coverings from fig leaves symbolizing their rift from Nature: "It was not cold, burning heat, or moisture that induced man to hit upon the device of dress, but rather the wish to hide from himself and from nature!" (MN, IX: 182, GSE 201). In the spirit of the early twentieth-century nudist movements, Gordon identifies the return to nature with being naked in nature. In this context he declares, "within nature and in relation to nature man feels himself completely free, free to himself, naked as the day he was born clinging to the very essence of nature without mediation ... without clothing ... " (MN, XV: 227).[88]

Gordon perceives language as something for man to hide behind, a kind of "garment to cover himself with, to cover his nakedness" (MN, IX: 182–183; GSE 202). The words that man uses impose a barrier between himself and the things in the world, as well as between himself and others, and even between him and himself. Culture, Gordon states, "does not tolerate total nudity" (MN, IX: 182–183; GSE 202). Language, as a branch of culture, expresses

---

[88] See MN, I: 29. Pioneers used to go out to work and guard barefoot in order to increase the sense of connection and unmediated contact with the soil of the Land of Israel. Bathing and immersion in water were also held as acts that provide direct contact with Nature. Tzvi Shatz (Russian Empire–Land of Israel, 1890–1921), the founder of the "intimate commune," describes in the following words his bathing experience in one of the rivers: "The stars shone, the water caressed me, and I felt happiness in 'the bosom of nature' as I united with it!"; Tzvi Shatz, "To R-H, on the Riverbank" [1920], in Shatz, *On the Edge of Silence: Writings* [Heb.], Tel Aviv: Mifaley Tarbut Vechinuch, 1967, p. 157. See also Neumann, *Land and Desire*, pp. 50–73; Muki Tsur, *Early Spring: Tzvi Shatz and the Intimate Commune* [Heb.], Tel Aviv: Am Oved 1984. Gordon's reference to nudity should be placed in the wider context of the broad spectrum of early twentieth-century nudist movements that highlighted the social and cultural crisis created by man's alienation from Nature. See, for example, John Alexander Williams, *Turning to Nature in Germany: Hiking, Nudism, and Conservation 1900-1940*, Stanford: Stanford University Press, 2007, pp. 23–65.

emotional "fortification, [as well as] man's disregard for nature, or at least distraction from it, and man's disregard for himself" (MN, IX: 182–183; GSE 202). According to Gordon, "Maeterlinck correctly observes that man does not know how to be silent; indeed, he actually fears silence. For when two men find themselves together, in close proximity, they talk, since speech serves directly to cover or to conceal something" (MN, IX: 182–183; GSE 202).[89]

According to Gordon, silence is man's ideal mode of communication not only with the Absolute and with his closest friends, but also with himself. However, Gordon admits that

> not even with itself can the soul always be silent, since with itself, too, it is not at all times free from those conventions which it has borrowed from society. In a fleeting moment man recalls some awkward word or deed— particularly one that embarrassed him before others. This depresses him so that he is unable to remain silent even within himself. Then there burst from his lips—unless his will checks him and he prevents their escape beyond the threshold of speech—words and comments that have no connection with his thought, that have but the one purpose of lifting the gloom from his spirit, of silencing his growing remorse. If man could fully maintain silence within himself, he would be able to communicate with his fellow man in the language of the soul, he would be able to maintain silence with him, too. (MN, IX: 182–183; GSE 202–203)[90]

[89] Maurice Maeterlinck, "Silence," in Maeterlinck, *The Treasure of the Humble*, trans. Alfred Sutro, New York: Dodd, Mead & Company, 1903, pp. 7–8. See also the discussion on Gordon's critique of language in the third chapter of this study. On the presence of Maeterlinck's writings in the Second Aliyah, see, for example, Eliezer Shochat, "Letter from Eliezer Shochat to His Wife" (August 16, 1923), in Shochat, *About Him*, pp. 142–143; Kushnir, *Men of Nebo*, pp. 196–197; Rachel Bluwstein, "Note on Maeterlinck's *The Life of the Ant*" [Heb.], in Bluwstein, *Shirat Rachel*, Jerusalem: Dvir, 1967 pp. 227–230.

[90] A description of silence as a means of intimate communication with the Other can also be found in Walden. Recalling his friendship with an old fisherman, Thoreau writes, "Once in a while we sat together on the pond, he at one end of the boat, and I at the other; but not many words passed between us, for he had grown deaf in his later years, but he occasionally hummed a psalm, which harmonized well enough with my philosophy. Our intercourse was thus altogether one of unbroken harmony, far more pleasing to remember than if it had been carried on by speech"; Thoreau, *Walden*, pp. 173–174.

6

Epilogue

What Is to Be Done?

Gordon's philosophy is a philosophy of life. It is no coincidence, therefore, that the word "life" appears more than a thousand times in MN. Indeed, a careful reading of MN reveals not one but, rather, two different yet complementary senses in which Gordon's philosophy is a philosophy of life. One sense is that the central theme of Gordon's philosophy is the phenomenon of life. The second sense is that Gordon's concrete daily life challenges and experiences are both the source and goal of his philosophy.

In my view the structure of Gordon's philosophy can be compared to a two-story house or building. On the ground floor Gordon meticulously presents a grand synoptic account of life in its entirety that unites ontology, epistemology, ethics, religion, politics, and aesthetics. On this floor Gordon reveals the dialectical basis of his metaphysics and suggests the principle of contradiction as the organizing principle of existence as well as the driving force of life. In addition, in his uniquely engaging spiral writing style Gordon introduces the key concepts of his philosophical system, such as "expansion" (*hitpashtut*), "contraction" (*tzimtzum*), and the "hidden intellect" (*sechel neelam*). The understanding of existence in its entirety, as well as man's place within it, is not a goal in itself for Gordon but, rather, a tool for reorienting man toward nature and pointing out for him the path to the good life.

On the second story of his philosophy Gordon applies the theoretical framework, principles, and concepts (developed in the first story) to the concrete issues of his life and the life of the pioneer community to which he belonged. Having constructed the ground floor of his philosophy with its organizing principles and concepts, Gordon dedicates the upper floor to the application of these principles and concepts to the concrete realities of his life and surroundings. It is on this floor where one can find the bulk of Gordon's writings, that is, short journals and newspaper essays as well as his extensive correspondence in which he responded to the pressing issues of his time,

The First Jewish Environmentalist. Yuval Jobani, Oxford University Press. © Oxford University Press 2024. DOI: 10.1093/oso/9780197617977.003.0006

such as the war of languages or the controversy surrounding volunteering for the Jewish legion during WWI.

The influence of the Russian intelligentsia is clearly apparent in Gordon's intense sense of commitment, as a man of letters, to issues of public interest and the pressing dilemmas of his time. As an autodidact who had spent most of his life in the Russian empire, Gordon sought an answer to the question posed by the Narodnik revolutionary Nikolay Chernyshevsky (Russia, 1828–1889) in the title of his inspirational utopian novel *What Is to Be Done?* [1863].[1] Indeed, Gordon shared the entire set of morals and convictions that characterized the Russian intelligentsia of his time, as summarized by Michael Confino,

> (i) a deep concern for problems and issues of public interest—social, economic, cultural, and political; (ii) a sense of guilt and personal responsibility for the state and the solution of these problems and issues; (iii) a propensity to view political and social questions as moral ones; (iv) a sense of obligation to seek ultimate logical conclusions—in thought as well as in life—at whatever cost (v) the conviction that things are not as they should be, and that something should be done.[2]

A systematic and thorough understanding of the relationship between the two stories in Gordon's philosophy requires a grounding in one of Gordon's most basic principles of life, according to which life is a volcanic outburst of singular and unique expressions of existence that constantly contends with the gravitational forces of social, religious, and cognitive forms that threaten to flatten life into rigid norms, dogmas, traditions, and rituals. Adhering to nature, according to Gordon, means living a life of constant change and renewal. He who wants to return to nature must avoid following others' tracks, even one's own, and time after time he must begin his life anew in the fullest and most radical sense (MN, I: 30; GSE 248).

---

[1] As Isaiah Berlin demonstrated in his classical essay on Russian populism, despite the numerous literary and philosophical flaws of Chernyshevsky's *What Is to be Done?* it had an epoch-making effect on the Russian intelligentsia. See Isaiah Berlin, "Russian Populism," in Berlin, *Russian Thinkers*, New York: Penguin Classics, 2013, 256–263. See also Andrew Michael Drozd, *Chernyshevskii's What Is to Be Done? A Reevaluation*, Evanston: Northwestern University Press, 2001. On Chernyshevsky as an ecological utopian thinker see Marco P. Vianna Franco, "Ecological Utopianism in Narodnik Thought: Nikolay Chernyshevsky and the Redemption of Land," *Capitalism Nature Socialism*, 32: 4 (2021), pp. 24–42

[2] Michael Confino, "On Intellectuals and Intellectual Traditions in Eighteenth and Nineteenth-Century Russia," *Daedalus*, 101: 2 (1972), p. 118.

Those who wish to follow me—Gordon seemingly declares—must follow themselves. At this point Gordon's position resonates with Nietzsche's call for self-affirmation, which was widely disseminated among and appropriated by Hebrew writers of the Russian empire as well as the young pioneers of the Second Aliyah.[3] "No one can construct for you the bridge upon which precisely you must cross the stream of life, no one but you yourself alone," writes Nietzsche in his *Schopenhauer as Educator* (1874).

> There are, to be sure, countless paths and bridges and demi-gods which would bear you through this stream; but only at the cost of yourself: you would put yourself in pawn and lose yourself. There exists in the world a single path along which no one can go except you.[4]

We can now better understand the distinction between the two stories in Gordon's philosophy. On the ground floor of his philosophy, Gordon limits himself to a philosophical exploration of the essential characteristics and fundamental principles of existence, such as the principle of constant and infinite renewal of nature, and the identification of the driving force of life with the dialectic interplay between opposites. These organizing principles must be followed by all who wish to live according to Nature. These same principles should, however, be sensitively adapted to each individual's circumstances of life.

In this spirit, on the upper floor of his philosophy, Gordon exemplifies his own implementations, as an individual, of the general principles presented on the ground floor. Impressive as these social, environmental, and political implementations are, Gordon did not expect us to embrace them as eternal truths, or as ultimate answers to the question "What is to be done?," but, rather, to inspire us in our own original implementations of the general principles of existence in our personal journey of life.

Let us turn now to a succinct exploration of Gordon's attitude regarding animals in order to illustrate how he concretely implements the principle of his philosophy that calls us to merge with nature rather than try to conquer

---

[3] Menachem Brinker, "Nietzsche's Influence on Hebrew Writers of The Russian Empire," in Bernice Glatzer Rosenthal (ed.), *Nietzsche and Soviet Culture: Ally and Adversary*, Cambridge: Cambridge University Press, 2010, pp. 393–413. See also the discussion in the second chapter of this study.
[4] Friedrich Nietzsche, "Schopenhauer as Educator" (1874), in Nietzsche, *Untimely Meditations (Cambridge Texts in the History of Philosophy)*, trans. R. J. Hollingdale, Cambridge: Cambridge University Press, 1997, p. 129.

nature. This exploration will further illustrate, later in the discussion, the anti-dogmatic nature of Gordon's philosophy.

Gordon became a vegetarian when he was fifty years old, shortly after immigrating to the Land of Israel.[5] His decision to become a vegetarian was influenced by the fact that many pioneers, upon immigrating to the Land of Israel, adopted vegetarianism as an integral part of their desire to live a more moral life in the Land of Israel.[6] Gordon may have also been influenced by Tolstoy's conversion to vegetarianism by the age of fifty, as well as by his well-known manifesto "The First Step" (1892), written as an introduction to the Russian translation of *The Ethics of Diet* by the English humanitarian and vegetarian activist Howard Williams (1837–1931).[7] Later in his life, Gordon converted from vegetarian to vegan, avoiding eggs and milk. Viewing his veganism as a private matter, Gordon rarely discussed it directly or thematically in his essays, letters, journal entries, or speeches. In the mess halls of the pioneer groups, he chose to join the regular dining tables where meat was also served, rather than eat at the tables designated for vegans. Nevertheless, Gordon's decision to adopt a vegan lifestyle was well-known among the young pioneers, and due to his iconic status in the Yishuv, he earned the title "'the father of Hebrew vegetarians' among the growing community of vegetarians in the Land of Israel."[8]

Purely ethical-philosophical principles bring Gordon to vehemently call for the liberation of animals from human cruelty and dominating oppression. In MN Gordon poses in great pain the following rhetorical question:

What is the beast, the animal, the fowl, and so on, to man? Either useful or harmful. The beneficial elements in nature provide meat for food, skins for

[5] Haim Tartakover, "A Conversation between Gordon and Buber on Vegetarianism," in Mordecai Kusnir (ed.), *A.D. Gordon: Reminiscences and Appreciations* [Heb.], Tel Aviv: Histadrut HaOvdim, 1947, pp. 75–76.

[6] Although we do not have accurate statistical information, we do have considerable evidence of there being a large vegetarian community in the Yishuv. See, for example, Zvi Suchovolsky, "On Vegetarianism and Higher Education" [Heb.], *Hapoel Hatzair*, vol. 23 (1964), p. 26; Abraham Mossel, *A Day Laborer from Holland in the Holy Land 1913-1914* [Heb.], trans. Itamar Prath, Jerusalem: publisher not indicated, 2002, p. 24.

[7] Leo Tolstoy "The First Step," in Tolstoy, *Essays and Letters*, trans. Aylmer Maude. New York: Funk and Wagnalls Company, 1904, pp. 53–93; Rina Lapidus, "Introduction to Gordon's Translation of Tolstoy's *What Is Art?*" [Heb.], *Iyunim Bitkumat Israel* (Thematic Series), 2008, pp. 357–361; Rafi Tsirkin-Sadan, "Tolstoy, Zionism, and the Hebrew Culture," *Tolstoy Studies Journal*, vol. 24 (2012), pp. 26–35.

[8] Suchovolsky, "On Vegetarianism and Higher Education," p. 26; Leah Pelled, *The Reception of Aharon David Gordon's Philosophy and Personality in Hebrew Literature and Periodicals (1904–1948)* [Heb.], PhD thesis, Jerusalem: The Hebrew University, 2004, pp. 52–53.

clothing, feathers for decorative purposes, power to wield, a means to satisfy the desire for spilling blood under the guise of hunting. . . . Are not men
ready to annihilate whole species of beasts merely for the sake of material
gains derived from them? . . . Where man holds beasts in his custody for
enjoyment, does he not treat them as he treats a machine? It is not enough
for him that he destroys their body, that to the last drop he extracts from
them all their strength, but one may say, he destroys their spirit as well. Take
the donkey, which does not mate except with a female of its kind. . . . Man
compels this creature by certain devices to mate with a mare in order to
bring forth a mule, a kind of unnatural, strange creature which yields no
offspring, but from which man derives much benefit . . . man, the jewel, the
crown of creation, deems a proud privilege: to devour, to eat of that which
is alive, to rob it of its freedom, to sap it of its strength (MN, XVI: 237; GSE
244–245).

Gordon's purely moral objection to the exploitation of animals and his call
for animals' liberation reflects and corresponds to his key philosophical distinction, explored in detail in the previous chapters, between two modes of
human existence. In the first mode, man stands *opposite nature* and regards
nature as a means for advancing his goals, while in the second mode man
stands *within nature* aspiring to merge with it. Gordon rejects the first mode
of existence, which he associates with the cold, human-centric, exploitative
approach to animals and urges us to adopt the second mode of existence,
which he associates with what he calls a "spiritual attitude" to animals (MN,
XVI: 237; GSE 244–245).

"Is there not really any spiritual affinity between man and the rest of living
beings?," Gordon rhetorically asks,

Is it not true, for example, that under conditions of complete isolation, of
utter estrangement from man, will not man be happy with any living creature near him? for example, a dog, a bird, even an ox, or a donkey, or a lamb?
Will he not then feel that the living creature is more to him than an object of
utilitarian gain? That first of all and above all, it is a living spirit that cannot
be evaluated in terms of profit? (MN, XVI: 238; GSE 245)

Indeed, it is the vulnerability and helplessness of animals, Gordon argues,
that turns our treatment of them into a litmus test of our morality. Our attitude toward living creatures, he declares,

is the most faithful . . . the clearest test of our attitude toward life and toward the world as it really is without artifice. The ethical regard toward living creatures that involves no hope of reward, no profitable motive—hidden or open, such as honor, and so on—shows us in a bright, unique mirror with almost tangible clarity what is the significance of righteousness and of all the other desired traits for which we pretend to give our lives.[9]

Gordon's reply to the abstract question "What is to be done?" is concrete and uncompromising. After he immigrated to the Land of Israel, as part of the new life he organized for himself in his new-old motherland, Gordon became a staunch vegetarian, and he ceased to wear phylacteries while praying because they are made of cow leather. It is important to emphasize, however, that Gordon's choice to avoid eating animals or wearing animal products does not pertain to what we labeled as the first floor of his philosophy. For vegetarianism is not necessarily mandatory or sufficient in all circumstances for all who wish to live according to Nature. Indeed, Gordon's vegetarianism is nothing but his own implementation, as an individual, of the general "new attitude that seeks, through work, to come ever closer to nature through an attempt to create a new life" (MN, XVI: 238; GSE, 274, slightly adapted from the original).

In his well-known letter on vegetarianism to the writer Nathan Bistritzky (1896–1980), Gordon argues that the avoidance of meat-eating, in itself, does not necessarily indicate a return to nature in the spirit of his philosophy. Gordon points out that some people's abstinence from eating meat is not grounded in a spiritual relationship with animals but is merely a bourgeois act of false refinement, distant and alienated from nature (GWA, V: 105; GSE, 278). Moreover, Gordon predicts that in the future man will feel empathy and compassion not only toward animals but also toward plants. Consequently, it will not be enough to refrain from meat-eating, for it will also be necessary to refrain from plant eating. Man will have to limit himself, Gordon opines, to the eating of fruits "that the plant itself offers him [man] to eat" (GWA, V: 102; GSE, 277). Hopefully, Gordon argues, scientific progress will lead to means that will allow man to support and sustain himself, to a large extent, if not entirely, with minerals (GSE, 277). In the realm of vegetarianism, as well as in all other realms of life, man's reunification with nature cannot be

---

[9] "A Letter to Nathan Bistritzky" (1920/1921) in GWA, V: 101; GSE, 275.

achieved through dogmatic, strict adherence to rules and instructions but only through sensitive attention to the particular circumstances of life.

The reunification of man with nature, as we saw earlier, occurs not in the social but, rather, in the private and personal realm. The personal realm, however, may harbor risks. Those situations in which the same person is the agent, as well as the witness, as well as the judge are deemed dangerous by the social and legal points of view.[10] However, from the point of view of the inner life, one should rather embrace these situations. Indeed, if the inner life is to be empowered, as Nietzsche argued, one should not avoid but, rather, seek to subject oneself to trials in which one is at once the agent, the witness, and the judge.[11]

However, when the act of self-examination or self-judgment involves self-deception, man may find himself not at the pinnacle of human existence but, rather, in its deepest abysses. Many sought to get closer to themselves but actually moved away from themselves. Nietzsche, who was one of them, boldly documented such failure: " 'I have done that,' says my memory. 'I cannot have done that,' says my pride, and remains inexorable. Eventually—memory yields.' "[12]

Self-deception is not merely an action of lying to oneself but, rather, a result of a principle and complete ignorance of the true motives of one's actions, even those actions most significant to one. If we take, for example, the feeling of merging with nature, which is especially important in the context of Gordon's philosophy, man does not know—for in principle he cannot know—whether the feeling of merging with nature expresses an actual mergence with nature, or not. It is quite possible that the sense of merging with nature expresses only man's eagerness for such mergence, or even only his desire to be perceived by others as one who has managed, through work in nature, to come into contact with the Absolute.

Gordon is well aware of the problem of self-deception that must concern anyone who seeks contact with the Absolute. When it comes to reporting on his own religious life Gordon is strict with himself even more than a "a maiden in her virgin's bower"—to borrow the metaphor of Søren

---

[10] See, for example, John Locke, *The Second Treatise*, in Locke, *Two Treatises of Government*, ed. Peter Laslett, Cambridge: Cambridge University Press, 1960, Chap. IX, p. 351.

[11] Friedrich Nietzsche, *Beyond Good and Evil*, trans. Walter Kaufmann, New York: Vintage Books 1966, §41, p. 51.

[12] Nietzsche, *Beyond Good and Evil*, §68, p. 80.

Kierkegaard (1813–1855), the eminent philosopher of religious existen-tialism.[13] Indeed, the protagonist of the "Return to Nature" speech is not identified with Gordon himself but, rather, with man, any man (*ben adam*) who has achieved direct contact with the Absolute.

Gordon applies his strict self-criticism not only to his personal life but to his philosophy as well. "Is there anything that unites me, in my innermost being, 'with this vast world in general, and with all its elements—with man, with whatever lives and exists?,'" Gordon asks himself while meticulously developing his metaphysical thoughts,

> Or perhaps this is nothing but an illusion, a figment of the imagina-tion . . . and I have no other relationship, no other account with all the world and all that is therein, beyond the relationship and the account of the struggle for existence. . . . Would it not be more fitting for me, a man-worm, with a brief span of life and full of troubles, to live . . . this short and insignificant life simply, without deceptive and vain rhapsodies which create worlds in mid-air, based on conscious self-delusions? (MN, III: 68, GSE 206)

As a distinctly existential philosopher Gordon refrains from mediating be-tween us and the world and demands that each of us answer for ourselves the great questions of existence.

---

[13] Søren Kierkegaard, *Fear and Trembling* in Kierkegaard, *Fear and Trembling; Repetition*, trans. Howard Hong Vincent and Edna Hatlestad Hong, Princeton: Princeton University Press, 1983, p. 75

Bibliography

Ahad Ha'am [Asher Zvi Hirsch Ginsberg], *Epistles* [Heb.], Tel Aviv: Dvir, 1956

Ahad Ha'am [Asher Zvi Hirsch Ginsberg], "Two Domains" [Heb.], in Ahad Ha'am, *Collected Writings*, Tel Aviv: Dvir, 1947, pp. 415–420

Aharonovich, Yoseph, "Biographical Notes on Gordon" [Heb.], *GWB*, I: 55–72

Aharonovich, Yoseph, *Collected Works of Yoseph Aharonovich* [Heb.], Tel Aviv: Am Oved, 1941

Almog, Shmuel, "From 'Muscular Jewry' to the 'Religion of Labor'" [Heb.], *Zionism - Studies in the History of the Zionist Movement and of the Jewish Community in Palestine*, vol. 9 (1984), pp. 137–146

Almog, Shmuel, "Pioneering as an Alternative Culture" [Heb.], *Zion: A Quarterly for Research in Jewish History*, 58: 3 (1993), pp. 246–329

Alroey, Gur, "Pioneers or Lost Souls? - The Issue of Suicide in the Second and the Third Aliya" [Heb.], *Contemporary Jewry*, vol. 13 (1999), pp. 209–241

Alroey, Gur, *An Unpromising Land: Jewish Migration to Palestine in the Early Twentieth Century*, Stanford: Stanford University Press, 2014

Aminur, Hezi, *Mixed Farm and Smallholding in Zionist Settlement Thought* [Heb.], Jerusalem: The Zalman Shazar Center, 2016

Amir, Eyal, "Ideology and Planning of the Kibbutz Dwelling" [Heb.], *Cathedra: For the History of Eretz Israel and Its Yishuv*, vol. 95 (2000), pp. 119–140

Anderson, Benedict, *Imagined Communities: Reflections on the Origin and Spread of Nationalism*, New York: Verso Books, 2006

Arakhin: An Anthology in Memory of Gordon [Heb.], editor not indicated, Tel Aviv: Gordonia Maccabi, 1942

Arieli, Yehoshua, "Modern History as Reinstatement of the Saeculum: A Study in the Semantics of History," *Journal of Jewish History*, vol. 8 (1994), pp. 205–228

Arkush, Allan, "Biblical Criticism and Cultural Zionism prior to the First World War," *Jewish History*, 21: 2 (2007), pp. 121–158

Artom, Elia Samuele, "Ben Adam" [Heb.], in *Encyclopaedia Biblica*, Jerusalem: Bialik Institute, 1971, vol. I, pp. 108–109

Augustine, *The Retractions*, trans. Mary Inez Bogan, Washington D.C.: Catholic University of America Press, 1968

Avinery, Solomon, "On the Canaanite Affair" [Heb.], *Hapoel Hatzair*, March 25, 1953, pp. 8–9

Avraham, Ben, "The Activities of the Academic Society for the Advancement of Nature Studies in Eretz Israel (special article)" [Heb.], *Hatzvi*, November 3, 1909, p. 2

Bacon, Francis, *Meditationes Sacrae* (1597), in James Spedding et al. (eds.), *The Works of Francis Bacon*, Boston: Brown, 1861, vol. 14, pp. 59–80

Bacon, Francis, *New Atlantis*, in Susan Bruce (ed.), *Three Early Modern Utopias*, New York: Oxford University Press, 1999, pp. 149–186

Bacon, Francis, *The New Organon*, eds. Lisa Jardine and Michael Silverthorne, Cambridge: Cambridge University Press, 2000

Barkan, Elazar, *Primitivism: Ideology and Desire in Modern Culture* [Heb.], Jerusalem: Israel Ministry of Defense Press, 2001

Bartal, Israel, *Exile in Israel: Pre-Zionist Settlement: A Collection of Studies and Essays* [Heb.], Jerusalem: The Zionist Library by the World Zionist Organization, 1994

Ben-Ari, Nitsa, *S. Yizhar: A Life Story* [Heb.], vol. 1, Tel Aviv: Tel Aviv University, 2013

Benglas, Hanit, *Judah Leib Metmann-HaCohen: Founder of The First Hebrew Gymnasium* [Heb.], MA thesis, Tel Aviv: Tel Aviv University, 2015

Benglas-Kaufman, Hanit, and Yuval Dror, "Dr. Yehuda Matman-Cohen: Founder of the Herzliya Gymnasium and Urban Zionist Entrepreneur of Hebrew Education and Culture in Europe and Israel (1869–1939)" [Heb.], *Dor Ledor - Studies in the History of Jewish Education in Israel and the Diaspora*, vol. LV (2021), pp. 38–84

Ben Yehuda, Baruch (ed.), *The Story of Herzliya Gymnasium* [Heb.], Tel Aviv: The Herzliya Gymnasium Publishing, 1970

Berdyczewski, Micha, "Destruction and Construction (Meditations)" [Heb., 1897], in Berdyczewski, *The Writings of Micha Berdyczewski*, ed. Avner Holtzman, Tel Aviv: Hakibbutz Hameuchad, 1996, vol. 5, pp. 110–114

Berger, Peter L., *The Sacred Canopy - Elements of a Sociological Theory of Religion*, New York: Anchor, 1990

Bergman, Samuel Hugo, "Introduction to *Man and Nature*," GWB, II: 13–27.

Bergman, Samuel Hugo, "On the Shaping of the Nation in Our State" [Heb.], *Hapoel Hatzair*, April 10, 1949, pp. 11–12

Bergson, Henri, *Creative Evolution: Humanity's Natural Creative Impulse*, trans. Arthur Mitchell, New York: The Modern Library, 1944 [1907]

Bergson, Henri, "Philosophical Intuition" in Bergson, *Key Writings*, eds. K. Pearson and J. Mullarkey, trans. Melissa McMahon, London: Bloomsbury, 2014, pp. 285–302

Berlin, Isaiah, "A Remarkable Decade" in Berlin, *Russian Thinkers*, pp. 114–210

Berlin, Isaiah, "Russian Populism," in Berlin, *Russian Thinkers*, pp. 240–272

Berlin, Isaiah, *Russian Thinkers*, New York: Penguin Classics, 2013

Bevir, Mark, "What Is Genealogy?," *Journal of the Philosophy of History*, 2: 3 (2008), pp. 263–275

Biale, David, *Not in the Heavens: The Tradition of Jewish Secular Thought*, Princeton: Princeton University Press, 2010

Bialik, Hayim Nahman, "The Explicit and Allusive in Language," trans. Avraham Holtz, *Literature East and West*, 15: 3 (1971), pp. 498–508

Biemann, Asher, *Inventing New Beginnings: On the Idea of Renaissance in Modern Judaism*, Stanford: Stanford University Press, 2009

Billington, James, *The Icon and Axe: An Interpretative History of Russian Culture*, New York: Vintage Books, 1970

Billington, James, *Mikhailovsky and Russian Populism*, London: Oxford University Press, 1958

Bistritzky, Nathan, *In the Secret of the Myth* [Heb.], Tel Aviv: Yachdav, 1980

Bloomfield, Samuel, "Gordon and His Thought in the Context of the Problems of Ecology in Our Time" [Heb.], in Menachem Zohary et al. (eds.), *Hebrew Thought in America*, Tel Aviv: Yavne, 1973, vol. 2, pp. 268–275

Brenner, Yosef Haim, "In Journals and in Literature [The Vision of Conversion]" [Heb.], in Brenner, *Yosef Haim Brenner: Complete Works*, Yitzhak Kafkafi (ed.), Tel Aviv: Hakibbutz Hameuchad, 1985, vol. 3, pp. 476–487

Brenner, Yosef Haim, [Zeira, B.], *Man and Nature* [Heb.], Jaffa: Laam, 1909–1910

Brenner, Yosef Haim, "The Missing Essence: Notes from Old Notebook" [Heb.], in Brenner, *Yosef Haim Brenner: Complete Works*, vol. 3, pp. 581–596

Brinker, Menachem, *Modern Hebrew Literature as European Literature* [Heb.], Jerusalem: Carmel, 2016

Brinker, Menachem, "Nietzsche's Influence on Hebrew Writers of the Russian Empire," in Bernice Glatzer Rosenthal (ed.), *Nietzsche and Soviet Culture: Ally and Adversary*, Cambridge: Cambridge University Press, 2010, pp. 393–413

Brinker, Menachem, *Up to the Tiberian Alley: Narrative, Art and Social Thought in Brenner's Work* [Heb.], Tel Aviv: Am Oved, 1990

Brunschwig, Jacques, "The Cradle Argument in Epicureanism and Stoicism," in Malcolm Schofield and Gisela Striker (eds.), *The Norms of Nature: Studies in Hellenistic Ethics*, Cambridge: Cambridge University Press, 2007, pp. 113–144

Brunschwig, Jacques, "Cradle Arguments," in Lawrence C. Becker and Charlotte B. Becker (eds.), *Encyclopedia of Ethics*, New York: Routledge, 2001, vol. 1, pp. 355–357

Buber, Martin, "Jewish Religiosity" [Heb.], in Buber, *Martin Buber: Selected Writings on Judaism and Jewish Affairs*, Jerusalem: The Zionist library, 1984, vol. I, pp. 70–79

Buber, Martin, "Jüdische Renaissance," *Ost und West*, 1: 1 (1901), pp. 1–10

Buber, Martin, "Leitwort Style in Pentateuchal Narrative," in Martin Buber and Franz Rosenzweig, *Scripture and Translation*, trans. Lawrence Rosenwald, Bloomington: Indiana University Press, 1994 [1936], pp. 114–128

Buber, Martin, "A Man Who Realizes the Idea of Zion (On A. D. Gordon)," in Buber, *On Zion: The History of an Idea*, trans. Stanley Godman, London: East and West Library, 1973, pp. 154–161

Buber, Martin, *Paths in Utopia* [Heb.], ed. Avraham Shapira, Tel Aviv: Am Oved, 1984

Buber, Martin, "The True Teacher: In Memoriam A. D. Gordon" [Heb., 1923] in Buber, *Paths in Utopia*, p. 253

Bulgakov, Valentin, *The Last Year of Leo Tolstoy*, trans. Ann Dunnigan, with an introduction by George Steiner, New York: Dial Press, 1971 [1911]

Burmil, Shmuel, and Ruth Enis, *The Changing Landscape of a Utopia: The Landscape and Gardens of the Kibbutz: Past and Present*, Worms: Wernersche Verlagsgesellschaft, 2011

Casanova, José, *Public Religions in the Modern World*, Chicago: The University of Chicago Press, 1994

Cassuto, Moshe David, "*Etz HaChaim*" [Heb.], in Benjamin Mazar (ed.), *Encyclopaedia Biblica*, Jerusalem: Bialik Institute 1971, vol. VI, pp. 328–330

Cavell, Stanley, *The Senses of Walden: An Expanded Edition*, Chicago: The University of Chicago Press, 1992

Chacham, Michal, "Herzlia's Crocodile: The Gymnasium's Art and Nature Classrooms" [Heb.], in Guy Raz (ed.), *Gymnasium Days: The Herzliya Hebrew Gymnasium 1905–1959*, Tel Aviv: Eretz Israel Museum, 2013, pp. 53–63

Chantrell, Glynnis (ed.), *The Oxford Dictionary of Word Histories*, New York: Oxford University Press, 2002

Charizman, Mordechai, "In Ein Ganim" [Heb.], in Mordecai Kushnir, *Reminiscences and Appreciations*, pp. 42–49

Chazan, Meir, "Activism and Moderation Regarding the Use of Force: Brenner, Gordon and Hapoel Hatzair" [Heb.], *Iyunim Bitkumat Israel: Studies in Zionism, the Yishuv and the State of Israel (Thematic Series)*, 2008, pp. 239–261

Chekhov, Anton, *Ten Early Plays by Chekhov*, trans. A. Szogyi, New York: Bantam Books, 1965

Cicero, Marcus Tullius, *On Moral Ends*, ed. Julia Annas, trans. Raphael Woolf, Cambridge: Cambridge University Press, 2001

Cohen, Shaye J. D., Robert Goldenberg, and Hayim Lapin (eds.), *The Oxford Annotated Mishnah*, New York: Oxford University Press, 2022

Costlow, Jane Tussey, *Heart-Pine Russia: Walking and Writing the Nineteenth-Century Forest*, Ithaca: Cornell University Press, 2013

Dekel-Chen, Jonathan, *Farming the Red Land: Jewish Agricultural Colonization and Local Soviet Power, 1924–1941*, New Haven: Yale University Press, 2008

De-Shalit, Avner, "From the Political to the Objective: The Dialectics of Zionism and the Environment" *Environmental Politics*, 4: 1 (1995), pp. 70–87

Dewey, John, *A Common Faith*, New Haven: Yale University Press, 1934

Diamond, James S., *Homeland or Holy Land? The "Canaanite" Critique of Israel*, Bloomington: Indiana University Press, 1986

Dobb, Fred, "Four Modern Teachers - Hirsch, Kook, Gordon, and Buber," in Arthur Waskow (ed.), *Torah of the Earth; Exploring 4,000 Years of Ecology in Jewish Thought*, Woodstock, VT: Jewish Lights Publishing, 2000, vol. 2, pp. 21–41

Drori, Hasia, "In Kfar Yehezkel" [Heb.], in Yehuda Erez (ed.), *The Book of the Third Aliya*, Tel Aviv: Am Oved, 1964, vol. 2, pp. 514–515

Durkheim, Emile, *The Division of Labor in Society*, trans. W. D. Halls, Basingstoke: Macmillan, 1984 [1893]

Durkheim, Emile, *The Elementary Forms of Religious Life*, trans. K. E. Fields, New York: Free Press, 1995 [1912]

Durkheim, Emile, *Incest: The Nature and Origin of the Taboo* [1897], in Edward Sagarin (ed. and trans.), Incest: The Nature and Origin of the Taboo *by Emile Durkheim and* The Origin and Development of the Incest Taboo *by Albert Ellis*, New York: Lyle and Stuart, 1963, pp. 11–119

Durkheim, Emile, *On Suicide*, trans. Robin Buss, London: Penguin, 2006 [1897]

Durkheim, Emile, "Preface to The Second Volume of L'Année Sociologique" [1899], in Wolff, Kurt H. (ed.), *Emile Durkheim, 1858–1917: A Collection of Essays with Translations and a Bibliography*, Columbus: The Ohio State University Press, 1960, pp. 347–353

Efrati, Nathan, *The Evolution of Spoken Hebrew in Pre-State Israel 1881–1922* [Heb.], Jerusalem: The Academy of the Hebrew Language, 2004, pp. 144–149

Elazari-Volcani, Yitzhak (I. Vilkanski), *The Communist Settlements in the Jewish Colonization in Palestine*, Tel Aviv: Palestine Economic Society, 1927

Elboim-Dror, Rachel, *Hebrew Education in Palestine - Vol.1: 1854–1914* [Heb.], Jerusalem: Yad Ben Zvi, 1986

Eldad, Israel, "Nietzsche and the Bible" [Heb.], in Jacob Golomb (ed.), *Nietzsche and Hebrew Culture*, Jerusalem: The Hebrew University Magnes Press, 2002, pp. 295–311

Eliade, Mircea, *Patterns in Comparative Religion*, Lincoln: University of Nebraska, 1996

Eliade, Mircea, *The Sacred and the Profane: The Nature of Religion*, New York: Houghton Mifflin Harcourt, 1987

Elias, Nobert, *The Civilizing Process: Sociogenetic and Psychogenetic Investigations*, trans. Edmund Jephcott, eds. Eric Dunning, Johan Goudsblom, and Stephen Mennell, Malden, Mass.: Blackwell, 2000 [1939]

Ely, Christopher David, *This Meager Nature: Landscape and National Identity in Imperial Russia*, DeKalb: Northern Illinois University Press, 2002

Englegardt, Aleksandr Nikolaevich, *Aleksandr Nikolaevich Engelgardt's Letters from the Country, 1872–1887*, trans. and ed. Cathy A. Frierson, New York: Oxford University Press, 1993

Fainholtz, Tzafrir, "A Mediterranean Vienna: The Work of Viennese Architects and the Presence of Central European Culture in the Haifa of the 1930s and 1940s," *The Leo Baeck Institute Year Book*, vol. *62* (2017), pp. 197–223

Feinberg, Absalom, *Absalom: Papers and Letters of the Late Absalom Feinberg* [Heb.], ed. Aharon Amir, Jerusalem: Shikmona, 1975

Feinstein, Nurit, *Repercussions of Identity: The Third Aliya Writers Yehudah Ya'ari, David Maletz and Others, as Thinkers and Identity-Molders in Pre-State Hebrew Literature* [Heb.], Tel Aviv: Hakibbutz Hameuchad, 2015

Fichman, Jacob, "First to Redemption" [Heb.], in Kushnir, *Reminiscences and Appreciations*, pp. 140–143

Fichman, Jacob, "Introduction to the Volume of Gordon's Letters and Notes" [Heb.], *GWB*, III: 9–25

Fisch, Menachem, "Introduction to *New Atlantis*" [Heb.], in Francis Bacon, *New Atlantis*, trans. Israel Cohen, Tel Aviv: Hakibbutz Hameuchad, 1986, pp. 5–18

Fischer, Kuno, *Franz Baco von Verulam*, Leipzig: publisher not indicated, 1856

Franco, Venturi, *Roots of Revolution: A History of the Populist and Socialist Movements in Nineteenth-Century Russia*, New York: Alfred A. Knopf, 1960

Frankel, Jonathan, *Prophecy and Politics: Socialism, Nationalism & the Russian Jews, 1862–1917*, Cambridge: Cambridge University Press, 1984

Frankenstein, Carl, and Baruch Sarel (eds.), *Akiba Ernst Simon - Educator in Thought and Action* [Heb], Jerusalem: Hebrew University Magnes Press, 1980

Franklin, Benjamin, "Advice to a Young Tradesman" [July 21, 1748], in Franklin, *The Papers of Benjamin Franklin - Vol. 3, January 1, 1745, through June 30, 1750*, ed. Leonard W. Labare, New Haven: Yale University Press, 1961, pp. 304–308

Frisby, David, "Bibliographical Note on Simmel's Works in Translation," *Theory, Culture & Society*, *8*: 3 (1991), pp. 235–241

Fuehrer, Ehud, *New Man in a Jewish Form: A New Reading in A. D. Gordon Philosophy* [Heb.], Ramat-Gan: Bar Ilan University Press, 2019

Funkenstein, Amos, "Maimonides: Political Theory and Realistic Messianism," in Funkenstein, *Perceptions of Jewish History*, Berkeley: University of California Press, 1993, pp. 131–155

Garber, Reuven, "Man and Nature: On Gordon's Doctrine of Sustainability and Its Application in Spiritual Education" [Heb.], *BaMichlala*, vol. *21* (2002), pp. 35–54

Gay, Peter, *Freud: A Life for Our Time*, New York: W. W. Norton & Company, 2006

Gay, Peter, *Modernism: The Lure of Heresy*, New-York: W. W. Norton & Company, 2010

Gay, Peter, *Weimar Culture: The Outsider as Insider*, New-York: W. W. Norton & Company, 2001

Geertz, Clifford, "Anti-Anti-Relativism," in Geertz, *Available Light: Anthropological Reflections on Philosophical Topics*, Princeton: Princeton University Press, 2000, pp. 42–67

Geuss, Raymond, "Nietzsche and Genealogy," *European Journal of Philosophy*, 2: 3 (1994), pp. 274–292

Ginzburg, Natalia, "Praise and Complaint of England," in Ginzburg, *The Little Virtues*, trans. Dick Davis, New York: Arcade Publishing, 2016, pp. 27–36

Glucker, John, "Introduction to Cicero's *On the Ends of Good and Evil*" [Heb.], in Marcus Tullius Cicero, *On the Ends of Good and Evil*, trans. Aviva Katzir, ed. John Glucker, Ramat-Gan: Bar-Ilan University, 1997, pp. 5–42

Golomb, Jacob, "The Agricultural Philosopher Aharon David Gordon Goes to Work" [Heb.], MN: 245–296

Golomb, Jacob, *Nietzsche and Zion*, Ithaca: Cornell University Press, 2004

Golomb, Jacob, *Nietzsche, Zionism and Hebrew Culture* [Heb.], Jerusalem: The Hebrew University Magnes Press, 2002

Gordon, Yael, "My Father prior to His Arrival to Eretz Israel" [Heb.], *T*, 2020, 28–38

Goultschin, Moshe, *Baruch Kurzweil as a Commentator on Culture* [Heb.], Ramat Gan: Bar Ilan University Press, 2009

Govrin, Nurit, *"The Brenner Affair" - The Fight for Free Speech* [Heb.], Jerusalem: Yad Ben Zvi, 1985

Govrin, Nurit, "Journalism in Embryonic Tel Aviv - The Story of Three Pioneering Periodicals" [Heb.], *Kesher*, vol. 39 (2009), pp. 39–49

Green, Arthur, "The Zaddiq as Axis Mundi in Later Judaism," *Journal of the American Academy of Religion*, XLV: 3 (1977), pp. 327–347

Gur (Grazowski), Yehuda, "In the Big World" [Heb.], in David Levontin (ed.), *Collective Associations in the World and in Our World*, Jaffa: England-Palestine Company in Jaffa, 1911, vol. III, pp. 2–9

Gurevitch, Zali, *On Israeli and Jewish Place* [Heb.], Tel Aviv: Am Oved, 2007

Halamish, Avivah, "The Dialectic Influence of A.D. Gordon on Hashomer Hatza'ir" [Heb.], *Cathedra: For the History of Eretz Israel and Its Yishuv*, vol. 114 (2004), pp. 99–120

Haramati, Shlomo, *The Pioneer Teachers in Eretz Israel* [Heb.], Tel Aviv: Israel Ministry of Defense Press, 2000

Harif, Hanan, *For We Are Brethren: The Turn to the East in Zionist Thought* [Heb.], Jerusalem: The Zalman Shazar Center, 2019

Harris, Jose, "Introduction to Community and Civil Society," in Tönnies, *Community and Civil Society*, 2001 [1887], pp. ix–xxx

Harshav, Benjamin, *The Meaning of Yiddish*, Berkeley: University of California Press, 1990

Hart, Ray, *God Being Nothing: Toward a Theology*, Chicago: The University of Chicago Press, 2016

Havens, George (ed.), *Voltaire's Marginalia on the Pages of Rousseau*, New York: Haskell House, 1966

Haviv-Lubman, Dov, "The Man Who Swam against the Current" [Heb.], *HaBoker*, April 6, 1939, p. 2

Helle, Horst Jurgen, "Introduction to Simmel's Essays on Religion," in Simmel, *Essays on Religion*, pp. xi–xx

Hevlin, Rina, *A Double Commitment: Jewish Identity between Tradition and Secularity in Ahad Ha'am's Thought* [Heb.], Tel Aviv: Hakibbutz Hameuchad, 2001, pp. 46–74

Hirschfeld, Ariel, *The Tuned Harp: The Language of Emotions in H. N. Bialik's Poetry* [Heb.], Tel Aviv: Am Oved, 2011

Hobbes, Thomas, *Leviathan, or the Matter, Forme, & Power of a Common-Wealth Ecclesiasticall and Civill Harmondsworth*, ed. C.B. Macpherson, London: Penguin, 1968

Hofmann, Klaus, "Canaanism," *Middle Eastern Studies*, *47*: 2 (2011), pp. 273–294

Horev, Shai, *A Man of Morals and of Labor: The Worldview and Ideological Place of Aharon David Gordon in the Context of the Ideological Leadership of the Labor Party* [Heb.], Haifa: Duchifat, 2013

Hotam, Yotam, *Modern Gnosis and Zionism: The Crisis of Culture, Life Philosophy and Jewish National Thought*, London: Routledge, 2013

Hoyt, Sarah F., "The Etymology of Religion," *Journal of the American Oriental Society*, vol. *32* (1912), pp. 126–129

Hubbs, Joanna, "The Worship of Mother Earth in Russian Culture," in James J. Preston (ed.), *Mother Worship: Theme and Variations*, Chapel Hill: University of North Carolina Press, 1982, pp. 123–144

Hunt, Priscilla, and Svitlana Kobets (eds.), *Holy Foolishness in Russia: New Perspectives*, Bloomington, Ind.: Slavica Publications, 2011

Ivanov, Sergey, *Holy Fools in Byzantium and Beyond*, New York: Oxford University Press, 2006

Jobani, Yuval, "Ethical or Political Religion? On the Contradiction between Two Models of Amended Religion in Spinoza's Theological-Political Treatise," *Hebraic Political Studies*, *3*: 4, 2008, pp. 396–415

Jobani, Yuval, "The Lure of Heresy: A Philosophical Typology of Hebrew Secularism in the First Half of the Twentieth Century," *The Journal of Jewish Thought and Philosophy*, *24*: 1 (2016), pp. 95–121

Jobani, Yuval, *The Role of Contradictions in Spinoza's Philosophy: The God-Intoxicated Heretic*, New York: Routledge, 2016

Jobani, Yuval, "The Secular University and Its Critics," *Studies in Philosophy and Education*, *35*: 4 (2016), pp. 333–351

Jobani, Yuval, "Three Basic Models of Secular Jewish Culture," *Israel Studies*, *13*: 3 (2008), pp. 160–169

Jobani, Yuval, "The True Teacher: Jewish Secularism in the Philosophy of A.D. Gordon," in Jan Woleńsky, Yaron M. Senderowicz, & Józef Bremer (eds.), *Jewish and Polish Philosophy*, Krakow: Austeria Publishing House, 2013, pp. 198–216

Jobani, Yuval, "What Led Gordon to Compose *Man and Nature*? Gordon's Neglected Criticism of Metmann's *Life and Nature* (1909)," *Jewish Quarterly Review*, *111*: 3 (2021), pp. 470–495

Jobani, Yuval, and Gideon Katz, "In the Convoy and alongside It: A Study of S. Yizhar's Works on Education and Literature," *Contemporary Jewry*, *36*: 2 (2016), pp. 203–224

Jobani, Yuval, and Nahshon Perez, *Governing the Sacred: Political Toleration in Five Contested Sacred Sites*, Oxford: Oxford University Press, 2020

Jobani, Yuval and Nahshon Perez, "Toleration and Illiberal Groups in Context: Israel's Ultra-Orthodox Society of Learners," *Journal of Political Ideologies*, *19*: 1, 2014, pp. 78–98

Jobani, Yuval, and Nahshon Perez, *Women of the Wall: Navigating Religion in the Public Sphere*, New York: Oxford University Press, 2017

Jowitt, Claire, "'Books Will Speak Plain'? Colonialism, Jewishness and Politics in Bacon's *New Atlantis*," in B. Price (ed.), *Francis Bacon's New Atlantis*, Manchester: Manchester University Press, 2018, pp. 129–155

Jung, Carl Gustav, *Memories, Dreams, Reflections*, New York: Vintage Books, 1989

Jung, Carl Gustav, "Psychological Aspects of the Mother Archetype," in Jung, *The Archetypes and the Collective Unconscious*, trans. R. F. C. Hull, Princeton: Princeton University Press, 1990, pp. 64–90

Kahana, Freddy, *Neither Town nor Village: The Architecture of The Kibbutz 1910–1990* [Heb.], Ramat Efal: Yad Tabenkin, 2011

Karmi, Moshe, "Segment" [Heb.], *HaAdama*, (1919–1920), vol. 1, p. 202

Katznelson, Berl, *Katznelson's Letters (1915–1918)* [Heb.], ed. Yehuda Sharett, Tel Aviv: Am Oved, 1961, vol. 1

Katznelson, Berl, *The Second Aliya: Lectures for the Socialist Youth (1928)* [Heb.], eds. Anita Shapira and Naomi Abir, Tel Aviv: Am Oved, 1990

Kedar, Benjamin Zeev, *The Changing Land between the Jordan and the Sea: Aerial Photographs from 1917 to the Present* [Heb.], Tel Aviv: Israel Ministry of Defense Press, 1999

Kierkegaard, Søren, *Fear and Trembling*, in Kierkegaard, *Fear and Trembling; Repetition*, Howard Hong Vincent and Edna Hatlestad Hong (trans.), Princeton: Princeton University Press, 1983, pp. 1–124

Klausner, Joseph, "The Creation of Life (On the Holiday of Tu Beshvat)" [Heb.], *Haaretz*, February 4, 1920, p. 3

Klausner, Joseph, "A World Come into Being (Part II)" [Heb.], *Hashiloah*, 28 (1913), pp. 531–542

Klausner, Joseph, "A World Come into Being (Part III)" [Heb.], *Hashiloah*, 29 (1913), pp. 201–227

Knaani, David, *The Labor Second Aliyah and Its Attitude Toward Religion and Tradition* [Heb.], Tel Aviv: Sifriat Po'alim, 1975

Knesset Protocols [Heb.], Jerusalem: Government Print, 1965, vol. 44

Kobets, Svitlana, "The Paradigm of the Hebrew Prophet and the Russian Tradition of Iurodstvo," *Canadian Slavonic Papers*, 50: 1–2 (2008), pp. 1–16

Kook, Avraham Yitzhaq Ha-Cohen, *Orot* [Heb.], Jerusalem: Mossad Ha-Rav Kook, 1950

Kosmin, Barry A. "Contemporary Secularity and Secularism," in Barry A. Kosmin and Ariela Keysar (eds.), *Secularism and Secularity: Contemporary International Perspectives*, Hartford, Conn.: Institute for the Study of Secularism in Society and Culture, 2007, pp. 1–13

Kremerman, Arie, *Buddhism in A.D. Gordon's Philosophy* [Heb.], MA thesis, Tel Aviv: Tel Aviv University, 2017

Kropotkin, Peter Alekseevich, *Mutual Aid: A Factor of Evolution*, London: Penguin, 1972

Kurzweil, Baruch, "The Essence and Origins of the Young Hebrews Movement (the Canaanites)" [Heb.], in Kurzweil, *Our New Literature—Continuity or Revolution?*, Jerusalem: Schocken Press, 1965, pp. 270–300

Kurzweil, Baruch, "Judaism as a Manifestation of the National-Critical Life-Will" [Heb.], in Kurzweil, *Our New Literature*, pp. 190–224

Kushnir, Mordecai (ed.), *A.D. Gordon: Reminiscences and Appreciations* [Heb.], Tel Aviv: Histadrut HaOvdim, 1947

Kushnir, Shimon, *Fatherland's Firstborn: A Tale of a Youth in the Days of the Second Aliyah* [Heb.], Tel Aviv: Ayanot, 1968

Kushnir, Shimon, *Men of Nebo* [Heb.], Tel Aviv: Am Oved, 2004

Laermans, Rudi, "The Ambivalence of Religiosity and Religion: A Reading of Georg Simmel," *Social Compass*, 53: 4 (2006), pp. 479–489

Laertius, Diogenes, *Lives of Eminent Philosophers*, trans. Robert Drew Hicks, Cambridge: Harvard University Press, 1925

Lahav, Hagar, "Postsecular Jewish Theology: Reading Gordon and Buber," *Israel Studies*, *19*: 1 (2014), pp. 189–213

Lang, Yosef, "The Agricultural School in Petach Tikva Headed by Dr. Pickholtz 1912–1925" [Heb.], *Dor Ledor: Studies in the History of Jewish Education in Israel and the Diaspora*, vol. *39* (2011), pp. 7–44

Lang, Yosef, *The Life of Eliezer Ben-Yehuda* [Heb.], Jerusalem: Yad Ben Zvi, 2008

Laor, Dan, "From 'The Sermon' to the Letter to the Hebrew Youth: Notes on the Concept of Negating the Diaspora" [Heb.], in Laor, *The Struggle for Memory: Essays on Literature, Society, and Culture*, Tel Aviv: Am Oved, 2009, pp. 233–249

Lapidus, Rina, "Introduction to Gordon's Translation of Tolstoy's *What Is Art?*" [Heb.], *Iyunim Bitkumat Israel: Studies in Zionism, the Yishuv and the State of Israel (Thematic Series)*, 2008, pp. 357–361

Lears, T. J. Jackson, *No Place of Grace: Antimodernism and the Transformation of American Culture 1880–1920*, Chicago: The University of Chicago Press, 1994

Lermontov, Mikhail, *Prose and Poetry*, trans. Avrahm Yarmolinsky et al., place of publication not indicated: Rusalka Books, 2020

Levin, Shalom, "Yehuda Leib Metmann-HaCohen" [Heb.], in I. Bartal, Y. Keniel, and Zev Tzachor (eds.), *The Second Aliyah,* Jerusalem: Yad Ben Zvi, 1997, vol. 3, pp. 523–524

Lewis, James R., and Olav Hammer (eds.), *The Invention of Sacred Tradition*, Cambridge: Cambridge University Press, 2017

Lieberson, Tehiya, *The Story of My Life* [Heb.], Tel Aviv: Mifaley Tarbut Vechinuch, 1970

Liebes, Yehuda, *Sections of the Zohar Lexicon* [Heb.], PhD thesis, Jerusalem: Hebrew University, 1976

Lorberbaum, Menachem, *Politics and the Limits of Law: Secularizing the Political in Medieval Jewish Thought*, Stanford: Stanford University Press, 2002

Lovejoy, Arthur O., "The Supposed Primitivism of Rousseau's Discourse on Inequality," *Modern Philology*, *21*: 2 (1923), pp.165–186

Lowenthal, David, *George Perkins Marsh: Prophet of Conservation*, Seattle: University of Washington Press, 2009

Luria, Yosef, *Education in the Land of Israel: Report (Booklet 2)* [Heb.], Tel Aviv: Education Department in Eretz Israel, 1921

Maeterlinck, Maurice, *The Treasure of the Humble*, trans. Alfred Sutro, New York: Dodd, Mead & Company, 1903

Maimonides, Moses, *The Guide of the Perplexed*, trans. with introduction and notes by Shlomo Pines, Chicago: The University of Chicago Press, 1963

Maletz, David, "With A.D. Gordon (10-Year Anniversary of Gordon's Death)" [Heb.], in Maletz, *Around the Essence - A Profile of a Generation*, Tel Aviv: Mifaley Tarbut Vechinuch, 1970, pp. 62–64, reprinted in Kushnir, *Reminiscences and Appreciations*, pp. 170–176

Maor, Yitzhak, "The Popular Revolutionaries ('Narodniks') and the Jews" [Heb.], in Maor, *The Jewish Question in the Liberal and Revolutionary Movement in Russia 1914–1890*, Jerusalem: Bialik Institute, 1964, pp. 105–115

Margolin, Ron, "The implicit Religiosity of Nietzsche's Heresy: On A. D. Gordon and Martin Buber's Reading of Nietzsche" [Heb.], *Iyyun: The Jerusalem Philosophical Quarterly*, vol. *64* (2015), pp. 418–430

Margolin, Ron, *Inner Religion in Jewish Sources: A Phenomenology of Inner Religious Life and Its Manifestation from the Bible to Hasidic Texts*, trans. Edward Levin, Boston: Academic Studies Press, 2021

Marsh, George P., *Man and Nature; Or, Physical Geography as Modified by Human Action*, New York: Charles Scribner, 1864; reprint, Cambridge, Mass.: Belknap, 1965

Marsh, Jan, *Back to the Land: The Pastoral Impulse in England 1880–1914*, London: Quartet Books Limited, 1982

Meitlis, Ofra, *On the Middle Path: David Yellin—A Life Story* [Heb.], Tel Aviv University: The Jaime and Joan Constantiner School of Education, 2015

Mendes-Floher, Paul, *From Mysticism to Dialogue: Martin Buber's Transformation of German Social Thought*, Detroit: Wayne State University Press, 1989

Merleau-Ponty, Maurice, *The Primacy of Perception: And Other Essays on Phenomenological Psychology, the Philosophy of Art, History and Politics (Studies in Phenomenology and Existential Philosophy)*, trans. Carleton Dallery, ed. James M. Edie, Evanston: Northwestern University Press, 1964

Metmann, Judah Leib, *Life and Nature* [Heb.], Jaffa: Atin, 1909

Metmann, Judah Leib, "Nature Study in High School" [Heb.], in Baruch Ben Yehuda (ed.), *The Story of Herzliya Gymnasium*, Tel Aviv: The Herzliya Gymnasium Publishing, 1970, pp. 87–93

Metmann, Leo, *Zur Regenerationsarbeit in Palästina: Vortrag gehalten im akademischen Zionistenverein Bern*, Bern: Verlag des A. Z. V., 1908

Michelson, Udi, and Aharon Lapidot (eds.), *One Hundred Years of Gymnasia* [Heb.], Tel Aviv: The Hebrew Gymnasia Herzliya, 2004

Midrash Ecclesiastes Rabbah [Heb., Vilna edition], Jerusalem: Vagshal, 2001

Mirsky, Yehudah, *Rav Kook: Mystic in a Time of Revolution*, New Haven: Yale University Press, 2014

Mirsky, Yehudah, *Towards the Mystical Experience of Modernity: The Making of Rav Kook, 1865–1904*, Boston: Academic Studies Press, 2021

Mishori, Daniel, "Signs and Sovereignty: Court Appeals against Highway Billboards as a Struggle over the Commons" [Heb.], *Maasei Mishpat: Tel Aviv University Journal of Law and Social Change*, 2008, vol. *1*, pp. 109–126

Moellendorf, Darrel, *The Moral Challenge of Dangerous Climate Change: Values, Poverty, and Policy*, New York: Cambridge University Press, 2014

Montagu, Basil, *The Life of Francis Bacon*, London: William Pickering, 1833

Morris-Reich, Amos, "Introduction" [Heb.], in Morris-Reich (ed.), *"How Is Society Possible?" and Other Essays by Georg Simmel*, trans. Miryam Kraus, Tel Aviv: Hakibbutz Hameuchad, 2012, pp. 7–68

Mossel, Abraham, *A Day Laborer from Holland in the Holy Land 1913–1914* [Heb.], trans. Itamar Prath, Jerusalem: publisher not indicated, 2002

Naor, Mordechai, "Working the Land in the Yishuv" [Heb.], *Zmanim: A Historical Quarterly*, vol. *25* (1987), pp. 94–101

Neumann, Boaz, *Land and Desire in Early Zionism*, trans. Haim Watzman, Waltham: Brandeis University Press, 2011

Nietzsche, Friedrich, *Beyond Good and Evil*, trans. Walter Kaufmann, New York: Vintage Books, 1966

Nietzsche, Friedrich, *The Gay Science: With a Prelude in German Rhymes and an Appendix of Songs*, trans. Josefine Nauckhoff and Adrian Del Caro, Cambridge: Cambridge University Press, 2001

Nietzsche, Friedrich, *The Portable Nietzsche*, trans. Walter Kaufmann, New York: Penguin, 1977

Nietzsche, Friedrich, "Schopenhauer as Educator" [1874], in Nietzsche, *Untimely Meditations (Cambridge Texts in the History of Philosophy)*, trans. R. J. Hollingdale, Cambridge: Cambridge University Press, 1997, pp. 125–194

Nietzsche, Friedrich, *Thus Spoke Zarathustra*, trans. Adrian Del Caro, Cambridge: Cambridge University Press, 2006

Nir, Dov, "Peter Kroptkin and the Israeli Utopia" [Heb.], *Studies in the Geography of Israel*, vol. *12* (1986), pp. 11–21

Ohana, David, *The Origins of Israeli Mythology: Neither Canaanites nor Crusaders*, trans. David Maisel, New York: Cambridge University Press, 2012

O'Hara, Kieron, *The Enlightenment: A Beginner's Guide*, London: Oneworld, 2012

Or, Iair, *Creating a Style for the Generation: Language Beliefs in the Hebrew Language Committee's Discussions, 1912-1928* [Heb.], Tel Aviv: Ov Press, 2016

Ornan, Uzzi, *The Claws of Asmodai* [Heb.], Kiryat Tivon: Enam Press, 1999

The Paths of Development of Degania: A Story of Fifty Years [Heb.], editor not indicated, Tel Aviv: Davar, 1961

Peled, Rina, *The "New Man" of the Zionist Revolution: Hashomer Hatzair and Its European Roots* [Heb.], Tel Aviv: Am Oved, 2002

Peled, Rina, and Sharon Gordon (eds.), *Vienna 1900: Blooming on the Edge of an Abyss* [Heb.], Jerusalem: Carmel, 2019

Pelled, Leah, "The Concept of Self-Education in A.D. Gordon's Teachings" [Heb.], *Hahinuch Usevivo*, vol. *1* (1989), pp. 27–37

Pelled, Leah, *The Reception of Aharon David Gordon's Philosophy and Personality in Hebrew Literature and Periodicals (1904-1948)* [Heb.], PhD thesis, Jerusalem: The Hebrew University, 2004

Penslar, Derek J., *Jews and the Military: A History*, Princeton: Princeton University Press, 2013

Pocock, J. G. A., "Perceptions of Modernity in Early Modern Historical Thinking," *Intellectual History Review*, *17*: 1 (2007), pp. 79–92

Pohatchevsky, Nechama, "Night and Day in the Rehovot (a kind of letter)" [Heb.], *Hapoel Hatzair 10,* July 30, 1908, p. 13

Porat, Yehoshua, *Weapon and Pen in His Hand: The Life of Uriel Shelah* [Heb.], Tel Aviv: Mahbarot le-sifrut, 1989

Potter, David M., *People of Plenty: Economic Abundance and the American Character*, Chicago: The University of Chicago Press, 2009 [1954]

Pryde, Philip Rust, *Conservation in the Soviet Union*, Cambridge: Cambridge University Press, 1972

Rabinovitz, Alexander Siskind, "On Four Things" [Heb.], in Kushnir, *Reminiscences and Appreciations*, pp. 130–137

Ramon, Einat, "A.D. Gordon (100-Year Anniversary of Gordon's Death)" [Heb.], *Makor Rishon*, January 26, 2022, Retrieved from https://www.makorrishon.co.il/opinion/450 649/, accessed July 3, 2023

Ramon, Einat, *A New Life: Religion, Motherhood and Supreme Love in the Works of Aharon David Gordon* [Heb.], Jerusalem: Carmel, 2007

Ramon, Einat, "Religion and Life: The Renewal of Halakhah and the Jewish Religion in the Works of Aharon David Gordon" [Heb.], *Zmanim: A Historical Quarterly*, vol. *72* (2000), pp. 76–88

Ramon, Einat, "A Woman-Human: A.D. Gordon's Approach to Women's Equality and His Influence on Second Aliya Feminists," in Ruth Kark, Margalit Shilo and Galit Hazan-Rokem (eds.), *Jewish Women in Pre-State Israel: Life History, Politics and Culture*, Waltham: Brandeis University Press, 2008, pp. 111–121

Ratosh, Yonathan, "Letter to the Hebrew Youth" [Heb.], in Ratosh, *The Beginning of Days: Hebrew Openings*, Tel Aviv: Hadar Press, 1982, pp. 32–37

Ratosh, Yonathan, "Opening Speech in the Committee of Groups' Envoys Assembly (first session)" [Heb.], in Ratosh, *The Beginning of Days: Hebrew Openings*, Tel Aviv: Hadar Press, 1982, pp. 149–203

Ratzabi, Shalom, *Anarchy in "Zion": Between Martin Buber and A.D. Gordon* [Heb.], Tel Aviv: Am Oved, 2011

Rechnitzer, Haim O., *Prophecy and the Perfect Political Order: The Political Theology of Leo Strauss* [Heb.], Jerusalem: Bialik Institute, 2012

Rechnitzer, Haim O., "Toward a Trans-Liberal Romanticism" [Heb.], in Jonathan Cohen and Elie Holzer (eds.), *Modes of Educational Translation*, Jerusalem: Hebrew University Magnes Press, 2008, pp. 91–100

Redler-Feldmann, Yehoshua, "Around" [Heb., 1908], in Redler-Feldmann, *On the Boundary: Notes and Articles*, Vienna: publisher not indicated, 1922 pp. 203–207

Redler-Feldmann, Yehoshua, "Rabbi Aharon David Gordon (the 25th Anniversary of His Death)" [Heb.], *HaTzofe, February* 14, 1947, p. 3

Reichel, Nirit, "The First Hebrew 'Gymnasiums' in Israel: Social Education as the Bridge between Ideological Gaps in Shaping the Image of the Desirable High School Graduate (1906–48)," *Israel Affairs, 17*: 4 (2011), pp. 604–620

Renan, Ernest, *Histoire générale et système comparé des langues sémitiques: Histoire générale des langues sémitiques*, vol. 1, Paris: Imprimerie impériale, 1863

Rio Declaration on Environment and Development, *International Legal Materials*, vol. *31* (1992), pp. 874

Ron-Feder-Amit, Galila, *A.D Gordon: A Life Narrative* [Heb.], Ben Shemen: Modan, 2017

Rosenow, Eliyahu, "On the Figure of The Pioneer in Zionist Thought: Ahad Ha'am's and A.D. Gordon's Concept of Education" [Heb.], in David Nevo (ed.), *The Educational Deed: Study and Research*, Tel Aviv: Tel Aviv University's School of Education, 1977, pp. 35–60

Rotenstreich, Nathan, "An Interview with Muki Tsur" [Heb.], *Sdemot: Literary Digest of the Kibbutzim Movement*, vol. *61* (1976), pp. 62–73

Rotenstreich, Nathan, *Issues in Philosophy* [Heb.], Tel Aviv: Dvir, 1962

Rotenstreich, Nathan, *The Nation in the Philosophy of Gordon* [Heb.], Jerusalem: World Zionist Organization, 1952

Rousseau, Jean-Jacques, "Discourse on the Origin and Basis of Inequality among Men," in Rousseau, *The First and Second Discourses*, trans. Victor Gourevitch, New York: Harper & Row, 1990, pp. 117–199

Rousseau, Jean-Jacques, *"The Discourses" and Other Early Political Writings (Cambridge Texts in the History of Political Thought)*, Cambridge: Cambridge University Press, 1997

Rousseau, Jean-Jacques, *Emile, or On Education*, trans. Allan Bloom, New York: Basic Books, 1979

Rousseau, Jean-Jacques, *Reveries of the Solitary Walker*, trans. Peter France, London: Penguin, 1980

Rubinstein, Arye, "The Concept of Cultura in Ahad Ha'am Thought" [Heb.], *Melilah: Manchester Journal of Jewish Studies*, vols. *3–4* (1950), pp. 289–310

Safranski, Rüdiger, *Nietzsche: A Philosophical Biography*, trans. Shelley Frisch, New York: W. W. Norton & Company, 2003

Sagi, Avi, "Are We Still Jews?" [Heb.], in Adi Ophir (ed.), *Fifty to Forty-Eight: Critical Moments in the History of the State of Israel*, Jerusalem: The Van Leer Jerusalem Institute, 1999, pp. 79–88

Sagi, Avi, *To Be a Jew: Joseph Chayim Brenner as a Jewish Existentialist*, trans. Batya Stein, London: Continuum, 2011

Sagi, Avi, "Tolerance and the Possibility of Pluralism in Judaism" [Heb.], *Iyyun: The Jerusalem Philosophical Quarterly*, vol. *44* (1995) pp. 175–200

Saposnik, Arieh Bruce, *Becoming Hebrew: The Creation of a Jewish National Culture in Ottoman Palestine*, New York: Oxford University Press, 2008

Schächter, Josef, *The Philosophy of Aharon David Gordon* [Heb.], Tel Aviv: Dvir, 1957

Schlanger, Jacques, *Sur la Bonne Vie - Conversations avec Épicure, Épictète et d'autres Amis*, Paris: Presses Universitaires de France, 2000

Schnell, Izhak, "Nature and Environment in the Socialist-Zionist Pioneers' Perceptions: A Sense of Desolation," *Ecumene*, 4: 1 (1997), pp. 69–85

Scholem, Gershom, "Contemplations on Science of Judaism" [Heb.], in Scholem, *Explications and Implications: Writings on Jewish Heritage and Renaissance*, Tel Aviv: Am Oved, 1976, vol. II, pp. 385–403

Schweid, Eliezer, "The Crazy Man of Spirit: The Prophetic Mission in Gordon's Life and Thought" [Heb.], in Schweid, *Prophets for Their People*, Jerusalem: Hebrew University Magnes Press, 1999, pp. 144–160

Schweid, Eliezer, *The Foundation and Sources of A.D. Gordon's Philosophy* [Heb.], Jerusalem: Bialik Institute, 2014

Schweid, Eliezer, *The Individual: The World of AD Gordon* [Heb.], Tel Aviv: Am Oved, 1970

Schweid, Eliezer, *New Gordonian Essays: Globalization, Post-Modernization and the Jewish People* [Heb.], Tel Aviv: Ha-Kibbutz Ha-Meuchad, 2005

Schweid, Eliezer, "The Philosophical-Educational Structure of the Thought of A. D. Gordon" [Heb.], *Iyyun: The Jerusalem Philosophical Quarterly*, vol. *46* (1997), pp. 393–414

Schweid, Eliezer, "The Reunion between the Scientific and the Existential Perspectives in Gordon's Thought" [Heb.], *Alpayim: Journal for Contemporary Thought and Literature*, vol. *23* (2002), pp. 153–178

Scott, Peter, and William T. Cavanaugh (eds.), *The Blackwell Companion to Political Theology*, Oxford: Blackwell Publishing, 2004

Scruton, Roger, *How to Think Seriously about the Planet: The Case for an Environmental Conservatism*, New York: Oxford University Press, 2014

Shamir, Eilon, *For the Sake of Life: The Art of Living According to Aharon David Gordon* [Heb.], Tel Aviv: Ha-Kibbutz Ha-Meuchad, 2018

Shamis, Asaf, "Reclaiming AD Gordon's Deep Eco-Nationalism," *Nations and Nationalism*, *29*:1 (2023), pp. 85–100

Shapira, Anita, *The Failed Struggle: Hebrew Work 1929–1939* [Heb.], Tel Aviv: Hakibbutz Hameuchad, 1977

Shapira, Anita, *Land and Power: The Zionist Resort to Force 1881–1948*, Stanford: Stanford University Press, 1999

Shapira, Anita, *Yosef Haim Brenner: A Life*, trans. Anthony Berris, Stanford: Stanford University Press, 2015

Shapira, Avraham, *The Kabbalistic and Hasidic Sources of A.D. Gordon's Thought* [Heb.], Tel Aviv: Am Oved, 1996

Shapira, Avraham, "Revival and Legacy: Martin Buber's Attitude to A. D. Gordon," *Journal of Israeli History: Politics, Society, Culture, 18*: 1 (1997), pp. 29–45

Shapira, Avraham, "Whole Systems in Twentieth-Century Jewish Thought: Buber and Gordon - Between Parallelism and Supposed Influence" [Heb.], *Teuda: Studies in Judaica*, vols. *16–17* (1990), pp. 697–722

Shapira, Yosef (ed.), *Eliezer Shohat: About Him, His Path, in His Memory* [Heb.], Tel Aviv: Mifaley Tarbut Vechinuch, 1973

Shavit, Ayelet, *One for All? Facts and Values in the Debates over the Evolution of Altruism* [Heb.], Jerusalem: The Hebrew University Magnes Press, 2008

Shavit, Yaacov, and Jehuda Reinharz, "Introduction" [Heb.], in Iganz Goldziher, *A Lecture on Orientalism: In Memory of Ernest Renan*, Yaacov Shavit and Jehuda Reinharz (eds.), Raanana: The Open University, 2016, pp. 9–58

Shavit, Zohar, "The Development of Hebrew Publishing in the Erets Yisra'el" [Heb.], in Shavit (ed.), *The History of the Jewish Community in Erets Yisra'el since 1882*, Jerusalem: Bialik Institute, 1998, vol. 1, pp. 199–262

Shoham, Hizky, *Israel Celebrates: Jewish Holidays and Civic Culture in Israel*, trans. Lenn Scharm and Diana File, Leiden and Boston: Brill, 2017

Shweder, Richard A., "Geertz's Challenge: Is It Possible to Be a Robust Cultural Pluralist and a Dedicated Political Liberal at the Same Time?," in Austin Sarat (ed.), *Law without Nations*, Stanford: Stanford University Press, 2010, pp. 185–231

Sigad, Ran, *Philo-Sopia: On the Only Truth* [Heb.], Jerusalem: Dvir, 1983

Simmel, Georg, "A Contribution to the Sociology of Religion" [1898] in Simmel, *Essays on Religion*, pp. 101–120

Simmel, Georg, *Essays on Religion*, Horst Jürgen Helle and Ludwig Nieder (trans. and eds.), New Haven: Yale University Press, 1997

Simmel, Georg, "Fundamental Religious Ideas and Modern Science: An Inquiry" [1909], in Simmel, *Essays on Religion*, pp. 3–6

Simmel, Georg, "The Metropolis and Mental Life," in Donald N. Levine (ed. and trans.), *Georg Simmel on Individuality and Social Forms*, Chicago: The University of Chicago Press, 1971, pp. 324–339

Simon, Akibah Ernst, *Are We Still Jews? Essays* [Heb.], Tel Aviv: Sifriat Poalim, 1983

Smith, Anthony D., "The Question of Jewish Identity," in Peter Y. Medding (ed.), *Studies in Contemporary Jewry VIII: A New Jewry? America since the Second World War*, New York: Oxford University Press, 1992, pp. 219–233

Smith, Barry, "On Place and Space: The Ontology of the Eruv," in C. Kanzian (ed.), *Cultures: Conflict - Analysis - Dialogue*, Frankfurt: Ontos Verlag, 2007, pp. 403–416

Somerville, John C., "Secular Society/Religious Population: Our Tacit Rules for Using the Term 'Secularization,'" *Journal for the Scientific Study of Religion*, vol. *37* (1998), pp. 249–253

Spinner, Samuel J., *Jewish Primitivism*, Stanford: Stanford University Press, 2021

Spinoza, Benedictus de, *The Collected Works of Spinoza*, vol. 1, trans. and ed. Edwin Curley, Princeton: Princeton University Press, 1985

Steiner, George, *Language and Silence*, London: Faber & Faber, 1967

Stevens, Anthony, *Jung: A Very Short Introduction*, New York: Oxford University Press, 2001

Strassberg-Dayan, Sara, *Individual, Nation and Mankind: The Conception of Man in the Teachings of A.D. Gordon and Rabbi Abraham I. Hacohen Kook* [Heb.], Tel Aviv: Hakibbutz Hameuchad, 1995

Struchkov, Anton Yu, "Nature Protection as Moral Duty: The Ethical Trend in the Russian Conservation Movement," *Journal of the History of Biology*, *25*: 3 (1992), pp. 413–428

Suchovolsky, Zvi, "The Man and the Friend" [Heb.], in Kushnir, *Reminiscences and Appreciations*, pp. 35–38

Suchovolsky, Zvi, "On Vegetarianism and Higher Education" [Heb.], *Hapoel Hatzair*, vol. *23* (1964), p. 26

Sunstein, Cass, *Laws of Fear: Beyond the Precautionary Principle*, Cambridge: Cambridge University Press, 2014

Tal, Alon, *All the Trees of the Forest: Israel's Woodland from the Bible to the Present (Yale Agrarian Studies Series)*, New Haven: Yale University Press, 2013

Tal, Alon, *Pollution in a Promised Land: An Environmental History of Israel*, Berkeley: University of California Press, 2002

Talmud Bavli: Berakhot, in Adin Steinsaltz (ed.), *Koren Talmud Bavli Noé*, Jerusalem: Koren Publishers, 2014, vol. 1

Tamir, Yael, "Two Concepts of Multiculturalism," *Journal of Philosophy of Education*, *29*: 2 (1995), pp. 161–172

Tanakh: The New JPS Translation According to the Traditional Hebrew Text, Philadelphia: Jewish Publication Society, 1985

Tartakover, Haim, "A Conversation between Gordon and Buber on Vegetarianism," in Kushnir, *Reminiscences and Appreciations*, pp. 75–76

Taylor, Charles, *A Secular Age*, Cambridge: Harvard University Press, 2007

Thompson, Ewa M., *Understanding Russia: The Holy Fool in Russian Culture*, Lanham, Md.: University Press of America, 1987

Thoreau, Henry David, *Walden*, Princeton: Princeton University Press, 1971

Thoreau, Henry David, *The Writings of Henry David Thoreau - Journal 1837–1846*, vol. 7, Boston and New York: Houghton, Mifflin, 1906

Tirosh-Samuelson, Hava (ed.), *Judaism and Ecology: Created World and Revealed Word: Religions of the World and Ecology*, Cambridge: Harvard University Press 2002

Tolstoy, Leo, *Anna Karenina*, trans. R. Pevear and L. Volokhonsky, New York: Penguin Classics, 2000

Tolstoy, Leo, *The Death of Ivan Ilyich*, trans. Lynn Solotaroff, New York: Random House, 2004

Tolstoy, Leo, "The First Step," in Tolstoy, *Essays and Letters*, trans. Aylmer Maude. New York: Funk and Wagnalls Company, 1904, pp. 53–93

Tolstoy, Leo, *What Is Art?*, trans. Aylmer Maude, Overland Park, Kans.: Digireads Publishing, 2020

Tönnies, Ferdinand, *Community and Civil Society* [1887], ed. Jose Harris, trans. Margaret Hollis and Jose Harris, Cambridge: Cambridge University Press, 2001

Troen, Ilan, *Imagining Zion: Dreams, Designs, and Realities in a Century of Jewish Settlement*, New Haven: Yale University Press, 2008

Tsabari, Udi, *Secularization, Secularism and Secularity in the Lives and Thought of Y. H. Brenner and A. D. Gordon* [Heb.], PhD thesis, Tel Aviv: Tel Aviv University, 2017

Tsahor, Ze'ev, "The Controversy amongst the Eretz-Israel Labor Parties Concerning Enlistment in the 'Jewish Legion'" [Heb.], *Cathedra: For the History of Eretz Israel and Its Yishuv*, vol. *3* (1977), pp. 30–39

Tsirkin-Sadan, Rafi, *Jewish Letters at the Pushkin's Library: Yossef Haim Brenner's Thought and Its Connection to Russian Literature and Thought* [Heb.], Jerusalem: Bialik Institute, 2013

Tsirkin-Sadan, Rafi, "Tolstoy, Zionism, and the Hebrew culture," *Tolstoy Studies Journal*, vol. *24* (2012), pp. 26–35

Tsur, Muki, *Doing It the Hard Way* [Heb.], Tel Aviv: Am Oved, 1976

Tsur, Muki, *Early Spring: Tzvi Shatz and the Intimate Commune* [Heb.], Tel Aviv: Am Oved, 1984

Tsur, Muki, *Studies in Kibbutz and Israeli Culture* [Heb.], Jerusalem: Yad Tabenkin, 2007

Tsur, Muki, and Yuval Danieli (eds.), *Mestechkin Builds Israel - Architecture in the Kibbutz* [Heb.], Tel-Aviv: Hakibbutz Hameuchad, 2008

Turner, Joseph Yossi, "National Individuality, Universal Humanity and Social Justice in the Thought of Aharon David Gordon" [Heb.], *Daat*, vol. *81* (2016), pp. 288–369

Turner, Joseph Yossi, "Philosophy and Praxis in the Thought of Aharon David Gordon," *The Journal of Jewish Thought and Philosophy*, *24*: 1 (2016), pp. 122–148

Turner, Joseph Yossi, *Quest for Life: A Study in Aharon David Gordon's Philosophy of Man in Nature*, Boston: Academic Studies Press, 2020

Turner, Victor, *The Ritual Process: Structure and Anti-Structure*, Ithaca: Cornell University Press, 1979

Tzur, Dvir, "Between Hallelujah and Requiem: Toiling of the Land in the Works of A.D. Gordon, S. Yizhar and Elie Shamir" [Heb.], *Alpayim Ve'Od: Rethinking Culture in Israel - A Biannual Journal*, vol. *2* (2019), pp. 175–197

Tzur, Dvir, *Between Home and the Field, between Man and Space: Space and Place in S. Yizhar's Novels Preliminaries and Tsalhavim* [Heb.], Jerusalem: Hebrew University Magnes Press, 2015

Ufaz, Gad, "The Source of the Concept of 'Self-Education' in AD Gordon's Thought" [Heb.], *Devarim*, vol. *2* (1999), pp. 59–71

Ufaz, Gad, "The Woman and the Family in the Philosophy of A. D. Gordon" [Heb.], *Iyunim Bitkumat Israel: Studies in Zionism, the Yishuv and the State of Israel*, vol. *8* (1998), pp. 602–613

"Uriah Village" [Heb.], author not indicated, *Ha-Tsfira*, January 8, 1913

Viñuales, Jorge E. (ed.), *The Rio Declaration on Environment and Development: A Commentary*, Oxford: Oxford University Press, 2015

Voltaire, François-Marie Arouet de, *Voltaire's Correspondence*, ed. Theodore Besterman, Geneva: Institut de Musee Voltaire, 1953–1966

Von Suffrin, Dana, "The Possibility of a Productive Palestine: Otto Warburg and Botanical Zionism," *Israel Studies*, *26*: 2 (2021), pp. 173–187

Walicki, Andrzej, *The Flow of Ideas: Russian Thought from the Enlightenment to the Religious-Philosophical Renaissance*, trans. Jolanta Kozak and Hilda Andrews-Rusiecka, Frankfurt am Main: Peter Lang, 2015

Walicki, Andrzej, *The Slavophile Controversy: History of a Conservative Utopia in Nineteenth-Century Russian Thought*, trans. Hilda Andrews-Rusiecka, New York: Oxford University Press, 1975

Walls, Dassow, *Henry David Thoreau: A Life*, Chicago: The University of Chicago Press, 2017

Walzer, Michael, Menachem Lorberbaum, Noam J. Zohar, and Ari Ackerman (eds.), *The Jewish Political Tradition: Membership*, vol. *2*, New Haven: Yale University Press, 2006

Weber, Marianne, *Max Weber: A Biography*, New Brunswick, NJ: Transaction, 1988

Weiner, Douglas R., *Models of Nature: Ecology, Conservation, and Cultural Revolution in Soviet Russia*, Pittsburgh: University of Pittsburgh Press, 2000

Weissblei, Gil, *The Revival of Hebrew Book Art in Weimar Germany* [Heb.], Jerusalem: Carmel, 2019

Weitz, Yosef, *First Pages* [Heb.], Tel Aviv: Gadish, 1958

Williams, John Alexander, *Turning to Nature in Germany: Hiking, Nudism, and Conservation 1900-1940*, Stanford: Stanford University Press, 2007

Wortman, Richard, *The Crisis of Russian Populism*, New York: Cambridge University Press, 2008

Yadin, Azzan, "A Web of Chaos: Bialik and Nietzsche on Language, Truth, and the Death of God," *Prooftexts*, 21: 1 (2001), pp. 179–203

Yanait-Ben-Zvi, Rachel, *We Ascend* [Heb.], Tel Aviv: Am Oved, 1959

Yanitski, Oleg, *Russian Environmentalism: Leading Figures, Facts, Opinions*, Moscow: Mezhdunarodnyje Otnoshenija Publishing House, 1993

Yeivin, Shemuel, "Work of the Land" [Heb.], in *Encyclopaedia Biblica*, Jerusalem: Bialik Institute, 1971, vol. VI. pp. 36–37

Yeshurun, Helit, "Telling the Finite with the Infinite - An Interview with S. Yizhar" [Heb.], *Hadarim - Journal on Poetry*, vol. 11 (1994), pp. 215–235

Yizhar, S., "The Courage to Be Secular" [Heb.], in Yizhar, *A Call for Education*, Tel Aviv: Sifriat Poalim, 1984, pp. 125–139

Yizhar, S., *On the Outskirts of the Negev* [Heb.], Tel Aviv: Hakibbutz Hameuchad, 1978

Yizhar, S., *Tsalhavim* [Heb.], Tel Aviv: Zmora Bitan, 1993

Yoreh, Tanhum, "Consumption, Wastefulness, and Simplicity in Ultra-Orthodox Communities," *Studies in Judaism, Humanities, and the Social Sciences*, 2: 2 (2018), pp. 137–152

Yoreh, Tanhum, "Recycling in Jerusalem: Right or Privilege?," *Local Environment*, 19: 4 (2014), pp. 417–432

Yovel, Yirmiyahu, *Dark Riddle - Hegel, Nietzsche, and the Jews*, University Park: Pennsylvania State University Press, 1998

Yovel, Yirmiyahu, "General Introduction" [Heb.], in Yirmiyahu Yovel, Yair Tzaban, and David Shaham (eds.), *New Jewish Time - Jewish Culture in a Secular Age: An Encyclopedic View*, Jerusalem: Keter Press, 2007, vol. 1, pp. xv–xxvi

Zalkin, Mordechai, "Can Jews Become Farmers? Rurality, Peasantry and Cultural Identity in the World of the Rural Jew in Nineteenth-Century Eastern Europe," *Rural History*, 24: 2 (2013), pp. 161–175

Zameret, Zvi, "Ahad Ha'am and the Shaping of Secular Education" [Heb.], *Studies in Zionism, the Yishuv and the State of Israel*, vol. 16 (2006), pp. 171–194

Zameret, Zvi, "Aharon David Gordon" [Heb.], in Ze'ev Tsahor (ed.), *The Second Aliya: Biographies*, Jerusalem: Yad Ben Zvi, 1997, pp. 121–131

Zeira, Moti, "Aharon David Gordon as a Shaper of Culture" [Heb.], *Iyunim Bitkumat Israel: Studies in Zionism, the Yishuv and the State of Israel (Thematic Series)*, 2008, pp. 345–355

Zeira, Moti, *Rural Collective Settlement and Jewish Culture in Eretz Israel during the 1920s* [Heb.], Jerusalem: Yad Ben Zvi, 2002

Zeira, Moti, "Shoshana, Valiant Girl, Where Are You?" [Heb.], *Sdemot: Literary Digest of the Kibbutzim Movement*, vol. 111 (1989), pp. 1–77

Zerubavel, Yael, *Desert in the Promised Land*, Stanford: Stanford University Press, 2018

Zerubavel, Yael, "The Forest as a National Icon: Literature, Politics, and the Archeology of Memory," *Israel Studies*, 1: 1 (1996), pp. 60–99

Ziolkowski, Margaret, *Hagiography and Modern Russian Literature*, Princeton: Princeton University Press, 2014

Zweig, Stefan, *The World of Yesterday: Memoirs of a European*, trans. Anthea Bell, Lincoln: University of Nebraska Press, 1964 [1942]

Index

For the benefit of digital users, indexed terms that span two pages (e.g., 52–53) may, on occasion, appear on only one of those pages.

Figures are indicated by *f* following the page number